# Current Issues in Workers' Compensation

James Chelius
*Editor*

Papers Presented at a
Conference Sponsored by:

The Institute of Management
and Labor Relations and the
Bureau of Economic Research,
Rutgers, The State University
of New Jersey

——

The New York State School
of Industrial and Labor Relations,
Cornell University

——

The Economics Department,
the University of Connecticut

1986

W. E. Upjohn Institute for Employment Research

**Library of Congress Cataloging in Publication Data**

Current issues in workers' compensation.

1. Workers' compensation—United States—Congresses.
I.   Chelius, James Robert.      II.   Rutgers University.
Institute of Management and Labor Relations
HD7103.6.U6C87   1986          368.4'1'00973        86-9267
ISBN 0-88099-037-6
ISBN 0-88099-036-8 (pbk.)

# Contents

# Editor's Note

In response to the 1972 recommendations of the National Commission on State Workmen's Compensation Laws, most states substantially broadened coverage and increased benefits for injured workers. The cost increases associated with these reforms have brought workers' compensation to the forefront in the debate over labor market regulatory policy. Substantial changes to workers' compensation continue, although the attention has shifted from the relatively straightforward issues of coverage and benefit levels to subtle and difficult matters such as permanent partial disability benefit arrangements, disease compensation, administrative efficiency, and competitive rate-making.

One of the alleged virtues of workers' compensation is the flexibility and learning from others afforded by the decentralized state-run programs. Unfortunately the ongoing reform debate in virtually every state is taking place in isolation from the experiences and lessons of others. The papers in this volume begin to fill that void by reporting and analyzing a range of workers' compensation issues that are key to every state's disability income policy. The emphasis is on what can be learned from the experience of other jurisdictions. The papers were presented at a conference held at Rutgers, The State University of New Jersey, in 1983.

James Chelius

# The Status and Direction of Workers' Compensation
## An Introduction to Current Issues

James R. Chelius
Institute of Management and Labor Relations
Rutgers University

The substantial increase in injury rates during the 1960s that gave rise to widespread federal involvement in occupational safety and health also spawned a period of significant change in the workers' compensation system. The Occupational Safety and Health Act of 1970 provided for a national commission to study workers' compensation.[1] This commission recommended that the states broaden coverage and increase benefits. Eighty-four specific suggestions were made, 19 of which were deemed essential to the commission's notion of a well-functioning workers' compensation system. If the states did not meet the 19 essential recommendations, the commission urged that federal standards be issued and the states forced to comply. Most states responded to either the commission's vision of the appropriate way to improve the workers' compensation system or perhaps to the threat of federal involvement. Substantial changes were made in both coverage and benefit levels. These changes, however, were not sufficient to meet all of the 19 essential recommendations. Several bills mandating federal standards were introduced in Congress but none passed.

The substantial changes of the 1970s in workers' compensation coverage and benefits, together with increased system usage by workers, resulted in dramatic increases in employer costs. Burton and Krueger (see chapter 7) estimate that workers' compensation costs as a percentage of payroll increased over 80 percent from 1972 through 1978, approximately double the increase from 1950 through 1972. Whereas the initial response to the commission's recommendations was a series of relatively straightforward changes in coverage and benefit levels, the resulting cost increases generated pressure for attention to the more subtle aspects of workers' compensation.

Issues such as eligibility for permanent partial benefits, pricing regulation, and administrative arrangements that were largely ignored in the initial round of reform following the commission's report became the focus of a second wave of reform that continues. Workers' compensation, therefore, is an increasingly important and changing aspect of the labor market regulatory environment. Every indication is that this importance and fluidity will continue.

Evaluation of any regulatory policy is desirable; however, it is usually difficult. One source of difficulty, particularly for recent labor market regulatory initiatives such as OSHA, is that they are uniformly applied throughout the country. Such a universal policy, whatever its advantages as a regulatory technique, does not provide for ready comparisons. One of the advantages of the state-based workers' compensation system is that one can compare the various state laws and evaluate their effectiveness and efficiency. This potential advantage of the state systems has not been utilized to any significant degree. The workers' compensation laws of each state tend to operate and even change in isolation from the experiences of others.

The conference from which this book arose is the first in a series examining the workers' compensation system. The goal is to provide scholars and practitioners with the insights of the workers' compensation experience in a variety of jurisdictions.

There are three main themes examined in this review of current issues in workers' compensation. We first describe and analyze the *process* of reforming workers' compensation with papers on a variety of states that have recently undergone attempts at significant change. While only some of these efforts have resulted in comprehensive change, there is much to be learned from failed as well as successful attempts. Of course, the process of change is not distinct from the attempted or actual outcome of the reform process. Several of the papers primarily focusing on the process of reform give us significant insight into the nature of the workers' compensation system in these states. A second group of papers examines the ongoing *operation* of several key states. These essays specifically examine the regulation of insurance rates, the differences in employer costs, and the administrative structure of New Jersey, New York, and Connecticut. The third section of the book deals with one of the most difficult of workers' compensation issues—*occupational disease*. These papers address how workers' compensation currently deals with this problem and suggest guidelines for directing future change.

In addition to these three basic themes, a final essay broadens our perspective by presenting information about the unusual accident compensation scheme used in New Zealand.

## *The Process of Workers' Compensation Reform*

The difference between reform and tinkering seems to depend on whether one is for or against the changes. Virtually every state makes some changes in its compensation statute annually; however, without getting more specific, the notion of reform as used here is of a fairly major change in the system with no connotation as to the desirability of the change.

The papers on the reform process examine a range of state experiences—California (Alan Tebb), Michigan (H. Allan Hunt), Minnesota (Steve Keefe), Florida, Louisiana, New Mexico, Delaware, and Alaska (John Lewis). While the political process is never a tidy one, several themes do emerge. First, research and the resulting insights into the specific problems of a state's system provide a necessary beginning to the reform process. Second, educating a wide range of individuals, including study commission members, key employer and labor leaders, and legislators, is also critical. Finally, substantive communication among the leaders of the various interest groups cannot be completely replaced by dialogue among their specialized representatives.

The necessary research for reform need not be sophisticated scholarly treatises; often the only requirement is that it adequately document what is happening in the system. The recurrent theme of research as a precondition for substantial change is well-illustrated by the Minnesota experience described by Keefe. For several years the high cost of workers' compensation made it an important political issue. However, no response to industry complaints was forthcoming, in part because the only publicized evidence for high costs was a series of anecdotes on payments to undeserving individuals. Only when credible data were developed, indicating that Minnesota was indeed a high cost state, did the reform effort develop momentum. Interestingly, the most cogent basis for cost comparison was with neighboring Wisconsin—a key competitor for many Minnesota industries. The research effort also pointed to the primary reason for the high costs. Whereas early reform pro-posals focused on general benefit levels, the analyses demonstrated that it was the amount of disability compen-sated rather than benefit levels that made Minnesota costs high.

The analyses documented that in Minnesota compared to Wisconsin: (1) the rate of permanent total disability per lost-time injury was 20 times higher; (2) the average duration of temporary total disability was 50 percent longer; (3) the fre-quency of permanent partial disability cases was 60 percent higher; (4) the average payment for partial disability was 20 percent higher even though the scheduled benefits were similar; and (5) the average medical cost per case was 50 per-cent higher. Based on these findings, it became obvious that the fundamental cost problem with the Minnesota system was not a high benefit schedule *per se.* The importance of such fundamental research is retold in the successful reform efforts of Florida and Louisiana and the failures of Delaware and New Mexico.

Educating key actors in the reform process is also crucial to success. One of the first requirements is to educate members of the ubiquitous study commissions as to the fun-damentals of workers' compensation. Without such knowledge, commission members tend to get locked into the specific proposals of the groups they represent. As events change and bargaining intensifies, such rigidity frequently blocks useful compromises. Legislators comprise another group that invariably requires such attention. An attempted workers' compensation reform that tries to reduce the long time frequently required for education is likely to be unsuc-cessful.

A closely related issue is the requirement of dialogue among the leaders of the affected interest groups. While this is perhaps obvious, the papers reviewing recent state changes reveal several interesting points. Because of the complexity of workers' compensation in general, and in particular the obscurity of the currently debated nonbenefit issues, many affected parties have delegated their role in the reform process to specialists. While this is typically not a problem, the papers note that in several states, labor unions frequently turned to their workers' compensation attorneys for advice on reform. However, since many of the proposed reforms include attempts at reducing the amount of litigation, the attorneys have an inherent conflict of interest and have often been a source of organized labor's opposition to reform. A similar delegation of authority on the employer's side was one of the reasons cited by Tebb as contributing to the languishing of reform efforts in California during the 1970s. Apparently senior management relied solely on trade associations to represent their interests just at the time when the associations lost many of their senior lobbyists. The point, therefore, is that it is desirable for leaders of business and labor to understand and communicate on workers' compensation.

One must not be so naive as to assume that once the "right" people begin a dialogue, all roadblocks to reform will be erased or even smoothed. However, there are many aspects of reform that can yield gains for both employers and employees. Taking advantage of these potential mutual gains, and fashioning optimal compromises on other aspects where both gains and losses are necessary, is greatly facilitated by the direct involvement of key leaders. Unfortunatly such attention is frequently lacking.

These papers on the reform process give us many insights into the dynamics of the states described, as well as providing evidence for the broad theme of what brings about reform. Anyone with an interest in substantial workers' compensation change must be prepared to deal with the issues addressed by these authors.

*The Regional Experience in Workers' Compensation*

Given the joint sponsorship of the conference by universities in the States of New Jersey, New York, and Connecticut, it was appropriate to focus the attention of one session on the operation of workers' compensation in these states. The issues addressed—cost differences, pricing regulation, and administration—are important concerns in all jurisdictions. The general context of the issues represents the bulk of the analysis, with the three states serving as examples.

The importance of thorough and well-documented research has already been noted. An excellent example of such analysis is the interstate cost comparison data presented by John F. Burton, Jr. and Alan Krueger. They begin by describing some inappropriate measures of cost differences among the states (earned premium-to-payroll ratios and average premiums per state). While the incorrectness of these measures may seem obvious once their inadequacies are demonstrated, such measures are in fact frequently used. The reason for the scarcity of valid data on costs becomes apparent upon examining the Burton and Krueger technique for constructing such measures—it is very complicated. The authors make a convincing case as to why such an elaborate procedure is necessary. Without attempting to summarize their technique, it should be noted that they take into account factors such as industry mix, payroll limitations, premium discounts, dividends, experience rating, expense and loss constants, and schedule rating.

The resulting cost data, across years and states, are then reviewed to demonstrate some of their more important uses. For example, it is noted that from 1950 through 1983 workers' compensation costs as a percentage of payroll almost tripled, with a particularly large increase in the period from 1972 through 1978. The apparent increase in the interstate variation of workers' compensation costs over time and even since the National Commission's recommendations is also an interesting finding, particularly in light of the commission's goal of greater equality across states.

While a formal statistical analysis of the reasons for these cost differences is beyond the scope of their paper, Burton and Krueger present some preliminary evidence on this important issue. Using New Jersey, New York, and Connecticut as examples, they compare the relative costliness of these states over time with the level of benefits available to injured workers. They conclude ". . . that changes in benefit levels are an important determinant of changes in the employers' costs of workers' compensation. . . ." The importance of other potential factors such as coverage, use of state insurance funds and self-insurance, and administration of the law are left for future analysis.

This paper also yields an interesting insight into a key aspect of the reform process. Certainly one of the important phases of this process is to determine changes that can yield gains for both workers and employers. Unfortunately, at least in the short run, many changes simply benefit one party at the expense of the other. However, data on the cost response to the New Jersey reform of 1979 indicate that benefits to most injured workers increased while employer costs declined. The thrust of the reform was to de-emphasize the role of minor permanent partial disability payments by requiring objective evidence of disability. While fewer workers are now receiving such benefits one would not imagine that, given the standard of eligibility, this is a significant problem for deserving individuals. Interestingly, the general level of benefits increased at the same time as relative employer costs were decreasing. This concern about the handling of permanent partial benefits is a key aspect of the reform debate in many states, including several of those discussed in the first section.

The paper discussing pricing is also quite timely as these issues are currently being debated in many states. Reflecting the general deregulatory trend in other lines of insurance as well as other sectors of the economy, the fundamental question is the appropriate role of competition in the pricing of workers' compensation insurance. Arthur Williams first provides a very readable account of the rate determination process—a review necessary for all but those thoroughly steeped in this arcane subject. The rate regulation process—ranging from prior governmental approvals to open competition—is then described. A final section of the paper summarizes three of the specific issues forming the heart of the debate on price regulation of workers' compensation insurance: the arguments for and against open competition, the appropriate role of investment income in regulated rates, and the use of excess profit statutes.

While most of the arguments for and against open competition are the same as those used in other areas of regulation, from bus fares to liquor prices, the unique aspect of the workers' compensation debate concerns whether the data base used to calculate rates will be less reliable under competition. Opponents of deregulation are concerned that competition will lead to a withering away of the rate-making data base pooled from most insurance companies. It is difficult to imagine why insurance companies would not want to maintain such a valuable pricing tool even if it were not mandated by regulation; however, in the spirit of neutrality, Williams chooses not to reveal his interpretation of the validity of the arguments.

The role of investment income in regulated rate-making is significant in workers' compensation because of the time lapse between collection of premiums and the dispersal of benefits. While the role of income earned on such investments would be moot under genuine open competition, its importance in the various regulated price environments will continue. The difficulties of determining a fair or efficient price without significant help from the marketplace are well illustrated by the debate on the appropriate role of investment income.

The final issue addressed by Williams is that of excess profits statutes. While only a minor part of the workers' compensation system, with only Florida currently having such a law, the issue may become more important if more states deregulate workers' compensation insurance. Such statutes can be used as a mechanism for easing into more competition in rate-making by serving as a guarantee that the deregulated firms will not generate "windfall" profits.

The efficient administration of workers' compensation is an important but extremely difficult issue addressed in the paper by Monroe Berkowitz. He reflects on the frustration of developing guidelines for how workers' compensation should be run, echoing the common theme of the "overuse" of litigation. It is ironic that most commentaries on workers' compensation emphasize the inefficiency of its extensive use of lawyers, while many other legal areas point to the "streamlined" workers' compensation system as a model to be emulated. Unfortunately, the characteristics of efficient administration remain illusive; Berkowitz, however, offers the hope that ongoing conferences and resulting books such as this one can provide a vehicle for invigorating the search process. Certainly excellent essays on the operation of workers' compensation such as the ones contained in this section will foster the process by which those concerned about workers' compensation will learn from the views and experiences of others.

## Occupational Disease

One of the most significant of workers' compensation problems is how to deal with occupational disease victims.

Unfortunately, the magnitude of the problem has only recently been appreciated. For many years occupational disease was seen largely as a phenomenon of the past with the major problems resolved.[2] The growing awareness of work-related health problems and in particular the asbestos issue have intensified the search for an effective and efficient mechanism to deal with these issues. There is currently a series of bills before Congress that propose to circumvent the state workers' compensation system by establishing a federal occupational disease compensation program.

The papers presented at the conference demonstrate the inadequacies of the current system as well as the difficulties of coming up with a solution. Donald Spatz illustrates the nature of the compensation problem with its most visible manifestation—asbestos. Most state workers' compensation laws have significant roadblocks that make it quite difficult for victims or survivors to collect benefits. These "artificial barriers" include recency of employment rules and statutes of limitations that are frequently inconsistent with the latency periods of occupational disease. The performance of workers' compensation within a state with no such barriers (New Jersey) illustrates that even at its best, the current system does not appear to be fairly compensating victims. The data on three groups of workers clearly indicate that the problem goes well beyond the law *per se.* Fewer than half of the victims or survivors of asbestos-associated diseases even filed a claim. The failure to claim benefits was particularly striking among a group of workers with typically short term exposures in a factory that closed in 1954. Only nine survivors of the 87 workers who died from asbestos-associated diseases filed workers' compensation claims. Apparently, the lack of recognition of the association between asbestos and disease was not as limiting a factor as was the lack of knowledge that the survivors were potentially eligible for benefits. Even among those filing claims, the settlements were frequently delayed and severely compromised. It is difficult to come to any other conclusion than that the workers' compensation system has difficulty coping with occupational diseases.

The papers by Donald Elisberg and Peter Barth present guidelines and suggestions for how the problem of occupational disease can be handled. Even if one does not agree with their solutions, the systematic discussion is very helpful since it presents the agenda with which any reform must cope.

Elisberg reviews five basic elements of any effective occupational disease compensation system. One of the issues that must be addressed is the appropriate role of the federal government. Elisberg argues for a federal preemption of disease compensation based on the advantages of uniformity, the difficulty of communicating complex issues of disease causality to state agencies, and the political problems of getting comprehensive legislation in many states. A second basic element is the appropriate role of presumptions for determining whether particular diseases should be automatically considered to arise out of and in the course of employment. Such presumptions are designed " . . . to eliminate the concept that in each individual case an entire system of proof need be offered to establish both the illness and its causal relationship to employment." It is argued that presumptions have gotten a bad name because of their politicization under the Black Lung law but that such subordination of medical criteria need not occur.

Another basic element of occupational disease compensation is benefit levels. Elisberg argues that pain and suffering should be compensated since work disincentives are not likely to be as troublesome as they are with injuries. It is then argued that claims handling could be made simple by the use of impartial medical panels to determine causality and the degree of disability. Adjudication would be further minimized under this proposal by funding the program with a mechanism such as a tax that does not give employers an incentive to challenge claims. Elisberg is concerned that any kind of an insurance mechanism would encourage employers or their associations to challenge legitimate claims in the hope of holding down premiums.

In addition to addressing some of the same basic issues, Barth raises several others, including the problem of exclusive remedy. Surely any occupational disease reform that bars tort suits must make the workers' compensation system ". . . more accessible to potential users." Barth feels such a *quid pro quo* is a useful element of disease compensation reform. One of the problems with achieving such a compromise—the reliance of organized labor on the advice of their attorneys—surfaced in the earlier discussion of the reform process. "The trial bar has no apparent interest in having future lawsuits by workers or survivors barred in disease cases. Any promise of a more effective workers' compensation system holds less interest for them than maintaining and expanding the right to sue." Whatever one's view of the optimal role of litigation, it is clearly an issue that needs to be addressed if victims and their survivors are to be fairly compensated.

### The New Zealand Experience

The final paper broadens our perspective on workers' compensation issues by reviewing the radically different New Zealand system. Barbara McIntosh begins her analysis by describing the legal arrangements by which all individuals are covered for 24 hours a day. The results of a survey of employer perceptions about the system are then analyzed. Three government funds are used to finance compensation—the Earner's Fund for all employed and self-employed persons (on and off the job), the Motor Vehicle Fund for all persons injured in motor vehicle accidents (including on-the-job injuries) and a Supplementary Fund for all others. The Earner and Motor Vehicle Funds are essentially self-supporting from levies on employers and vehicle owners respectively. The Supplementary Fund is financed from general tax revenues. The employer levies for work injuries and diseases vary by industry although they are sharply constrained by minimums and maximums. The quite minor Safety Incentive Bonuses are the only version of experience rating used. The costs of earners' nonwork injuries are spread among all employers. Benefits are generous, with 100 percent of earnings up to $600 (NZ) per week currently covered.

The results of extensive interviews with New Zealand senior executives indicate that the compensation scheme is not perceived as a key factor influencing safety decisions. More significant influences were government safety rules, employee concerns, and local union demands. While the executives did not feel the legislation was a hindrance to their operations, they did feel that more accidents are reported and longer time taken off as a result of the compensation scheme.

## Conclusion

The very fact that workers' compensation has lasted for over 70 years indicates it has strengths as a device for dealing with an important social problem. Similarly it is hard to deny that it has significant weaknesses. Whatever one's view of the balance of these strengths and weaknesses, the papers in this volume will provide insights into the current state and desirable directions for workers' compensation.

## NOTES

1. *The Report of the National Commission on State Workmen's Compensation Laws* (Washington: Government Printing Office, 1972).

2. A classic study published in 1954 stated ". . . for industry as a whole, problems of air pollution, industrial poisoning, silicosis, dermatitis, or other occupational health hazards are less pressing today than disability and absenteeism due to general illness." Herman Somers and Anne Somers. *Workmen's Compensation* (New York: John Wiley, 1954) p. 218.

# 2

# The Minnesota Experience with Workers' Compensation Reform*

Steve Keefe

Commissioner, Department of Labor and Industry
State of Minnesota

## The Problem and the Political Environment

From 1975, when it first became a hot political issue, the debate over workers' compensation in Minnesota has been characterized by more heat than light. Employers' complaints about high costs were initially supported mainly by anecdotal information about abuses in individual cases, and proposed solutions were more intuitive than based on any particular strategy of addressing high cost impact areas. Upon examination, anecdotal stories of abuses frequently turned out to have been exaggerated. One collection of 25 "horror stories" presented by employers to a legislative committee in 1977 as evidence of the excessive liberality of Minnesota judges led to an investigation which discovered that 14 of the 25 cases had never been before judges but had rather been decided without litigation by insurance companies on their own motion. Intuitive solutions frequently turned out, upon adoption, not to have any substantial im-

---

*This paper was originally scheduled to be presented at the conference, however, the final legislative debate on the reforms coincided with the conference and Mr. Keefe was unable to make the presentation.

pact on costs of the system. A list of proposals by the insurance industry in 1979 had all been adopted by 1981 without any apparent substantial impact on costs. While complaints tended to focus on payments to undeserving individuals, proposed solutions tended to focus on across-the-board benefit cuts.

By the early 1980s, analytical understanding of what was different about the Minnesota system and whether that system was actually more costly began to become available. A legislative study in 1979,[1] a study by the insurance division in 1981,[2] and a study by the Citizens League in 1982[3] began to point at key aspects of the nature of Minnesota's workers' compensation problem. In addition, the studies identified another problem, perhaps equally severe, of poor service to injured workers.

Comparisons of average workers' compensation rates from state to state were at first used to determine the degree of the Minnesota problem. It was quickly discovered that these comparisons were misleading because of the important effects of differences in industrial mix from state to state and from socio-economic differences which lead to differences in litigation and system utilization from state to state. Furthermore, parallel state-to-state comparisons ignored the real competitive problems which individual businesses face. Nationwide average workers' compensation rates are far less important to employers than the actual workers' compensation rates in similar classifications in states where the employers' competition is found.

More detailed examination of rates on a classification-by-classification basis by Insurance Commissioner Michael Markman in 1981[4] showed that Minnesota workers' compensation rates were indeed substantially higher than rates in surrounding states, even though not particularly higher than rates in some more heavily industrialized states on the East and West Coasts. In fact, the study showed workers' compensation rates averaging 70 percent higher in Minnesota than in our neighboring state of Wisconsin, which has a quite similar industrial and socio-economic mix as well as a somewhat similar average benefit level. Furthermore, the Markman study showed that differences in compensation rates tend to be more pronounced in those industries with the highest rates, particularly in classifications containing large numbers of small businesses. This creates particular economic problems because those are the very businesses which find their competition in the neighboring State of Wisconsin, and in which workers' compensation rates are a more important competitive factor. For example, the lumbering industry, found heavily in both northern Minnesota and northern Wisconsin, has a workers' compensation rate of almost $50 per $100 of payroll in Minnesota. Although the average increase in Minnesota over Wisconsin rate levels is 70 percent, a number of rate classifications had differences of as much as 200 or 300 percent.

Analysis of the reasons for these differences in Minnesota as compared to Wisconsin turned up interesting information about the impact of benefit levels. Maximum weekly benefit levels in both states are quite similar. The Citizens League study showed that scheduled awards for various bodily parts turned out to be quite similar for an average wage earner in each state, although there is a broader range and therefore a higher maximum (and a lower minimum) in Minnesota than in Wisconsin. The Minnesota cost-of-living escalator turns out to have an impact on rates of only approximately 1 percent or 2 percent once investment income is taken into consideration as it is in the Minnesota rating structure (although not yet in the Wisconsin rating structure).

The 1977-79 legislative study[5] suggested one reason for these differences when it found a strong correlation between average workers' compensation rate levels and litigation rates in various states, including Minnesota and Wisconsin. As of 1979, the Minnesota litigation rate was approximately three times that of Wisconsin (petitions for hearing amounted to approximately 10 percent of first reports of an injury in Minnesota as opposed to barely 3 percent in Wisconsin). The Markman report zeroed in more precisely on the reasons for the substantially higher costs in Minnesota when it discovered that the Minnesota system has the following important differences from Wisconsin in frequency and severity of disability:

- The rate of permanent total disability cases per lost time injury is approximately 20 times as high in Minnesota as it is in Wisconsin (63 permanent total cases per 10,000 lost time injuries in Minnesota as opposed to 3 in Wisconsin).

- The average duration of temporary total disability in Minnesota is approximately 50 percent longer than it is in Wisconsin.

- The frequency of permanent partial disability cases is approximately 60 percent higher in Minnesota than it is in Wisconsin.

- The average payment for partial disability is 20 percent higher in Minnesota than it is in Wisconsin (in spite of the apparent similarity in the two state schedules).

- The average medical cost per case is approximately 50 percent higher in Minnesota than it is in Wisconsin.

Analysis of the two state systems seems to show that the major reason for the difference in the cost of compensation for work-related disability in Minnesota as compared to Wisconsin is not the level of compensation so much as it is the amount of disability compensated.

In order to determine the reasons for the difference in the amount of disability actually being compensated in Minnesota, a great deal of attention has been given to comparisons of the state's system with that used in the State of Wisconsin and to the methods used by a number of businesses in Minnesota that have managed to substantially reduce the costs of their own workers' compensation program within the structure of the existing Minnesota laws and benefit levels by changing their internal company practices.

In Minnesota, a significant number of private companies, usually larger self-insuring employers (although larger companies purchasing insurance have also enjoyed these improvements), have recently reformed their internal workers' compensation programs and accomplished savings of anywhere from 20 percent to 50 percent of their workers' compensation costs. These company-sponsored programs usually contain an important safety component. Companywide commitments to preventing accidents in the first place are extremely effective in dealing with the workers' compensation costs.

More modern loss control methods adopted after the fact also seem to have a substantial impact on reducing the actual disability that needs to be compensated. By instituting vigorous early intervention and return-to-work programs, aggressive Minnesota employers have found that they can substantially reduce the disability resulting from even serious injuries. Such programs also seem to result in improved employer-employee relations and substantially reduced litigation rates.

The State of Wisconsin seems to accomplish similar results by having an active early intervention philosophy of state administration of the workers' compensation law. This administration seems to accomplish the same kinds of substantially better return-to-work rates and substantially lower litigation rates that are accomplished individually by certain companies in Minnesota.[6]

This analysis of the workers' compensation problem in Minnesota suggests a possible solution to the political problem surrounding workers' compensation as well as to the policy problem of how to control workers' compensation costs for employers and, incidentally, how to improve the system from the point of view of workers at the same time. Since attention to the amount of disability in the system seems to offer much more promise for controlling workers' compensation rates, and since the level of disability is just as much a problem for employees and, therefore, their union representatives, it should be possible to develop a coalition of business and labor support for certain programs designed to both reduce costs and improve service.

This political strategy was suggested by the Citizens League study in Minnesota and adopted by the new administration of Governor Rudy Perpich, elected in November 1982, which, incidentally, hired the chairman of the Citizens League study as Commissioner of Labor and Industry to take responsibility for the administration's workers' compensation legislative program.

The strategy adopted by the administration was to develop a workers' compensation program which would reform the workers' compensation system in order to improve service, reorganize the benefit structure to encourage return-to-work programs, both on the part of employers and injured employees, and reduce the costs to the employers by reducing the amount of disability that needs to be compensated. The point was to change the conception of the system from a closed, win/lose system where, if premiums are to go down, benefits must go down, to an open system where a win/win solution is possible with premium costs going down while injured workers enjoy an increase in the sum of benefits and wages as a result of less frequent and severe duration of disability.

It was believed that the amount of political warfare that had been engaged in over the past several years over the problems in the system was actually contributing to the problem by exaggerating the perception of employers and employees of the system as an adversary system where employees and employers are necessarily at odds. Successful workers' compensation administrators insisted on the necessity of good employer-employee relationships and a mutual sense of trust in order to accomplish effective rehabiliation and return-to-work programs, particularly in the case of serious or difficult injuries such as back conditions.

Although major reform legislation was adopted by the legislature[7] incorporating the concepts recommended by the administration, a major part of that political strategy, that of getting business-labor agreement in support of the changes, was a failure, at least in part. The state's major labor organization actively opposed the legislation, at least its key provision, and few other labor organizations were willing to come forward in any public way to support the legislation. At first, however, prospects seemed much better. The initial strategy was begun by seeking out a wide variety of key leaders among business, labor, insurance, legal, medical, and rehabilitation groups and trying to sell the concept of a reorganization of the system based on good activist management like that of Wisconsin and a redesign of the benefit structure which would maintain overall benefit levels but provide increased incentives for employers to provide return-to-work programs and for employees to accept jobs offered. The relatively good credibility of the recent studies of workers' compensation and the implications of their analyses of the nature of the Minnesota problem were particularly helpful in gaining business and insurance support for the administration strategy.

The studies were viewed with a great deal more suspicion by organized labor, but preliminary agreement with the strategy of developing a business-labor compromise proposal was obtained from that quarter as well. Various service groups involved in workers' compensation, i.e., defense attorneys, rehabilitation consultants, medical personnel, and so on, were particularly receptive to the approach suggested by the administration with the exception of the Trial Lawyers Association, which viewed proposed changes in benefit structure with suspicion.

In an attempt to follow the Wisconsin model, the Workers' Compensation Advisory Council was reactivated and populated with appointments representing key leaders from business, labor and insurance groups as well as a sprinkling of expertise from the medical and legal communities. This group spent many hours working over detailed proposals to reform and improve administration, introduce nonadversarial means of resolving disputes and provide more objective means for establishing compensation for permanent partial disabilities. This commission was not, however, able to face in any constructive way the very difficult benefit issues that most students of workers' compensation felt needed to be addressed in order to accomplish a major reform of the system. The public nature of the advisory council forum, combined with the high degree of hostility and mistrust engendered by recent bitter political battles, seemed to make it impossible for the Advisory Council to come to grips with these issues.

As a result, talks were opened between a key spokesman for business and a key spokesman for labor in an attempt to put together a compromise package on the benefit issues that would make the rest of the compromise being worked on by the Advisory Council acceptable to both sides. These talks proceeded productively for some time but eventually broke down over a fundamental quandry in the political positions of the two groups. Labor felt obliged to resist any benefit cuts but was prepared to make moderate compromises if it could accomplish in the same legislation a state compensation insurance fund. Business was vigorously opposed to the idea of a state compensation insurance fund but was willing to consider it if substantial benefit reform was offered. Labor was unable to face substantial benefit cuts even in return for a state compensation insurance fund.

The solution proposed at that time by the administration was a recommendation of the Citizens League study designed to be a major reform in the benefit structure without being a major cut in benefit levels. This so-called two-tiered benefit system (an attempt at a synthesis of the strong points of wage loss compensation for permanent partial disability and more traditional schedule-type systems) was first considered of academic interest only. It became clear, however, that it provided the only possible solution to the fundamental political problem of business demanding major benefit change and labor unable to agree to major benefit cuts. Talks proceeded on the details of the two-tiered benefit structure system for some time, with most parties hopeful that some solution could be reached. At one point most people believed an agreement over the whole package had been reached, but when the parties sat down the next morning to ratify the agreement, it turned out that labor was not prepared to accept the two-tiered system without a further substantial benefit increase which was clearly unacceptable to the administration as well as to business and insurance interests.

It was widely believed at that time that vigorous opposition to the two-tiered benefit structure system from the plaintiffs' attorneys was instrumental in convincing labor of the inadvisability of supporting that concept. Although invited by the administration to participate in the development of the two-tiered system, plaintiffs' attorneys refused and instead fought it vigorously, mainly by lobbying key leaders in organized labor. Although AFL-CIO leaders denied being influenced by attorney pressure, it was well known that the key labor spokesman had been embarrassed two years earlier when trial lawyers used their wide influence in local unions to attack a business-labor compromise bill.

Even without labor support, business groups approached the administration and offered to support the administration's compromise package as a balanced approach to solving the workers' compensation problem. The governor and significant majorities in both houses in Minnesota are Democrats, and it was believed that even though a compromise could not be reached with labor, any legislation would have to be perceived as moderate and friendly to labor in order to have a chance at passage.

As a matter of fact, the administration-sponsored legislation with the support of business and insurance groups as well as the medical association and other support organizations, not only passed both houses by overwhelming votes, but actually received a majority of the Democratic votes in each house as well as all of the Republican votes. Some smaller union groups expressed public and private support for the so-called compromise legislation, including the most radical steelworkers' union on the Minnesota Iron Range, home territory of Governor Perpich.

Although labor vigorously opposed the two-tiered system for compensating permanent partial disability, they did continue to support the rest of the bill, including some modest benefit reductions, and the state compensation insurance fund which passed in separate legislation. Although the battle to pass the legislation was extremely hard-fought and at times quite bitter, there seemed to be a general agreement to avoid tampering with the noncontroversial sections of the bill as long as the political dispute could be limited to the two-tiered system. As a result, the product of the Workers' Compensation Advisory Council, even though not formally agreed on by them, was maintained essentially intact.

## The Two-Tiered System for Compensating Permanent Partial Disability

The most controversial and unusual aspect of the legislation finally passed in Minnesota was the new two-tiered system for compensating permanent partial disability which developed out of the Citizens League study of workers' compensation completed in 1982. The system attempts to be a synthesis of the advantages of wage loss systems and traditional schedule systems for compensating permanent partial disability.

In my view, a view ultimately shared by the Citizens League study committee which I chaired, the most compelling arguments for wage loss systems are the equity arguments raised against schedule systems. Studies of the amount of workers' compensation benefits paid as compared to actual economic losses in wages and medical costs by various workers in certain states have clearly shown that some employees are compensated much more than their actual economic loss while others are compensated much less. This inequity tends to be consistent in that those employees with the most serious injuries and the highest economic losses are paradoxically those who are most undercompensated by typical schedule systems.

On the other hand, rehabilitation experts argue that systems for compensating disability of any sort tend to contribute to the degree of disability by reducing the normal economic incentives for return to work. Schedule systems seem to offer an advantage over wage loss systems in that they discontinue the dependency relationship between the worker and the insurance company at the earliest possible opportunity. That minimizes the effect of compensation on functional overlay and incentives for return to work. Schedule systems also minimize the necessity for insurance companies to maintain relatively large numbers of open reserves against the potential of future wage loss, a very expensive proposition in the current insurance rating system.

Wage loss systems are also touted as reducing litigation by eliminating the attraction of large lump-sum payments to litigants and their attorneys.

These claims have not been established in practice as yet. It is still too early to assess the impact of wage loss on Florida's litigation problem. Michigan and Pennsylvania, two states which have had wage loss systems for some time, have not enjoyed low litigation rates although the litigation problems in those states may be, in part, the result of socio-economic factors. Litigation rates tend to be higher in more heavily industrialized, urbanized areas as compared to socially conservative rural areas.[8] Nevertheless, wage loss has not resulted in low litigation rates in those states. It can be argued that the ongoing dependency relationship between the insurance company and the claimant inherent in the wage loss system creates an endless source of reasons for litigation. If the only way of preventing that litigation is by not providing adequate money to support fees for the claimant to hire expert help, that is not a fair way to control litigation.

The state that has the best success at avoiding litigation, given its socio-economic makeup, is probably the State of Wisconsin, with a relatively high degree of industrialization and a startlingly low litigation rate.[9] The Wisconsin system benefits from a very detailed set of disability schedules which avoid litigation over degree of disability by minimizing the grounds for dispute over degree of disability.

The Minnesota two-tiered system for compensating permanent partial disability attempts to resolve the equity issues raised against scheduled systems by wage loss supporters. John Burton, for example, has shown that in Wisconsin, Alabama and Florida (before wage loss), with systems similar in structure to permanent partial disability systems, workers with more serious injuries tend to have their actual economic losses less well-compensated than those with less serious injuries. The new Minnesota system attempts to correct this equity problem by distinguishing between minor and serious injuries, and by distinguishing between those workers who are able to return to employment quickly and easily and those who are unable to do so.

Litigation control is accomplished through authority of the Department of Labor and Industry to develop detailed disability schedules to eliminate causes for dispute. Testimony from the medical community indicates that disputes over degree of disability tend not to reflect disputes over diagnoses but rather differences in medical opinions over what disability results from a given medical condition. The Medical Association is providing substantial support to the Department in developing schedules which will list specific conditions (e.g., laminectomy with good result—15 percent) by the effective date of the Act—January 1, 1984.

The system provides better equity for more serious injuries through a sliding scale of compensation for degree of disability (see appendix 1). As a result, 60 percent disability of the body pays substantially more than four times as much as 15 percent of the body.

In addition, the employer is liable for a lower permanent partial disability award if he makes the employee a suitable job offer within 90 days after the date of maximum medical improvement. The job offered need not be the employee's old job, but it must meet rehabilitation standards which include such aspects as permanency, benefits, salary levels and so on. The basic rehabilitation test is that the new job help the employee to recover an economic status as close as possible to the one that he enjoyed before the accident. Temporary partial disability payments to make up partial wage loss are available indefinitely. The job offered need not be with the old employer. Any job found by the employee during a 90-day period after maximum medical improvement qualifies.

If the job offer is made within the prescribed time period, the employee is entitled to an impairment award which is somewhat smaller than the current permanent partial disability award. The impairment award is based on a dollar amount for the whole person, with no difference resulting from differences in wage levels. This provides the same compensation for a rich person's hand as a poor person's hand if each is able to return to his old job or another job like it.

If the job offer is not made during the prescribed time period, the employee is entitled to a substantially larger economic recovery benefit which is based on the degree of disability and his wage at the time of the injury. That benefit vests on the expiration of the 90-day period and the employee is entitled to it regardless of whether he finds a job or not in the future.

On the other hand, either the impairment or the economic recovery benefit is paid to the employee as a lump sum only when he goes to work (the impairment benefit when he accepts the job offer, the economic recovery benefit when he finds a job on his own). If the employee does not choose to go to work for whatever reason, he begins receiving either award as a weekly benefit replacing temporary total disability payments.

Under the old Minnesota system, temporary total disability benefits continue for an unlimited period of time as long as a worker suffers disability as a result of his injury. This gives Minnesota, in effect, a wage loss system in addition to a fairly generous schedule system. Cost control is only accomplished by insurers working with employees to make sure that they continue to make a diligent effort to seek work. Lack of cooperation with a rehabilitation plan or lack of a diligent effort to seek work is grounds for termination, but suits over termination of benefits are frequently lost by employers and insurers. This system results in a constant train of cutoffs followed by litigation followed by reinstatement followed by cutoffs, making effective rehabilitation unlikely and contributing to the relatively high incidence of permanent total disability and the relatively long duration of temporary total disability in Minnesota as compared to Wisconsin.

The new two-tiered system replaces the stick of the employer's threats to cut off benefits with the economic incentive of lump-sum payment when the employee finds a job on his own. Rehabilitation services are available to the employee during that time, but the insurance company no longer has any substantial economic interest in forcing the employee to look for work. The employee's incentive to look for work is the same as the incentive which makes most of us work—simple financial gain.

The details of the Minnesota two-tiered benefit system are discussed in more detail in the Appendices.

## Other Major Provisions in Minnesota Legislation

### Medical Monitoring System

To get control of medical costs and medical utilization under the workers' compensation system in Minnesota, a substantial system of medical monitoring has been established based on peer review systems in use in other sectors.

A panel consisting of medical providers, employer representatives, employee representatives, and the general public will review charges for medical services as well as utilization of those services, and relative quality of clinical results, and establish standards which will serve as maximums for what insurance companies will be required to reimburse. Providers who are found to be abusing the system, either by overcharging or overtreating without good clinical results, will be disqualified from reimbursement by the system.

Medical testimony over degree of disability in litigated cases will be submitted by report only unless the workers' compensation judge orders the doctor to testify in court. Standardized medical report forms will be designed which provide the information necessary to determine where the injury fits in the disability schedules to reduce the need for substantial judgmental issues to be considered in court.

## Mandatory Rehabilitation in Minnesota

Under the new law, insurers will be required to do an assessment of whether there is a need for rehabilitation after 60 days of lost time in the case of most injuries and 30 days of lost time in the case of back injuries. A study of the rehabilitation system had shown that a number of fairly serious back cases were going one to two years before being referred to rehabilitation as a result of conservative treatment practices by inexperienced providers. Any employee who is not able to return to his former job will be entitled to rehabilitation services. When there is a dispute over primary liability, rehabilitation services will be provided by the state and charged to the insurer if primary liability is established.

## Nonadversarial Methods of Resolving Disputes

Substantial increases in staffing of the Department of Labor and Industry patterned after staffing levels in Wisconsin will provide much more extensive assistance to injured employees, employers and claims adjusters who require help under the new law. Department employees, both compensation specialists and rehabilitation specialists, will be trained in mediation techniques so that they can help to resolve disputes. Departmental attorneys who had filed claims petitions against employers on behalf of employees will be phased out over a period of years and replaced with nonadversarial support for injured workers. Employees whose disputes with insurance companies cannot be resolved by normal departmental procedures will be referred to a new full-time mediation department which will attempt to accomplish settlement. Settlement judges will examine claim petitions submitted for cases where settlement out of court seems probable, and will require the parties to come in to settlement conferences even before the normal pre-trial conferences. The major emphasis upon nonadversarial methods of resolving litigation is intended not only to avoid the cost associated with litigation but also to avoid the bitterness engendered by adversarial methods and their resulting detrimental effects on rehabilitation and return-to-work programs.

## Deregulation of Workers' Compensation Insurance Rates

Effective January 1, 1984, there will be no further state regulation of workers' compensation rates. The new system is essentially a "file and use system" similar to the regulation system for other lines of insurance in Minnesota. This deregulation is a result of a phased-in process that began two years ago as a result of 1981 legislation. The Workers' Compensation Rating Association (Minnesota's industry-supported rating bureau) will not be permitted to publish proposed rates. Normal anti-trust laws will apply to the insurance industry in spite of federal exemptions, and information available from the Rating Association will be limited to pure premium determinations. Competition between insurance companies under partial deregulation has already resulted in substantial discounts to more attractive employers. It is widely believed that the increased competition resulting from deregulation will encourage insurers to experiment in rehabilitation and return-to-work programs, as well as to reward those employers who are successful with such programs with lower premiums.

There is considerable evidence that these effects are present already. Testimony from employers to legislative committees in 1983 indicated that a wide variety of discount plans are being offered by insurers in an attempt to gain market share. Over 20 insurers have filed plans offering discounts of from 5 to 20 percent off manual rates, and more are expected to do so.

## Conclusion

There is no question that it is easier politically for organized labor to oppose reforms in workers' compensation systems designed to control costs. Workers' compensation is a complicated technical area, and most laymen assume that costs and premiums are directly linked. Although that is not necessarily true, as the experience in Wisconsin has clearly shown, it is certainly easier for labor to oppose those changes which offer promise of reducing costs. Such opposition has the side effect of increasing the credibility of the legislation with businessmen who also assume that benefits must be cut in order to save premium dollars.

In spite of the relatively acrimonious political debate over workers' compensation in Minnesota, there is some reason to believe that the initial strategy of developing a rapprochement between business and labor may still be possible. The Workers' Compensation Advisory Council is being consulted extensively by the department in the development of administrative rules to implement the new act, and there is some reason to hope that the substantial improvements in service to injured workers may win friends in organized labor as the act becomes effective.

The two-tiered system may be of some interest to students of workers' compensation in other states as an attempt to meet the equity issues so correctly raised by wage loss proponents as well as providing a system which minimizes its contribution to the total disability to be compensated.

Even if the theory of the two-tiered system is sound, it may not work unless case law decisions are consistent with the philosophy of the new system. Having noticed that previous Supreme Court decisions relied heavily on a law review article by Senate Counsel after the passage of the major 1979 legislation, the Department of Labor and Industry is preparing a detailed law review article with a wide variety of hypothetical cases in order to provide guidance both for practitioners in the field as well as (we hope) for judges faced with difficult precedent-setting decisions.[10]

It is hoped that the new system will offer a way that the state can provide a generous system of compensation for injured workers at a cost which permits its employers to be sufficiently competitive with their counterparts in other states, that they can maintain the jobs for those employees, both before and after they have been injured.

**NOTES**

1. Report of the Minnesota Workers' Compensation Study Commission, February 1979.

2. *Workers' Compensation in Minnesota: An Analysis with Recommendations,* Minnesota Insurance Division, January 1982.

3. *Workers' Compensation Reform: Get the Employees Back on the Job,* Citizens League, December 15, 1982.

4. Workers' Compensation in Minnesota, pp. 45-49.

5. Report of the Minnesota Study.

6. Workers' Compensation Reform, pp. 11-15, 22-23.

7. Laws, Minnesota, 1983, Chapter 290.

8. Report of the Minnesota Study, pp. 199-212.

9. Ibid.

10. *William Mitchell Law Review,* Vol. 6, No. 3-1980 Mack v. City of Minneapolis, 35 W.C.D. 732. In re: matter David Mack, Finance and Commerce 5/13/83.

# Appendix 1
# Overview of the 1983 Workers' Compensation Law
# H.F. No. 274*

This summary deals with the major provisions of Minnesota Laws 1983, Ch. *290,* the amendments to Minnesota's Workers' Compensation Law.

The 1983 amendments are intended to restructure and redistribute benefits, to improve the administration of the system, and to lower the workers' compensation costs of Minnesota employers. A schematic of events and benefits is presented in appendix 2.

## Permanent Partial Disability

Sections 44-64. Economic recovery compensation and impairment compensation replace permanent partial disability benefits and eliminate temporary total benefits after maximum medical improvement is reached. Whether impairment or economic recovery is payable for permanent partial disability depends on whether the employer makes a job offer meeting statutory criteria. Impairment compensation is paid if a job offer is made; the payment is a lump sum if the offer is accepted, and is weekly if the offer is rejected. Economic recovery compensation is paid weekly if no job offer is made. The total economic recovery compensation payable is intended to be greater than the lump-sum impairment compensation, creating an incentive for the employer to make a job offer. The new system does not become effective until the Commissioner of Labor and Industry has promulgated rules for establishing the percentage of loss of function to a body part. Greater detail is provided in the section-by-section analysis which follows.

Section 59. Economic recovery compensation for permanent partial disability is payable where no suitable job offer has been made within 90 days after the employee has reached maximum medical improvement or has completed an approved retraining program. Temporary total compensation cannot be paid concurrently with economic recovery compensation. Minn. Stat. § 176.101, subd. 3p.

Section 44. The amount of economic recovery compensation is 66⅔ percent of the weekly wage at the time of injury, subject to the statutory

---

*This summary was prepared by Joan Volz, vice president and general counsel, Workers' Compensation Reinsurance Association.

maximum. The number of weeks of compensation is determined by multiplying the percent of disability to the body as a whole by the number of weeks set forth in the new statutory schedule. The new schedule is presented in appendix 3. For example, a 25 percent disabiilty is multiplied by 600 weeks to give 150 weeks of compensation. A 100 percent disability is multiplied by 1,200 weeks, giving a maximum of 1,200 weeks of economic recovery compensation. The amendment does not become effective until the Commissioner of Labor and Industry has adopted rules scheduling the percent of disability to the body as a whole caused by the loss of particular members. Minn. Stat. § 176.101, subd. 3a.

Section 60. Economic recovery compensation is paid weekly. If an employee who is receiving economic recovery compensation returns to work for at least 30 days, remaining economic recovery benefits are paid in a lump sum. The periodic payments are not subject to the annual adjustment of Minn. Stat. § 176.645. Minn. Stat. § 176.101, subd. 3q.

Section 48, 49, 65. Impairment compensation for permanent partial disability is payable where a job offer meeting the statutory criteria has been made. Temporary total compensation cannot be paid concurrently with impairment compensation.

The job offer must be made within 90 days after the employee has reached maximum medical improvement or has completed a retraining program. The job offered must be within the employee's physical capabilities and must result in an economic status similar to that which the employee would have had without the disability.

The job offer may come from an employer other than the employer at the time of injury. If the job differs from the employee's old job, the offer must be in writing. The employee must act upon the job offer within 14 days. Minn. Stat. § 176.101, subd. 3e. The job offer may be made prior to reaching maximum medical improvement. Minn. Stat. § 176.101, subd. 3f. Whether a job offer meets the statutory criteria may be resolved in an administrative conference. Minn. Stat. § 176.101, subd. 3v.

Section 45. The amount of impairment compensation is determined by multiplying the percent of disability to the body as a whole by the statutorily scheduled amount. The new schedule for impairment compensation is listed in appendix 4. For example, a 25 percent disability is multiplied by $75,000, giving an impairment amount of $18,750. A 100 percent disability is multiplied by $400,000, making the maximum impairment compensation $400,000. As with economic recovery compensation, the impairment compensation provisions are not effective until rules have been adopted. Minn. Stat. § 176.101, subd. 3b.

Section 50. Impairment compensation is paid in a lump sum 30 days after the employee returns to work. Minn. Stat. § 176.101, subd. 3g.

Sections 47, 48, 59, 63. Temporary total compensation is payable until 90 days after reaching maximum medical improvement or ending an approved retraining program, whichever is later. It ceases when the employee returns to work. If there is no permanent partial disability, the employee receives 26 weeks of economic recovery compensation in the absence of a job offer. Minn. Stat. § 176.101, subds. 3d, 3e, 3p, 3t(b).

Sections 55-57. Refusal of a job offer affects the type and timing of benefit payments. Impairment compensation is paid weekly rather than in a lump sum, although a subsequent return to work entitles the employee to a lump-sum payment of the balance. Temporary total compensation ceases. The amount of the weekly impairment compensation is equal to the amount of temporary total compensation the employee was receiving. An employee who refuses a job offer but later works at a lower paying job cannot receive temporary partial compensation or rehabilitation. Minn. Stat. § 176.101, subds. 31-3n.

Section 58. Permanent total disability entitles the employee to both permanent total benefits and impairment compensation. The impairment compensation is paid at the same interval and amount as permanent total compensation. Impairment compensation ceases when the total amount to which the employee is entitled has been paid. As under current law, permanent total compensation under the new law is paid weekly and is subject to annual escalation and the social security offset. The weekly impairment compensation, however, cannot be escalated or offset by social security. Permanent total compensation cannot be offset by any impairment or economic recovery compensation the employee may have received. Economic recovery compensation ceases when an employee is determined to have permanent total disability. Minn. Stat. § 176.101, subd. 3o.

Sections 52, 54, 63. Monitoring period compensation is payable to an employee who accepts a job offer, returns to work, and is later laid off because of economic conditions. The layoff must occur prior to the expiration of the monitoring period, which begins to run upon the employee's return to work. The amount of weekly monitoring period compensation is equal to the amount of weekly temporary total benefits the employee was receiving. The compensation is paid during the balance of the monitoring period, or, if it is less, the monitoring period minus impairment compensation already paid. For this purpose, impairment compensation is converted to weeks by dividing it by the employee's compensation rate for temporary total disability. Minn. Stat. § 176.101, subds. 3i and 3t(a). Where the layoff is due to seasonal conditions, the employee may continue receiving temporary partial disability compensation and may, if eligible, also receive unemployment compensation. Minn. Stat. § 176.101, subd. 3k.

Sections 46, 62. The maximum impairment and economic recovery compensation payable cannot exceed the maximum payable for a disability to the body as a whole. After receiving maximum economic recovery or impairment compensation, an employee is entitled to further economic recovery or impairment compensation only if a greater permanent partial disability is sustained. Minn. Stat. § 176.101, subds. 3c and 3s.

Section 63. The maximum economic recovery compensation is at least 120 percent of the impairment compensation that would be received if impairment compensation were payable. Minn. Stat. § 176.101, subd. 3t.

# Appendix 2

## Summary of New Temporary Total, Permanent Partial, and Permanent Total Benefits

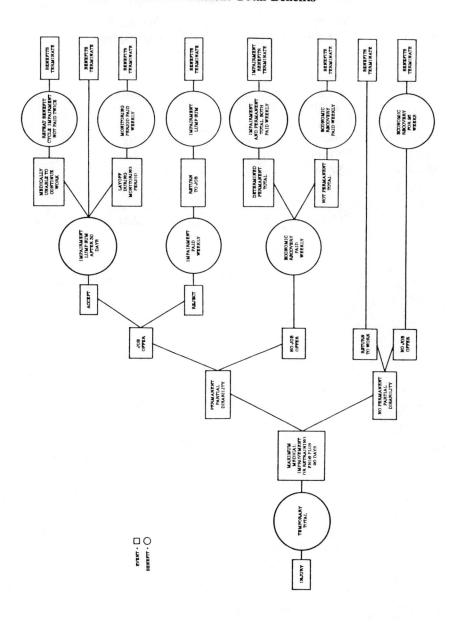

# Appendix 3
## Schedule for Economic Recovery Compensation

### Multiply Percent of Disability by Scheduled Weeks

| Percent of disability | Weeks of compensation |
|:---:|:---:|
| 0-25 | 600 |
| 26-30 | 640 |
| 31-35 | 680 |
| 36-40 | 720 |
| 41-45 | 760 |
| 46-50 | 800 |
| 51-55 | 880 |
| 56-60 | 960 |
| 61-65 | 1,040 |
| 66-70 | 1,120 |
| 71-100 | 1,200 |

# Appendix 4
# Schedule for Impairment Compensation

**Multiply Percent of Disability by Scheduled Amount**

| Percent of disability | Amount |
|:---:|:---:|
| 0-25 | $ 75,000 |
| 26-30 | 80,000 |
| 31-35 | 85,000 |
| 36-40 | 90,000 |
| 41-45 | 95,000 |
| 46-50 | 100,000 |
| 51-55 | 120,000 |
| 56-60 | 140,000 |
| 61-65 | 160,000 |
| 66-70 | 180,000 |
| 71-75 | 200,000 |
| 76-80 | 240,000 |
| 81-85 | 280,000 |
| 86-90 | 320,000 |
| 91-95 | 360,000 |
| 96-100 | 400,000 |

# 3

# The 1982 Changes in California

Alan Tebb

General Manager
California Workers' Compensation Institute

## Background

It is my pleasure to discuss the 1982 amendments to the California workers' compensation law. The planning committee has asked that I summarize those changes and describe why the law was amended, the short term results of the legislated changes, and the potential long-range consequences of that action.

It is inappropriate, however, to characterize the 1982 legislative changes in California as "reform," the central theme of this conference. There were changes in the California law—indeed, massive changes—but with minor exceptions, the 1982 amendments did little to make the California compensation program more equitable, effective, or efficient. Instead, my remarks might more properly be labeled, "The Political Realities of Workers' Compensation Reform," an object lesson in what happens when employees and employers abrogate their responsibility to participate in the establishment of public policy in the workers' compensation arena.

By way of background, the California law extends to about 600,000 employers employing 11 million covered workers. Compensable injuries approximate 1.3 million annually, of which 375,000 are "disabling," i.e., one or more days lost time, and of that latter number perhaps 70,000 work injuries result in permanent residual impairment. The state agency's role has been essentially passive, in large part limited to adjudication after a dispute has developed, and the bulk of its $30 million-plus budget pays for 120 referee teams resident in 23 offices throughout the state. Given this emphasis, litigation is pervasive in the California workers' compensation system, marked by a high degree of involvement by attorneys and forensic physicians.

California Workers' Compensation Institute research studies establish that the costs of workers' compensation litigation in California exceeded $350 million in 1981. That total includes attorneys' fees for employee and employer, expenses of medical testimony and other direct out-of-pocket costs incident to the litigation, but excludes benefits paid to workers. My purpose in mentioning this is to underscore the interests of other players when workers' compensation reform is considered, and the difficulty in making any changes that are perceived to affect these interests.

## The 1982 Amendments

The 1982 amendments to the California workers' compensation law were the first substantive changes in 10 years. There had been some procedural modifications during this period, but attempts at major revision were frustrated by the balance of power among the special interest groups. The practical effect was that organized labor's drive for higher benefits could be stalled by the employer lobby unless labor accepted the employers' demand for a *quid pro quo,* which labor was unwilling to do. Similarly, changes sought by the employer community were not possible without including a substantial benefit package, and the dominant employer groups thought the price too high. Both labor and management had veto power and exercised it.

The balance shifted in 1982, due more to the entry of some additional players, specifically, the trial bar, than any change in political power, and the result was enactment of a workers' compensation benefit-reform package. The most visible feature of the package is a sharp increase in benefits. Over a two-year period, benefit levels will rise $660 million, while costs to employers will increase by nearly $1 billion. That represents the largest benefit increase in California history, if not the largest benefit increase in the history of workers' compensation.

I have no particular problem with the size of the benefit increase, but I do have concerns with its distribution. More than 90 percent of the new benefit dollars will increase indemnity levels for permanent partial disability—the benefit sector most fraught with litigation and, accordingly, most fruitful for trial attorneys and forensic doctors—while leaving maximum weekly benefits for total disability, both temporary and permanent, woefully inadequate (i.e., less than 60 percent of the statewide average wage). The 1982 benefit increases magnify the maldistribution of California workers' compensation benefits, a maldistribution I feel confident in predicting will require wrenching change within the current decade.

The reform part of the package—the *quid pro quo* for the employer community—included enactment of a provision requiring factual issues in litigated claims to be determined by a preponderance of the evidence. Trial judges and the appellate courts over time had accepted the liberal construction imperative too literally in the view of many employer observers, and this change was an attempt to restore balance. The law still must be construed liberally, but the facts must be determined by a preponderance of evidence.

Second, the legislation provided a statute of limitations on the vocational rehabilitation benefit. In 1974 California became the first state to adopt mandatory vocational rehabilitation as part of its workers' compensation law. The 1974 enactment, however, was something less than a paragon of clarity, and there was a substantial question as to whether the benefit was open-ended or had to be exercised within a specific period of time after the injury. The benefit-reform package opted for certainty.

The most important of the reform elements was a buttressing of the exclusive remedy doctrine. A series of court decisions held that the employment relationship did not shield an employer from civil liability if the employee's injury was attributable to the employer's other "capacity," e.g., as a manufacturer. Thus, a California employee injured in the course of employment by a defective product produced by the employer was entitled to workers' compensation benefits and, additionally, could bring a civil action for damages against the employer as a manufacturer. The 1982 legislation overturned these holdings, restoring the reciprocal concessions of employees and employers to their original balance—and, according to one estimate, saving employers $1 billion in additional costs over the next five years.

That in general was the package. It resulted from the interplay of a number of factors:

- No significant benefit increases in 10 years;
- A series of adverse appellate decisions;
- The growing political influence of the trial bar;
- The decline in the legislative muscle of the employer community and, to a lesser degree, statewide labor;
- Sharp differences in the priorities of the principal players and an inability to resolve the differences.

It was an interesting exercise in pragmatic politics, albeit one which requires looking backward.

## The Politics of Workers' Compensation

In 1971, the dominant employer organization and the insurance industry were instrumental in negotiating a significant revision to the California workers' compensation system through an "agreed bill" that granted substantial benefit increases in exchange for major concessions by organized labor. Five years later, in 1976, another modest reform package was enacted, but this time the negotiating parties were limited to organized labor and the insurance industry. No employer group was actively involved in the effort—not because employers didn't have a stake, but mainly because of a collective inability to agree upon any pressing reforms in exchange for increased benefit levels.

What had happened in that five-year period? At the risk of oversimplifying, the major change was the end of involvement by chief executive officers and other senior management types representing employers. For whatever reason, responsibility for social insurance issues was transferred to middle level managers and, ultimately, the entire subject was left in the hands of the institutional employer organizations. At the same time employers who had been legislatively active (and their trade associations) lost their senior professional lobbyists to death and retirement and thus lost their input to legislative leaders.

Organized labor's role also underwent a change with the legislative emergence of local unions. Many of the locals relied heavily upon the advice of local compensation claimants' attorneys whose interests, vis-a-vis labor's, were not always consonant in workers' compensation issues. Statewide labor was still a force, but its positions were increasingly muted or neutralized by what local unions were telling legislators.

Some indication of the shifting in relative strength came in 1977 when the insurance industry secured passage of controversial legislation that altered the allocation of liability among multiple defendants in cumulative injury and occupational disease claims over the *combined* opposition of the employer community and organized labor. The key to its enactment may have been that the economic interests of the trial bar were unaffected.

By the 1980 session, the employer community had become inflexible. In theory, employers continued to adhere to the strategy of no benefit increases without commensurate reform. In reality, however, they had become entrenched around a policy of no change whatsoever. So the insurance industry and statewide labor, with the governor's office as marriage broker, began discussions leading to a major overhaul of the compensation system. The package included substantial benefit increases (totaling only about half the cost of the 1982 bill) in exchange for building more certainty and objectivity into the determination of permanent partial disability, and thereby sharply curtailed the system's dependence upon lawyers and forensic doctors. It was a game but unsuccessful effort because the trial bar, working through local union officials, was able to present the appearance of a divided labor camp; because employers were unwilling to pay higher benefits; and because of the unreconstructed egos of some of the parties.

Nevertheless, the pressure continued to build. The courts began to respond to benefit inadequacy through a series of decisions eroding the exclusivity of workers' compensation. During the 1981 legislative session, the employer and insurer lobby introduced a measure to restrict the courts' expanded definition of the "dual capacity" doctrine. It passed the Senate, but the Assembly Speaker would not permit its passage without a large increase in benefits, a price employers were unwilling to pay. In November, after the session recessed, the Supreme Court handed down its decision in *Bell vs. Industrial Vangas,* 30 Cal 3d 268, which transmuted dual capacity into double jeopardy for employers.

As the 1982 session opened, the real parties weren't talking. Organized labor refused to consider an amendment to the dual capacity issue "because that's not a comp issue." Employers were reluctant to negotiate with labor without dual capacity being considered, and were unwilling to negotiate directly with the trial bar because of the magnitude of the benefit increases being advanced. That left the insurance industry and the trial bar as the only players with an ostensible community of interest, so their discussions began.

Originally the insurer representatives functioned as surrogates for the employer groups, keeping them informed of developments while attempting to convince them of the need for movement, given the Assembly Speaker's commitment to pass a benefit bill—with or without other reforms. Over time, however, the insurer-employer relationship broke down because of a series of economic decisions made by the employer association:

- First, a decision not to support the permanent partial disability reforms proposed by the insurance industry (and bitterly resisted by the trial bar) because the expected savings couldn't be quantified. Throughout, the thinking seemed to be, "If benefits are increased by X million dollars, we need Y million back in reforms."

- Second, a decision to forego legislative repeal of the dual capacity doctrine and wait until the next session when the political climate might be more favorable, a wistful vision that never came to pass. This approach conflicted with the priorities of compensation insurers which felt, I think correctly, that the real reason for backing off was the high price tag associated with dual capacity repeal.

- And, finally, the employer trade associations were limited in the amount to be included in the benefit package. They couldn't make the ante. And in politics, as in poker, the rules dictate that when you fold your hand, you don't get any more cards.

With employers dropping out of the game, a series of amendments were drafted by the remaining principals, incorporated into an Assembly-passed bill in the Senate, and enacted into law within two weeks after surfacing.

## The Impact of the Amendments

The immediate results—good news or bad news, depending upon your perspective—include containment of the dual capacity doctrine and removal of a threat to the legal underpinnings of the workers' compensation system, a change that will result in significant savings in loss and legal costs. The limitation on the vocational rehabilitation benefit similarly will save some unnecessary expense and permit insurers and employers to close files. Binding the trier of fact to a preponderance of evidence test has the potential to make workers' compensation more professional by introducing a standard of judicial objectivity where one didn't exist before. And the upgrading of disability benefits may convince the civil courts that it isn't necessary to create legal fictions to accomplish substantial justice for injured workers.

On the other hand, California employers are faced with escalating costs, upwards of 30 percent, without any meaningful substantive change in the workers' compensation law. More litigation, fueled by higher benefit levels, can be expected. Minimum weekly benefits were adjusted dramatically and the result may be longer periods of disability for the low wage earner. Moreover, the higher benefits may signal a change in benefit utilization and an acceleration in the assertion of so-called "stress" claims once the economic recovery is achieved.

The long term consequences of the 1982 legislation are more difficult to divine. All I can do is speculate, but I believe there will be at least two observable effects—or noneffects, as the case may be.

- First, no real changes in the California workers' compensation system in the immediate future, despite the extant inequities, leakages and waste. Legislators have an excuse—"we dealt with comp last year"—and many find compensation legislation politically unattractive. Absent an agreed bill, comp is a "bad" vote for one or more of a legislator's constituencies. Legislators generally would prefer to avoid the issue unless they're pushed, and there's no one pushing them—which brings me to my second, equally dour projection.

- There will be no meaningful changes until the real stakeholders—organized labor and employers—initiate the movement.

Organized labor, in many instances, has permitted its role to be co-opted by attorneys. The complexities of workers' compensation are little understood by labor leaders, particularly at the local union level, and there is a tendency in what appears to be a highly legalistic system to yield to the "expert," that is, a lawyer. The interests of organized labor in workers' compensation legislation are not always consonant with the interests of claimants' attorneys, protestations of the latter to the contrary notwithstanding. Unfortunately, the dichotomy hasn't been recognized, much less acknowledged.

The other factor in the formula, the employer community, is at least as troubling. Today employers complain about being frozen out of the legislative negotiations, but the truth is that they voluntarily isolated themselves. Unless they demonstrate a willingness to participate in the political arena where the workers' compensation policy decisions are made, the legislative decisions will continue to be dictated by the scorekeepers and linesmen.

## Conclusion

Obviously, my remarks are pertinent only to California. I suggest, however, that the 1982 experience in California may have application to other jurisdictions, and the differences are more of degree than substance.

If there is a lesson, it is that workers' compensation is a statutory creature. Changes, no matter how well-reasoned and researched, cannot be accomplished in academe, by studies, or by the imprimatur of blue ribbon commissions. Real change requires *legislative* action in a *political* environment. Until that lesson is accepted, reform—that is, improvement—of the workers' compensation system cannot be realized.

# 4

# Two Rounds of Workers' Compensation Reform in Michigan

H. Allan Hunt
Manager of Research
W. E. Upjohn Institute
for Employment Research

By the mid-1970s Michigan's workers' compensation system for workers disabled by injuries or illnesses arising out of their employment was approaching a crisis.[1] Relative to neighboring states, Michigan's workers' compensation insurance rates had risen alarmingly after 1958 according to John Burton's employer cost statistics. Table 1 shows that from 1958 to 1975 workers' compensation insurance rates nearly tripled in Michigan, while they doubled in Illinois and Ohio and held relatively constant in Wisconsin and Indiana. Over this period Michigan's rates rose from 20 percent below average to 35 percent above average for the 28 states for which consistent data are available.[2]

Of course there was another reason to be considering reform in workers' compensation systems in the mid-70s. The *Report of the National Commission on State Workmen's Compensation Laws* was published in 1972. The appointment of that National Commission had reflected substantial congressional dissatisfaction with the status of state workers' compensation systems. The Commission, after due consideration, found that state laws generally did *not* provide adequate, prompt, or equitable systems for compensating disabled workers. It offered a set of 84 recommendations for the improvement of these systems; 19 of these were deemed so important as to be "Essential Recommendations." The National Commission urged that if the states had not complied with this restricted list by July 1, 1975, Congress should take steps to guarantee compliance.[3]

### Table 1
### Standardized Insurance Manual Rates for
### Workers' Compensation Insurance, East North Cental States
### 1958-1975[a]

| State | 1958 | 1962 | 1965 | 1972 | 1975 |
|-------|------|------|------|------|------|
| Illinois ........ | .514 | .609 | .624 | .657 | 1.002 |
| Indiana ....... | .410 | .398 | .430 | .385 | .417 |
| Michigan ...... | .450 | .694 | .715 | .914 | 1.238 |
| Ohio.......... | .627 | .813 | .820 | .885 | 1.109 |
| Wisconsin ..... | .523 | .556 | .603 | .505 | .581 |
| Region average[b] | .505 | .614 | .638 | .669 | .869 |
| 28-state average[c] | .571 | .630 | .676 | .692 | .914 |

SOURCE: John F. Burton, Jr., *Workers' Compensation Cost for Employers,* Research Report of the Interdepartmental Workers' Compensation Task Force, Vol. 3, U.S. Department of Labor, Employment Standards Administration, June 1979, table 12, p. 28.

a. For 45 selected insurance classes, weighted by U.S. payroll distribution. Entries represent the standardized percentage of payroll that would be charged for workers' compensation insurance coverage.

b. Unweighted.

c. Unweighted average for 28 states where NCCI data are available for each of the listed years.

This reform atmosphere was reflected in the appointment by William G. Milliken of a Governor's Workmen's Compensation Advisory Commission in 1974 to: (1) review the report of the National Commission and other federal initiatives in the occupational safety and health area;

(2) evaluate the adequacy of the Michigan system; and (3) "recommend legislation to alter or amend the existing laws to ensure a just, fair and equitable workmen's compensation program for Michigan."[4] Unfortunately, it did not prove to be a feasible assignment. The letter of transmittal from Dean St. Antoine, Chairman of the Governor's Advisory Commission, began with the following paragraph:

> It is with regret that I must inform you that your Workmen's Compensation Advisory Commission has been unable to reach agreement upon a comprehensive set of recommendations for the improvement of workers' compensation in Michigan. Every effort was made, but the obstacles were insurmountable.[5]

In essence, the report of the Commission consisted of a discussion of the issues, accompanied by recapitulations of the positions adopted by employer and employee representatives. The document does not suggest a "near miss" on negotiating workers' compensation reform; the parties were far apart on issues ranging from the definition of disability to the statute of limitations.

After this failure to negotiate reform in face-to-face confrontations on the Governor's Advisory Commission, efforts to forge a labor/management compromise on workers' compensation reform continued in the legislature. The most notable of these was Senate Bill 1285, introduced in December 1977 after extensive private discussions. This bipartisan proposal made a broad attack on alleged abuses of workers' compensation as well as altering the benefit formula to reflect after-tax earnings and instituting a retrospective inflation adjustment plan. However, the compromise coalition eventually collapsed when the Senate Labor Committee began amending the package, and no legislation was enacted. As will be seen later, this bill contained many of the elements of the eventual reforms enacted in 1980.[6]

Assessing the situation as it existed in 1978, a number of observations can be made. First, the cost of workers' compensation in Michigan was very high. According to Professor Burton's results displayed in table 2, Michigan ranked 3rd highest nationally in standardized workers' compensation insurance rates for manufacturing employers, more than 80 percent above the average figure for other states. For a group of general employers (table 3), Michigan ranked 7th highest, 44 percent above average.[7]

Manual rates are sometimes viewed with suspicion in Michigan because of the large proportion of self-insureds in the state. In recent years, approximately 40 percent of indemnity payments have been made by self-insured employers. For that reason, it is also valuable to look at total benefit payments in the workers' compensation programs.

Table 4 shows that according to data published by Daniel Price of the Social Security Administration on actual benefits paid by all employers in the various states, Michigan ranked 12th in benefit cost relative to payroll, 21 percent above the average for the nation as a whole.[8] The cost of workers' compensation in Michigan was undeniably high.

Ironically, Michigan's benefit schedule in 1978 was quite low. In that year, the maximum benefit available to Michigan claimants (if their earnings and number of dependents were sufficient to warrant it) was $171 a week. As shown in table 5, this maximum benefit ranked 28th highest among the states, i.e., lower than the median. When the maximum benefit is expressed as a proportion of each state's average weekly wage, Michigan actually ranked even lower, 39th in the nation.[9] Results from the Michigan Closed Case Survey (an Upjohn Institute data base of 2,200 Michigan workers' compensation cases closed in 1978) confirm these figures on income replacement levels in Michigan's system. The average weekly payment case in 1978 received 58 percent of weekly earnings, not the nominal 67 percent called for in the statute.[10] Thus it is also undeniable that benefit levels in Michigan, at least as measured by weekly payments, were low.

Table 2
Adjusted Manual Rates (per $100 of payroll)
25 Types of Manufacturing Employers-1978

| State | Rank | Adjusted manual rate ($) | Ratio to unweighted average |
|-------|------|--------------------------|-----------------------------|
| Alabama | 36 | 1.674 | 0.60 |
| Alaska | 20 | 2.857 | 1.03 |
| Arizona | 5 | 4.548 | 1.64 |
| Arkansas | 25 | 2.479 | 0.89 |
| California | 6 | 4.241 | 1.53 |
| Colorado | 23 | 2.590 | 0.93 |
| Connecticut | 21 | 2.816 | 1.02 |
| Delaware | 19 | 2.906 | 1.05 |
| District of Columbia | 1 | 6.612 | 2.39 |
| Florida | 4 | 4.701 | 1.70 |
| Georgia | 28 | 2.366 | 0.85 |
| Hawaii | 8 | 4.149 | 1.50 |
| Idaho | 30 | 2.307 | 0.83 |
| Illinois | 27 | 2.431 | 0.88 |
| Indiana | 47 | 0.910 | 0.33 |
| Iowa | 33 | 1.734 | 0.63 |
| Kansas | 35 | 1.690 | 0.61 |
| Kentucky | 17 | 3.064 | 1.11 |
| Louisiana | 13 | 3.302 | 1.19 |
| Maine | 18 | 2.929 | 1.06 |
| Maryland | 26 | 2.476 | 0.89 |
| Massachusetts | 15 | 3.226 | 1.16 |
| Michigan | 3 | 5.035 | 1.82 |
| Minnesota | 7 | 4.167 | 1.50 |
| Mississippi | 39 | 1.561 | 0.56 |

**Table 2 (continued)**

| State | Rank | Adjusted manual rate ($) | Ratio to unweighted average |
|---|---|---|---|
| Missouri | 41 | 1.452 | 0.52 |
| Montana | 31 | 2.280 | 0.82 |
| Nebraska | 45 | 1.290 | 0.47 |
| Nevada | – | – | – |
| New Hampshire | 29 | 2.364 | 0.85 |
| New Jersey | 12 | 3.484 | 1.26 |
| New Mexico | 16 | 3.138 | 1.13 |
| New York | 9 | 3.836 | 1.38 |
| North Carolina | 46 | 1.077 | 0.39 |
| North Dakota | – | – | – |
| Ohio | 22 | 2.697 | 0.97 |
| Oklahoma | 11 | 3.542 | 1.28 |
| Oregon | 2 | 6.430 | 2.32 |
| Pennsylvania | 24 | 2.563 | 0.92 |
| Rhode Island | 14 | 3.262 | 1.18 |
| South Carolina | 34 | 1.717 | 0.62 |
| South Dakota | 42 | 1.414 | 0.51 |
| Tennessee | 32 | 1.918 | 0.69 |
| Texas | 10 | 3.557 | 1.28 |
| Utah | 37 | 1.640 | 0.59 |
| Vermont | 38 | 1.637 | 0.59 |
| Virginia | 43 | 1.349 | 0.49 |
| Washington | – | – | – |
| West Virginia | 44 | 1.313 | 0.47 |
| Wisconsin | 40 | 1.519 | 0.55 |
| Wyoming | – | – | – |
| Unweighted average | | 2.771 | |

SOURCE: Calculated from Martin W. Elson and John F. Burton, Jr., "Workers' Compensation Insurance: Recent Trends in Employer Costs," *Monthly Labor Review,* March 1981, table 1.

## Table 3
### Adjusted Manual Rates (per $100 of payroll)
### 79 Types of Employers-1978

| State | Rank | Adjusted manual rate ($) | Ratio to unweighted average |
|---|---|---|---|
| Alabama | 35 | 1.062 | 0.62 |
| Alaska | 11 | 2.070 | 1.20 |
| Arizona | 4 | 3.023 | 1.75 |
| Arkansas | 25 | 1.560 | 0.90 |
| California | 5 | 2.655 | 1.54 |
| Colorado | 28 | 1.486 | 0.86 |
| Connecticut | 19 | 1.755 | 1.02 |
| Delaware | – | – | – |
| District of Columbia | 1 | 4.181 | 2.42 |
| Florida | 3 | 3.086 | 1.79 |
| Georgia | 29 | 1.340 | 0.78 |
| Hawaii | 6 | 2.650 | 1.53 |
| Idaho | 24 | 1.608 | 0.93 |
| Illinois | 22 | 1.649 | 0.96 |
| Indiana | 44 | 0.585 | 0.34 |
| Iowa | 30 | 1.286 | 0.74 |
| Kansas | 34 | 1.064 | 0.62 |
| Kentucky | 16 | 1.816 | 1.05 |
| Louisiana | 13 | 1.934 | 1.12 |
| Maine | 21 | 1.671 | 0.97 |
| Maryland | 26 | 1.526 | 0.88 |
| Massachusetts | 17 | 1.776 | 1.03 |
| Michigan | 7 | 2.493 | 1.44 |
| Minnesota | 8 | 2.296 | 1.33 |
| Mississippi | 32 | 1.096 | 0.63 |
| Missouri | 41 | 0.932 | 0.54 |
| Montana | 20 | 1.692 | 0.98 |
| Nebraska | 42 | 0.834 | 0.48 |
| Nevada | – | – | – |
| New Hampshire | 27 | 1.517 | 0.88 |

## Table 3 (continued)

| State | Rank | Adjusted manual rate ($) | Ratio to unweighted average |
|-------|------|--------------------------|-----------------------------|
| New Jersey | 12 | 1.983 | 1.15 |
| New Mexico | 18 | 1.775 | 1.03 |
| New York | 10 | 2.164 | 1.25 |
| North Carolina | 43 | 0.680 | 0.39 |
| North Dakota | – | – | – |
| Ohio | 15 | 1.839 | 1.07 |
| Oklahoma | 14 | 1.880 | 1.09 |
| Oregon | 2 | 3.772 | 2.18 |
| Pennsylvania | – | – | – |
| Rhode Island | 23 | 1.641 | 0.95 |
| South Carolina | 36 | 1.055 | 0.61 |
| South Dakota | 39 | 1.002 | 0.58 |
| Tennessee | 31 | 1.177 | 0.68 |
| Texas | 9 | 2.220 | 1.29 |
| Utah | 33 | 1.083 | 0.63 |
| Vermont | 38 | 1.039 | 0.60 |
| Virginia | 37 | 1.052 | 0.61 |
| Washington | – | – | – |
| West Virginia | – | – | – |
| Wisconsin | 40 | 0.963 | 0.56 |
| Wyoming | – | – | – |
| Unweighted average | | 1.727 | |

SOURCE: Calculated from Martin W. Elson and John F. Burton, Jr., "Workers' Compensation Insurance: Recent Trends in Employer Costs," *Monthly Labor Review,* March 1981, table 1.

Table 4
Workers' Compensation Benefit Costs by State

| State | 1978 workers' compensation payments[1] ($1,000) | 1978 UI wage and salary payments[2] ($1,000) | Absolute cost | Rank | Cost relative to U.S. average |
|---|---|---|---|---|---|
| Alabama | $84,624 | $10,879,577 | .0078 | 31 | 0.80 |
| Alaska | 56,924 | 2,305,023 | .0247 | 1 | 2.52 |
| Arizona | 87,162 | 7,818,303 | .0111 | 19 | 1.13 |
| Arkansas | 56,283 | 5,744,458 | .0098 | 23 | 1.00 |
| California | 1,246,813 | 93,891,538 | .0133 | 10 | 1.36 |
| Colorado | 73,789 | 10,389,967 | .0071 | 37 | 0.72 |
| Connecticut | 89,033 | 13,776,612 | .0065 | 42 | 0.66 |
| Delaware | 16,379 | 2,557,399 | .0064 | 44 | 0.65 |
| District of Columbia | 51,138 | 3,768,672 | .0136 | 9 | 1.39 |
| Florida | 307,868 | 26,572,254 | .0116 | 14 | 1.18 |
| Georgia | 129,879 | 17,378,132 | .0075 | 32 | 0.77 |
| Hawaii | 39,710 | 3,087,630 | .0129 | 11 | 1.32 |
| Idaho | 29,873 | 2,607,410 | .0115 | 15 | 1.17 |
| Illinois | 490,010 | 53,390,139 | .0092 | 26 | 0.94 |
| Indiana | 89,708 | 22,428,476 | .0040 | 51 | 0.41 |
| Iowa | 71,457 | 9,578,298 | .0075 | 33 | 0.77 |
| Kansas | 56,210 | 7,511,565 | .0075 | 34 | 0.77 |

Table 4 (continued)

| State | 1978 workers' compensation payments[1] ($1,000) | 1978 UI wage and salary payments[2] ($1,000) | Absolute cost | Rank | Cost relative to U.S. average |
|---|---|---|---|---|---|
| Kentucky | 102,594 | 10,392,526 | .0099 | 22 | 1.01 |
| Louisiana | 198,838 | 13,786,265 | .0144 | 8 | 1.47 |
| Maine | 44,494 | 2,906,767 | .0153 | 4 | 1.56 |
| Maryland | 133,186 | 13,222,553 | .0101 | 21 | 1.03 |
| Massachusetts | 191,494 | 23,051,196 | .0083 | 29 | 0.85 |
| Michigan | 496,987 | 41,928,554 | .0119 | 12 | 1.21 |
| Minnesota | 173,523 | 15,112,317 | .0115 | 16 | 1.17 |
| Mississippi | 42,074 | 5,902,652 | .0071 | 38 | 0.72 |
| Missouri | 92,170 | 18,005,281 | .0051 | 49 | 0.52 |
| Montana | 29,403 | 1,992,955 | .0148 | 6 | 1.51 |
| Nebraska | 28,129 | 4,570,370 | .0062 | 45 | 0.63 |
| Nevada | 50,379 | 3,478,725 | .0145 | 7 | 1.48 |
| New Hampshire | 30,914 | 2,885,609 | .0107 | 20 | 1.09 |
| New Jersey | 268,441 | 30,298,748 | .0089 | 28 | 0.91 |
| New Mexico | 36,638 | 3,226,503 | .0114 | 17 | 1.16 |
| New York | 496,606 | 71,151,726 | .0070 | 40 | 0.71 |
| North Carolina | 93,668 | 18,358,568 | .0051 | 50 | 0.52 |
| North Dakota | 12,856 | 1,601,984 | .0080 | 30 | 0.82 |

| | | | | | |
|---|---|---|---|---|---|
| Ohio | 531,518 | 45,356,196 | .0117 | 13 | 1.19 |
| Oklahoma | 82,865 | 8,859,462 | .0094 | 25 | 0.96 |
| Oregon | 224,398 | 9,290,901 | .0242 | 2 | 2.47 |
| Pennsylvania | 407,135 | 45,071,677 | .0090 | 27 | 0.92 |
| Rhode Island | 36,027 | 3,172,627 | .0114 | 18 | 1.16 |
| South Carolina | 52,192 | 8,799,377 | .0059 | 46 | 0.60 |
| South Dakota | 9,058 | 1,528,375 | .0059 | 47 | 0.60 |
| Tennessee | 95,890 | 14,723,793 | .0065 | 43 | 0.66 |
| Texas | 506,255 | 51,710,551 | .0098 | 24 | 1.00 |
| Utah | 28,394 | 4,057,701 | .0070 | 41 | 0.71 |
| Vermont | 10,446 | 1,434,307 | .0073 | 35 | 0.74 |
| Virginia | 119,615 | 16,412,456 | .0073 | 36 | 0.74 |
| Washington | 224,770 | 14,906,610 | .0151 | 5 | 1.54 |
| West Virginia | 125,599 | 6,413,352 | .0196 | 3 | 2.00 |
| Wisconsin | 123,333 | 17,427,533 | .0071 | 39 | 0.72 |
| Wyoming | 9,603 | 1,777,748 | .0054 | 48 | 0.55 |
| Total | $8,086,352 | $826,501,418 | .0098 | | |

SOURCES:
1. Daniel N. Price, "Workers' Compensation: Coverage, Benefits, and Costs, 1979," *Social Security Bulletin*, September 1981, Vol. 44, No. 9, table 2.

2. Unemployment Insurance Program Letter No. 41-80, *Handbook of Unemployment Insurance Financial Data, 1978, Taxable*, p. 1, U.S. Department of Labor, Employment and Training Administration.

Table 5
Maximum Weekly Benefit for Temporary Total Disability-1978

| State | Rank | Maximum weekly benefit[1] | UI average weekly wage[2] | Maximum weekly benefit ratio to UI average weekly wage |
|---|---|---|---|---|
| Alabama | 40 | $128.00 | $208.10 | 0.62 |
| Alaska | 1 | 607.85 | 394.53 | 1.54 |
| Arizona | 34 | 153.85 | 218.43 | 0.70 |
| Arkansas | 51 | 87.50 | 186.53 | 0.47 |
| California | 33 | 154.00 | 243.15 | 0.63 |
| Colorado | 25 | 173.60 | 226.99 | 0.76 |
| Connecticut | 36 | 147.00 | 243.61 | 0.60 |
| Delaware | 32 | 154.50 | 257.87 | 0.60 |
| District of Columbia | 2 | 367.22 | 264.82 | 1.39 |
| Florida | 41 | 126.00 | 199.41 | 0.63 |
| Georgia | 46 | 110.00 | 209.22 | 0.53 |
| Hawaii | 16 | 189.00 | 208.00 | 0.91 |
| Idaho | 47 | 109.80 | 206.25 | 0.53 |
| Illinois | 3 | 321.50 | 259.54 | 1.24 |
| Indiana | 43 | 120.00 | 242.65 | 0.49 |
| Iowa | 4 | 265.00 | 215.94 | 1.23 |
| Kansas | 39 | 129.06 | 211.27 | 0.61 |

| | | | | |
|---|---|---|---|---|
| Kentucky | 45 | 112.00 | 219.60 | 0.51 |
| Louisiana | 38 | 130.00 | 229.81 | 0.57 |
| Maine | 5 | 231.72 | 185.77 | 1.25 |
| Maryland | 12 | 202.00 | 224.14 | 0.90 |
| Massachusetts | 35 | 150.00 | 224.21 | 0.67 |
| Michigan | 28 | 171.00 | 288.96 | 0.59 |
| Minnesota | 14 | 197.00 | 226.97 | 0.87 |
| Mississippi | 49 | 91.00 | 182.91 | 0.50 |
| Missouri | 44 | 115.00 | 226.20 | 0.51 |
| Montana | 17 | 188.00 | 201.87 | 0.93 |
| Nebraska | 30 | 155.00 | 199.78 | 0.78 |
| Nevada | 10 | 212.02 | 227.34 | 0.93 |
| New Hampshire | 20 | 180.00 | 196.14 | 0.92 |
| New Jersey | 37 | 146.00 | 250.31 | 0.58 |
| New Mexico | 26 | 172.46 | 202.37 | 0.85 |
| New York | 21 | 180.00 | 259.47 | 0.69 |
| North Carolina | 29 | 168.00 | 192.30 | 0.87 |
| North Dakota | 22 | 180.00 | 200.70 | 0.90 |
| Ohio | 8 | 216.00 | 255.64 | 0.84 |
| Oklahoma | 42 | 121.00 | 219.25 | 0.55 |
| Oregon | 6 | 224.16 | 232.45 | 0.96 |
| Pennsylvania | 9 | 213.00 | 233.96 | 0.91 |
| Rhode Island | 23 | 176.00 | 194.55 | 0.90 |

## Table 5 (continued)

| State | Rank | Maximum weekly benefit[1] | UI average weekly wage[2] | Maximum weekly benefit ratio to UI average weekly wage |
|---|---|---|---|---|
| South Carolina | 27 | 172.00 | 192.01 | 0.90 |
| South Dakota | 31 | 155.00 | 175.99 | 0.88 |
| Tennessee | 48 | 100.00 | 201.23 | 0.50 |
| Texas | 50 | 91.00 | 230.93 | 0.39 |
| Utah | 15 | 197.00 | 211.85 | 0.93 |
| Vermont | 19 | 181.00 | 191.88 | 0.94 |
| Virginia | 18 | 187.00 | 205.76 | 0.91 |
| Washington | 24 | 175.30 | 251.49 | 0.70 |
| West Virginia | 7 | 224.00 | 243.84 | 0.92 |
| Wisconsin | 13 | 202.00 | 228.46 | 0.88 |
| Wyoming | 11 | 211.15 | 241.26 | 0.88 |

SOURCES:

1. U.S. Department of Labor, Employment Standards Administration, Division of State Workers' Compensation Standards, July 1978.

2. Unemployment Insurance Program Letter No. 41-80, *Handbook of Unemployment Insurance Financial Data, 1978, Taxable*, p. 1, U.S. Department of Labor, Employment and Training Administration.

Furthermore, since Michigan had experienced no major changes in statute while other states had been moving to implement some of the National Commission recommendations, Michigan's standing relative to those other states was steadily deteriorating. In 1972, when the average state compliance score with the 19 essential recommendations of the National Commission stood at 6.9, Michigan had complied with 11 of the 19, ranking 4th among the states. Table 6 shows that by 1978 the average compliance score had risen to 11.7 and Michigan, still with only 11, had fallen to a rank of 27th.[11]

By 1979, even those who might have preferred to do nothing rather than moving in the direction of reform along the lines of the National Commission recommendations were frustrated. There was no shortage of opinions as to what reforms were needed to cope with Michigan's problems.[12] What was missing was a spirit of compromise, or a feeling of sufficient urgency to overcome old adversarial attitudes and patterns.

When the Governor and the legislative leadership announced a joint Workers' Compensation Reform Task Force in May of 1979, it seemed that the lessons of the past would enable the Task Force to effectively negotiate around the shoals of previous failures and bring workers' compensation reform to reality. Unfortunately it was not to be. Agreement was reached on changes in the benefit formula and on maximums and minimums, but progress was ended when it could not be established whether the savings from coordination of benefits (which employers wanted) would truly offset the cost of inflation protection (which organized labor sought for employees). There were recriminations over the available data and accusations about the fairness of the analysis; more fundamentally there was insufficient sentiment for compromise, and neither side could impose its will on the other.

## Table 6
## Full Compliance Scores Based on the 19 Essential Recommendations
### January 1, 1972 through January 1, 1980

|  | 1972 | 1974 | 1976 | 1978 | 1980 |
|---|---|---|---|---|---|
| Mean score | 6.9 | 8.6 | 11.2 | 11.7 | 12.1 |
| Standard deviation | 3.07 | 3.03 | 2.96 | 2.42 | 2.40 |
| Alabama | 2.00 | 6.00 | 9.00 | 9.00 | 9.00 |
| Alaska | 5.50 | 5.50 | 14.00 | 14.00 | 14.00 |
| Arizona | 7.50 | 13.50 | 11.50 | 11.50 | 11.50 |
| Arkansas | 2.50 | 2.50 | 3.50 | 8.50 | 7.50 |
| California | 7.00 | 7.00 | 11.00 | 11.00 | 12.00 |
| Colorado | 10.00 | 11.00 | 12.00 | 12.50 | 16.00 |
| Connecticut | 10.50 | 10.50 | 10.50 | 10.75 | 13.75 |
| Delaware | 8.00 | 8.00 | 11.00 | 11.00 | 11.00 |
| District of Columbia | 11.00 | 14.00 | 14.00 | 14.00 | 14.00 |
| Florida | 5.00 | 6.00 | 6.50 | 6.50 | 10.50 |
| Georgia | 5.00 | 8.50 | 9.50 | 9.50 | 9.50 |
| Hawaii | 12.00 | 12.00 | 14.50 | 14.50 | 14.50 |
| Idaho | 9.00 | 9.00 | 9.00 | 9.00 | 9.00 |
| Illinois | 4.00 | 4.00 | 14.00 | 14.00 | 14.00 |
| Indiana | 7.00 | 7.00 | 11.00 | 11.00 | 11.00 |
| Iowa | 8.50 | 11.50 | 14.50 | 14.50 | 14.50 |
| Kansas | 1.00 | 1.00 | 9.50 | 9.50 | 9.50 |
| Kentucky | 6.00 | 8.50 | 9.50 | 11.50 | 11.50 |
| Louisiana | 1.50 | 1.50 | 10.75 | 11.25 | 11.25 |
| Maine | 9.00 | 10.00 | 13.50 | 13.50 | 13.50 |
| Maryland | 8.50 | 10.75 | 14.25 | 14.25 | 14.25 |
| Massachusetts | 6.50 | 9.00 | 9.50 | 9.50 | 11.50 |
| Michigan | 11.00 | 11.00 | 11.00 | 11.00 | 11.00 |
| Minnesota | 6.75 | 8.25 | 10.50 | 12.50 | 12.75 |
| Mississippi | 7.00 | 7.00 | 7.00 | 7.00 | 7.00 |
| Missouri | 6.00 | 6.00 | 10.25 | 10.25 | 10.75 |
| Montana | 3.00 | 14.25 | 14.50 | 14.50 | 15.50 |
| Nebraska | 10.25 | 13.00 | 14.00 | 13.50 | 13.50 |

**Table 6 (continued)**

|                      | 1972  | 1974  | 1976  | 1978  | 1980  |
|----------------------|-------|-------|-------|-------|-------|
| Mean score           | 6.9   | 8.6   | 11.2  | 11.7  | 12.1  |
| Standard<br>  deviation | 3.07 | 3.03  | 2.96  | 2.42  | 2.40  |
| Nevada               | 3.00  | 8.00  | 14.00 | 14.00 | 14.00 |
| New Hampshire        | 11.75 | 13.75 | 18.50 | 18.50 | 18.50 |
| New Jersey           | 10.50 | 10.50 | 10.50 | 10.50 | 10.50 |
| New Mexico           | 2.00  | 8.00  | 8.00  | 9.50  | 12.50 |
| New York             | 9.00  | 9.00  | 9.00  | 10.00 | 10.00 |
| North Carolina       | 3.00  | 6.00  | 12.50 | 12.50 | 12.50 |
| North Dakota         | 8.75  | 8.75  | 13.75 | 13.75 | 13.75 |
| Ohio                 | 8.50  | 10.50 | 16.50 | 16.50 | 16.50 |
| Oklahoma             | 4.50  | 6.50  | 6.50  | 9.75  | 9.75  |
| Oregon               | 10.50 | 11.50 | 13.50 | 13.50 | 13.50 |
| Pennsylvania         | 8.00  | 8.00  | 13.00 | 13.00 | 13.00 |
| Puerto Rico          | 11.75 | 11.75 | 11.75 | 11.75 | 11.75 |
| Rhode Island         | 10.00 | 10.00 | 13.50 | 13.50 | 13.50 |
| South Carolina       | 3.00  | 4.00  | 8.00  | 11.00 | 11.00 |
| South Dakota         | 6.50  | 8.50  | 9.00  | 9.25  | 13.25 |
| Tennessee            | 2.00  | 4.50  | 5.50  | 8.50  | 8.50  |
| Texas                | 4.50  | 9.50  | 9.50  | 9.50  | 9.50  |
| Utah                 | 8.00  | 11.00 | 12.00 | 12.00 | 12.00 |
| Vermont              | 5.00  | 7.50  | 7.75  | 11.75 | 13.75 |
| Virginia             | 3.50  | 7.50  | 10.50 | 10.50 | 10.50 |
| Washington           | 10.00 | 10.00 | 10.00 | 9.00  | 9.00  |
| West Virginia        | 6.00  | 6.50  | 14.50 | 14.50 | 14.75 |
| Wisconsin            | 10.50 | 10.50 | 16.00 | 15.00 | 15.00 |
| Wyoming              | 7.00  | 7.00  | 9.00  | 9.00  | 9.00  |

SOURCE: U.S. Department of Labor, Employment Standards Administration, Division of State Workers' Compensation Standards, January 1981.

After meeting intermittently from June through December 1979, the Workers' Compensation Reform Task Force collapsed as well.

During 1980 there were occasional rumors of progress, especially when the Democratic Chairman of the Senate Labor Committee announced that a new coalition of small business and the AFL-CIO had agreed on a compromise package. Hearings were held on this package, and it was reported out by the Committee, but the lack of enthusiasm from the state's largest employers and its largest union (i.e., the auto industry) doomed the effort. Finally, in December of 1980, the Governor and the legislative leadership held a series of closed-door meetings and hammered out a minimal reform package very similar to old S.B. 1285 from 1977. When this bill (S.B. 1044) was subsequently passed and signed into law without major amendment, the long legislative log jam in Michigan was finally broken. Round one was at last completed.

The goal of the 1979-80 effort had been not simply to reform Michigan's workers' compensation system, but to make improvements in the system without imposing any substantial cost penalty on Michigan's already burdened employers. However, the 1980 package when evaluated by the actuarial consulting firm of Tillinghast, Nelson & Warren, was found to meet these goals only for those employers who purchased commercial insurance coverage. Estimates were that S.B. 1044 would increase the workers' compensation costs for this group of employers by just 0.7 percent overall. For larger employers who self-insure the increase would be in the range of 25 to 35 percent.[13] This uneven impact resulted primarily from past inequities in income replacement rates between high-wage and low-wage workers. The old benefit formula severely capped weekly benefits for high-wage workers while sometimes giving more than 100 percent wage replacement to low-wage workers. Thus when the benefit formula was rationalized, by making the replacement of lost wages at a more consistent rate for many more workers, employers who had formerly been paying at the relatively low maximums would experience the most significant cost increases.

This is demonstrated in table 7, developed from the Michigan Closed Case Survey. It shows that 98 percent of weekly payment cases from the big three auto producers were paid the maximum benefit for their dependency class in 1978. Over 73 percent of other self-insured cases and 52 percent of carrier-insured cases also received the maximum benefit. On the other hand, no big three cases at all received the minimum benefit while 9 percent of other self-insured and 22 percent of carrier cases qualified for minimum payments.

As a result there was a massive outcry from employer groups throughout the State of Michigan. Insistent demands for workers' compensation *cost reductions* became an important part of the political climate in 1981 in many legislative districts. The pressure from employer groups, together with the general pro-business swing in the nation and in the state, resulted in another series of amendments to the workers' compensation system at the end of 1981; most of these were designed simply to reduce the cost of workers' compensation coverage for all employers large and small. These changes were enacted over the outraged objections of both the UAW and AFL-CIO.

The reform coalition this time consisted of a unanimous Republican caucus and a dozen or so "renegade" Democrats who risked the wrath of organized labor to secure leadership positions in this round of workers' compensation reform. The result was that the legislative leadership for the 1981 reforms was almost totally new; the "old hands" at workers' compensation issues were generally excluded from the pro-

Table 7
Benefit Rate by Insurer Type

| Benefit rate | Total | | Carrier | | Insurer type Big three | | Other self-insurers | |
|---|---|---|---|---|---|---|---|---|
| | Number | Percent | Number | Percent | Number | Percent | Number | Percent |
| Minimum benefit | 546 | 15.6 | 467 | 21.9 | 0 | 0 | 79 | 8.8 |
| Two-thirds of wage | 719 | 20.5 | 551 | 25.9 | 8 | 1.7 | 160 | 17.7 |
| Maximum benefit | 2,244 | 63.9 | 1,110 | 52.2 | 470 | 98.3 | 664 | 73.5 |
| Total | 3,509 | 100.0 | 2,127 | 100.0 | 478 | 100.0 | 904 | 100.0 |
| Missing cases | 1,134 | | | | | | | |
| Grand total | 4,642 | | | | | | | |

Chi-square (unweighted) = 197.07** with 4 degrees of freedom.
Unlitigated cases are inflated by a factor of 3.583 to compensate for the smaller sampling ratio in the unlitigated sample.
Columns may not add to total due to rounding.

cess. Round two of reform in Michigan thus had a very different flavor.

While these two separate reform packages had very different objectives and mechanisms of attack, it seems appropriate to discuss all the new provisions together to provide a better feel for the magnitude of change enacted in Michigan's workers' compensation system. Most of these new provisions went into effect either on January 1 or April 1, 1982.[14]

## Benefit Formula

The most significant change in the workers' compensation system is clearly the change in the benefit formula. This will have a direct impact on claimants and is also the single biggest cost item of all the reforms. The old benefit formula provided replacement of two-thirds of *gross* earnings (including fringe benefits not continued during disability). The new law calls for a basic benefit of 80 percent of *after-tax* earnings (deductions to include federal and state income tax and OASDHI taxes). These 1980 changes were amended in 1981 to provide that fringe benefits are to be included in the calculation of the benefit only if the level of the benefit is less than the old maximum benefit.[15]

## Maximum Benefit

The old maximum benefit was two-thirds of the state average weekly wage (SAWW), but less if fewer than five dependents were claimed. As noted above, this resulted in a majority of claimants receiving less than two-thirds replacement of their gross earnings in workers' compensation benefits.[16] The new maximum benefit is set at 90 percent of the SAWW without regard to dependency. Currently the number of dependents influences the benefit level only through its effect on deductions, and thus after-tax earnings.

The net result is that most workers who earn more than the SAWW will qualify for higher benefits than they would have under the old law.

## Minimum Benefit

The old minimum benefits (which were very high due to an earlier court decision that indexed them along with the maximums) were eliminated.[17] There is now no minimum benefit for general disability cases; low-wage workers simply receive 80 percent of their after-tax earnings. Exceptions are made for fatality claims and specific loss claims, where minimum benefit levels are set at 50 percent and 25 percent of the SAWW respectively.

## Coordination of Benefits

The second most significant area of reform is the coordination of benefits between different income maintenance programs paid for, in part or in total, by the disabled worker's employer. The basic approach here is to put the workers' compensation benefit dollar *last* in the queue in those cases where multiple benefits are received by the claimant. The Michigan approach is very broad; the offset against other benefits applies to unemployment insurance, other state workers' compensation benefits for the same condition, private disability, wage continuation or pension plans, Old Age and Survivor's Insurance (OASI), and "other" income maintenance plans. It is also provided that, if and when it becomes possible again, Michigan's workers' compensation benefits will be coordinated with federal Disability Insurance payments.

In each case, the workers' compensation benefit under Michigan law is reduced by benefits in these other programs according to the proportion of the benefit financed by employer payments. Thus in the case of OASI, the employer is allowed a credit of 50 percent of the monthly OASI benefit against the workers' compensation benefit, since the employer provided 50 percent of the tax payments to the OASI program. These benefit coordination provisions do not apply to benefits for specific loss claims, or to payments from disability pension plans that were in operation previous to the effective date of the statute. However, the statute specifically allows that such existing plans may be modified to allow coordination if the parties wish. These coordination of benefits provisions are expected to lead to significant cost savings for Michigan employers, particularly larger employers with extensive fringe benefit plans.

## Retiree Claims

In addition to the coordination of benefits described above, there was another attack on what many had regarded as the most flagrant abuse of Michigan's workers' compensation system—claims from retired workers. The 1980 package introduced a new presumption of no loss of earnings or earning capacity on the part of a claimant who is receiving nondisability pension or retirement benefits (including OASI). While this presumption can be rebutted by a preponderance of the evidence, it should help to reduce claims from retired workers, especially when considered in conjunction with the offset for other retirement benefits provided under the coordination of benefits provisions.

## Inflation Protection

The 1980 reforms also included the addition of a new retrospective inflation protection plan applying to all cases with injury dates before January 1, 1980. A state-financed Compensation Supplement Fund was established for this purpose. A benefit supplement equal to the increase in the SAWW (not to exceed 5 percent for any year) is to be paid to all continuing claims from these years. The benefit adjustment payments are made by the insurers directly to claimants, with quarterly reimbursements from the Compensation Supplement Fund. This provision is an attempt to maintain a major share of the original purchasing power of workers' compensation benefits for existing long term disability cases. There are no provisions for additional adjustments in the future for these or other claimants, but the Director of the Bureau of Workers' Disability Compensation is ordered to conduct biannual studies of the general adequacy of benefits, specifically including the impact of inflation.

## Statute of Limitations

Both the 1980 and 1981 reform packages addressed the statute of limitations under the workers' compensation law. The old statute of limitations had been rendered ineffective by a requirement that if the employer did not give notice of the injury to the Bureau of Workers' Disability Compensation, the time period did not begin to toll. The 1980 reforms resurrected by the statute by striking the employer notice requirement and simply providing that the claim must be entered within two years of the occurrence of the injury, the date the disability manifests itself, or the last day of employment. The 1981 reforms recomplicated this by adding a new requirement that the *employee* must give notice to the employer within 90 days of the injury. If this requirement is not met, the employer can contest the case on the grounds that the failure by the employee to provide notification of the injury prejudiced the employer's defense against the claim.[18]

## Definition of Disability

Both packages also attacked the issue of the definition of disability. The 1980 reforms contained language designed to tighten up on claims involving mental disabilities, conditions resulting from the aging process, and social and recreational injuries. The 1981 reform went much deeper into the substance of the law. It defined disability in terms of a general field of employment, rather than a specific job as in the old law. It also separated the issue of disability from that of wage loss in an attempt to further tighten eligibility standards. There is a new provision for disqualification if the claimant refuses a bona fide offer of reasonable employment. A significant complication was introduced concerning reemployment and favored work. If an injured employee has returned to work for more than 100 weeks and subsequently loses that job, only partial disability payments can be paid. If fewer than 100 weeks of new work experience are obtained, full disability eligibility is maintained on the basis of the original job.

There is also a requirement for notification to the Michigan Employment Security Commission when disabled workers are unemployed. That agency is directed to give priority treatment to such referrals. The intent was to urge partially disabled workers to return to work, but the statute is so complex it will take some sorting out by the courts. Meanwhile, the entire definition of disability section is slated to expire at the end of 1984.

## Logging Industry

The 1980 package expanded the Silicosis and Dust Disease Fund to the Silicosis, Dust Disease, and *Logging Industry* Compensation Fund (emphasis added). This imposes a $12,500 insurer liability limit on each workers' compensation claim arising in the logging industry. Any benefits above $12,500 per claim will be paid by the Fund rather than the individual insurer. This has the effect of transferring the burden of expensive claims in the logging industry to the general employer population, since the Fund is financed by proportional assessment on all employers. This special fund is due to expire at the end of 1985.

## Medical Costs

Another complicating provision is the imposition of a medical cost regulation scheme into the workers' compensation system. The Bureau of Workers' Disability Compensation is directed to establish fee schedules for medical treatment under the workers' compensation statute. In addition, they are to monitor the performance of providers of service and establish utilization review procedures for individual workers' compensation cases. This reflects the interest of one of the major Democratic participants in the 1981 reform coalition.

## Redemptions

The 1981 reform package also included an outright prohibition of redemptions (compromise and release settlements) for any petitions filed after January 1, 1984. Inasmuch as 70 percent of all litigated cases are redeemed in Michigan (settled with a lump sum), this provision could have enormous significance for the way the Michigan workers' compensation system really works.[19] No one is yet able to predict what this will mean, however.

## Rate-making

Last, but by no means least, reform of the workers' compensation insurance procedures should also be reported here. Even though this provision was not enacted until 1982, it was under discussion with the 1981 reforms, and everyone understood it to be a part of the total package. The legislature mandated a 20 percent rollback for the 1982 policy year in the average manual premium rate for workers' compensation insurance coverage in the state. They also directed that Michigan should move to "open competition" in workers' compensation insurance rates effective January 1, 1983.

Michigan's system provides for a "file and use" procedure with a new public body, the Workers' Compensation Data Collection Agency, responsible for collecting and disseminating the pure premium data to be used by the individual insurance companies to set their rates. Undoubtedly, the way that workers' compensation insurance carriers do their business will be altered; it is not clear exactly what impact this change in procedures will have on the system as a whole. Those who promoted this reform felt that it would lead to lower prices for workers' compensation insurance as the competitive pressures of the free market were felt in the insurance industry.[20]

There are many smaller changes that have been omitted from this discussion, some of which may turn out to have greater significance than is evident now. The most important point to make may be that many of these enactments will depend on court decisions for their specific content. Obviously, it will be some years before the true impact of this entire set of reforms will be apparent. At the moment, one must be content to point out the significant changes that have been accomplished: (1) the benefit structure has been rationalized considerably; (2) some of the most serious abuses cited by employer groups have been addressed; and (3) part of the loss imposed on the long term disabled by inflation in the last decade has been restored.

Early in 1982, commercial insurance carriers through the Workers' Compensation Rating and Inspection Association of Michigan (WCRIAM) filed for a rate reduction of 22 percent in the average workers' compensation premium. As was discussed earlier, this was not the result of an actuarial evaluation, but was WCRIAM's response to a legislatively mandated rollback of at least 20 percent in premium levels. Thus it is not at all clear that this represents the actual anticipated cost impact of the reforms.

Even if some of the reforms turn out to have been ill-advised, any errors were the natural by-product of the pressure-cooker legislative environment that was required to break the stalemate that had developed in Michigan. It is to be hoped that necessary updating will not prove as difficult in the future. Taken as a whole, the two rounds of reform appear to constitute a significant improvement in Michigan's workers' compensation system.

## NOTES

1. H. Allan Hunt, *Workers' Compensation in Michigan: Problems and Prospects* (Kalamazoo, MI: W. E. Upjohn Institute for Employment Research, May 1979).

2. In each case these cost measurements are for adjusted insurance manual rates as reported in the analysis of Professor John F. Burton, Jr., of Cornell University. Professor Burton has published a series of articles on interstate cost comparisons. The most recent was coauthored by Martin W. Elson, "Workers' Compensation Insurance: Recent Trends in Employer Costs," *Monthly Labor Review,* Vol. 104, March 1981, pp. 45-50.

3. See *The Report of the National Commission on State Workmen's Compensation Laws* (Washington, DC: Government Printing Office, 1972).

4. Governor's Workmen's Compensation Advisory Commission, *Workers' Compensation in Michigan* (Ann Arbor, MI: The Commission, 1975), p. 5.

5. Letter of transmittal, *op. cit.,* p. 1.

6. See Hunt, *Workers' Compensation in Michigan: Problems and Prospects,* for a more complete discussion of the S.B. 1285 story.

7. Data from Elson and Burton, "Workers' Compensation Insurance: Recent Trends in Employer Costs," *Monthly Labor Review,* March 1981.

8. Daniel N. Price, "Workers' Compensation: Coverage, Benefits, and Costs, 1979," *Social Security Bulletin,* Vol. 44, September 1981, table 2, p. 11.

9. Data from U.S. Department of Labor, Employment Standards Administration, Division of State Workers' Compensation Standards.

10. See Hunt, *The Workers' Compensation System in Michigan: A Closed Case Survey* (Kalamazoo, MI: W. E. Upjohn Institute for Employment Research, 1982), especially chapter 4, for a more adequate account of Michigan benefit levels.

11. *State Compliance with the 19 Essential Recommendations of the National Commission on State Workmen's Compensation Laws, 1972-1980,* U.S. Department of Labor, Employment Standards Administration, Division of State Workers' Compensation Standards, January 1981, table 1, p. 18.

12. See "A Report to the People of Michigan, Workers' Compensation in Michigan: Report of the House Republican Task Force on Workers' Compensation" (mimeo, no date), or "Areas for Reform in the Workers' Disability Compensation System in the State of Michigan," published by the Business and Industry Compensation Reform Coalition in March 1979.

13. Actuarial evaluation of S.B. 1044 prepared for Workers' Compensation Rating and Inspection Association of Michigan.

14. See also the separate description of the legislative changes published by the Michigan Department of Labor. The 1980 reforms were described in "Workers' Compensation Changes Explained," *LABORegister,* February 1981, pp. 28-30. The 1981 package was presented in "Workers' Compensation Changes Summarized," *LABORegister,* February 1982, pp. 22-23.

15. In other words, an injured worker shall not be deprived of the previous benefit level by the elimination of fringe benefits from the wage base. This elimination was a reaction to the very significant increase in the effective maximum benefit.

16. According to the Upjohn Institute's Michigan Closed Case Survey, 64 percent of all claimants qualified for the maximum benefit, i.e., received less than two-thirds gross wage replacement in their weekly workers' compensation benefit. See Hunt, *The Workers' Compensation System in Michigan: A Closed Case Survey,* table 2-13, p. 50.

17. Indexing was extended to minimum benefits by *Jolliff v. American Advertising,* 49 Mich App 1 (1973). This decision was reversed in *Gussler v. Fairview,* 412 Mich 270 (1981).

18. There is a great deal of confusion about the meaning of this provision. Some contend that reintroduction of any notice requirement may lead to nullifying the statute of limitations once again.

19. See Hunt, *The Workers' Compensation System in Michigan: A Closed Case Survey,* chapter 3, for a discussion of the influence of litigation in the Michigan system.

20. Reports from Kentucky and Oregon, based on the first six months of experience under their open-competition systems, indicate savings in premiums ranging from 8 to 40 percent. In addition, there are reports that the price competition among carriers is making some inroads on the self-insured market share as well. See *Business Insurance,* January 10, 1983, January 3, 1983 and September 20, 1982.

# 5

# The Politics of Workers' Compensation Reform

John H. Lewis
Attorney
Coconut Grove, Florida

According to the program, this presentation deals with legislative efforts concerning workers' compensation laws in the States of Louisiana and New Mexico. Both of these states are a long way from Rutgers, and may appear to have little relevance to a program the avowed purpose of which is to focus on the workers' compensation systems of three northeastern states. Relevance may now appear to take more of a beating, since it is my intention to also discuss the States of Florida, Delaware and Alaska, which are at least as remote, in the political if not the physical sense, from the states which are to be the subject of our concern as the two previously mentioned.

Actually, the topic is better described as "Workers' Compensation Reform and How to Get It." Now, reform is a difficult subject to discuss, since it is to a great extent in the eye of the beholder. It may not even be excessively cynical or egotistical to say that reform is what I do, as opposed to whatever it is the rest of you do. However, to avoid controversy, for today's purposes, the term "reform" will refer to significant changes in a workers' compensation law intended to provide long term solutions to perceived defects or deficiencies in the system—as opposed to what is best described as tinkering, which, unfortunately, is the usual legislative response to workers' compensation problems.

Given this unilateral change of topic, the relevancy of the states previously mentioned becomes apparent. All of these states have been involved, or are involved, in workers' compensation reform efforts. The patterns of success versus failure, and the events which led to the respective conclusions, are remarkably similar in these states, and as a result highly instructive for any state wishing to institute the long and difficult process of workers' compensation reform.

As distasteful and/or redundant as it may be to many of you, the first portion of our discussion will deal with the no longer recent Florida reform effort, which culminated with the legislation passed in 1979. Most aspects of the Florida experience have been talked to death and, fortunately, need not even be mentioned. What is of importance is how the forces in Florida arrived at what they believed to be a solution to the state's workers' compensation problems.

Most people in the compensation community are aware of the events of the 1979 Florida legislation session, and some are aware of the efforts made during the 1978 session, which resulted in some temporary patchwork and the famous "sunset" provision, which, theoretically, would have eliminated Florida's workers' compensation law in 1979 if new legislation had not been passed. Very few are aware of the years of work which went into preparing the state and the legislature to deal with workers' compensation on a meaningful basis. A significant amount of research was performed by a wide variety of groups and individuals, including Dr. John Burton, Associated Industries of Florida, the Florida Association of Insurance Agents, and myself. This research furnished the bedrock for the reform effort, since it provided everyone involved in the process with factual information as to what was going on in the system. In addition, the Florida Workers' Compensation Advisory Council had spent several years looking at the compensation system and discussing the problems of all the interests involved, each of which was represented on the Council by individuals who were initially or took the time and trouble to become knowledgeable in workers' compensation matters. The Council itself was somewhat remarkable in that its activities were devoid of the public posturing and recriminations which often mark similar attempts at compromise. As a result, the Council was able to deal with substance, rather than illusion, and virtually all of its recommendations were adopted without internal dissent.

Another ingredient in the process was education. Through the activities of the trade groups mentioned above and others, numerous newspaper articles, including an influential series by the *Miami Herald,* a major legislative conference, and many months of study by a legislative joint committee, the general public and many members of the legislature were made aware of what the compensation system was all about and how it was performing or failing to perform. Most important, and perhaps by coincidence, one member of each house of the legislature became extremely well-educated as to the workings of the system, as well as the various reform proposals and their probable impact. As a result, they were able to provide leadership in legislative discussions and to keep the basic reform program together during the various committee and floor debates and through the critical late-night negotiating sessions.

The final component of the reform process was the cooperation between labor and management, which in terms of political reality left the legislature and the governor with little choice when the agreed upon package came to them for approval, despite the opposition of other, usually powerful, interests. This coalition may not appear unique, but to the extent to which it was based upon the best interests of the two groups involved to the exclusion of peripheral interests in the compensation system, it is unique. It is interesting to note that many of the critics of the new Florida system fault the act of cooperation by the AFL-CIO leadership, rather than praise it. In reality, organized labor in Florida gained far more than it lost in 1979, and certainly benefited from the coalition, as compared to what most likely would have happened had the bill been structured through normal confrontation politics. In fact, if one compares what has happened to the workers' benefit package as the result of less publicized "reform" efforts in other states, the result in Florida looks better and better for the injured worker.

By way of comparison, we can look at the State of Delaware, which, in spite of significant political effort and what I believe to be the best of intentions on the part of most of those involved in the reform effort, repeatedly turned back a proposal far more financially generous than that which was passed in Florida, as well as in other states.

Delaware's reform effort grew out of an official study commission, which, near the end of its deliberations, became aware of the new Florida law and decided to emulate it. Unfortunately, the effort did not include, nor, for reasons of time, could it, the research and education portion of the Florida experience. In addition, the proponents of the bill which was drafted were faced with the knee-jerk reaction of some interest groups to any proposal that even looked like Florida's, which, as you well know, has been the subject of some of the least informed criticism of any workers' compensation law in history. As a result, numerous mistakes were made which, in retrospect, virtually guaranteed the failure of the reform effort. Certain interest groups were made to appear to be the source of all of the system's problems, which insured their opposition. Because of the lack of factual information about the system and its shortcomings, broad support for change did not develop. The business community split, primarily as the result of internal political maneuvering. Organized labor was equally as divided, despite early support for the proposal, apparently because of outside influences having little to do with the merits of the legislative proposal. Finally, there was virtually no workers' compensation expertise within the legislature, so that opponents were able to sway votes by actually asserting that the only thing wrong with the system was the fact that insurance companies were taking in around $50,000,000.00 a year in premium, and paying out about $5,000,000.00 in benefits. The lack of knowledge on the part of many of those involved in the legislative debate was highlighted by Senate floor debate, which included fierce opposition to portions of the bill which merely recodified existing law, the very law which they claimed was virtually fault free. All of these problems and mistakes were probably aggravated by a political decision to go right back to the legislature after the bill's initial defeat instead of taking a year or two to do the basic work required to make a strong case for reform and for the proposal. Against this background of success and failure we can now look at and evaluate the recent developments in Louisiana and New Mexico.

## Louisiana

From a political standpoint, Louisiana is a very interesting state in that virtually all aspects of government are highly politicized, with administrative appointments on many levels and virtually all legislative action based on interest group pressure and power politics. Contrary to popular belief, organized labor plays a significant role in this process and often can lay claim to "owning" one or the other house of the legislature, or both, as well as the governor's office. Please understand that the use of the term "own" is in the political sense, and not the literal sense. The extent to which this state of affairs affects the actions of those involved in the political process was brought home to me on one of my first trips to the state, for a meeting with a broad spectrum of the business community. Several representatives of major, national employers expressed reservations about a proposal to create an administrative body to run the compensation program, on the grounds that at some point the political power held by "the other side" would result in a totally employee-oriented administration. Although this view was eventually rejected, it does illustrate how even major players in the political arena can be inhibited in efforts to improve a workers' compensation system.

The Louisiana effort, which was successful, parallels Florida in many respects. The impetus for reform came from the state's major business organization, the Louisiana Association of Business and Industry (LABI). Unlike most business associations, LABI is headed by an individual with a strong background in research. As a result, any legislation sponsored by LABI in areas such as workers' compensation is based upon well-documented facts, rather than opinion or gut-reaction. This was extremely important in two respects. First, no public pronouncements were made until the dimensions and cause of the problem were known, and until the efficacy of proposed solutions had been investigated. Through this process, it was found that the perceived source of the dual problems of high costs and low benefits was not the area of permanent total disability benefits, but rather the usual villain—permanent partial disability benefits. In addition, the viability of an income replacement system as a reform measure was confirmed, and the inadequacy of the court-administered system, which resulted in virtually no administration and an overwhelming reliance on compromise and release agreements to keep the system under control, was demonstrated.

Second, when the time for public and legislative debate came, the LABI position could be defended on a factual, rather than emotional, basis. As will be seen, this factor may have been the most critical in the entire process.

Once it was determined that problems truly existed, and that there were reasonable solutions available, LABI and the business community committed themselves to a true reform effort. Although there was legislation introduced rather quickly without the long lead time employed in Florida, it was with the understanding that it would almost certainly take two legislative sessions (in reality it also took a special session) in order to achieve the final goal. However, the first session could also be used as part of the educational effort, and it was. With the strong financial and political support of the business community, the entire project was handled on a professional basis, with the emphasis on establishing to the satisfaction of the voters and the legislature the need for change and the validity of the proposed reform. Both were accomplished, partly because of research efforts previously described, and partly because LABI did not take the all too common approach of simply proposing a reduction in benefits as a way to reduce costs. Instead LABI arrived at a package of benefit and administrative changes geared towards reallocating the premium dollar to areas in which it was needed, avoiding duplication of benefits and decreasing the cost of litigation. The latter was most significant in that, unlike Florida, Louisiana was unable to put together a coalition of labor and management. While I cannot even attempt to speak for organized labor in Louisiana, there is a widely held belief that because of inaccurate comparisons of the Louisiana proposal and the then recent Florida reform, as well as long-standing ties with the trial bar which did stand to lose if the proposals passed, labor could not, from a political standpoint, afford to be perceived as having cooperated or agreed with any management position. As a result, all attempts at compromise failed, and unfortunately the benefit package eventually enacted into law was smaller than that which could have been obtained through negotiation.

As you must have already surmised, the first legislative proposal did not pass. As an aside, this "failure" was, in retrospect, for the best, since later drafts were, in my opinion, far superior and better suited for local conditions. However, the attempt did serve its purpose, since it brought the issue of workers' compensation to the forefront and raised the issues which would have to be faced. During the 10 months between legislative sessions, additional educational efforts were made, with particular emphasis on the members of the legislature. These efforts included a special legislative conference with speakers from both inside and outside the state, as well as special efforts with key legislators and potential sponsors. As was the case in Florida, several members of each house became totally conversant with the problems and the proposed solutions, thereby maintaining control of the debate process and influencing other, less knowledgeable legislators.

The modified package passed the House on its second attempt, in the regular session of 1982, but was amended many times in a labor-dominated Senate committee. Interestingly enough, virtually all the amendments were stripped by the full Senate, which was generally considered to be highly sympathetic to the labor/trial lawyer position. However, the operative word was "virtually," since the failure to strip *all* of the amendments meant that the bill had to go to conference committee. There, as a result of a weekend of political maneuvering, a compromise was reached *without* the consent of the business community and announced approximately 15 minutes before the end of the legislative session. The compromise included language which had not been previously offered, in areas not directly related to the reform effort (third-party actions) apparently in the belief that

LABI and the other backers of the bill would "settle" for what was sure to pass. To their credit, the business community stuck to its program of no action without a complete understanding of all implications of the proposal. Since this was impossible given the short time involved, the sponsors asked the representatives who supported them to kill the bill, and this was done. Once again, in retrospect this was the correct step to take, but the decision was not unanimous, and LABI was accused by some legislators and newspapers of being "greedy." In fact, LABI had already compromised the bill to a considerable extent on the basis of what might best be described as informed consent. The attempt to add new features at the last minute was a mistake from all standpoints. Last minute changes, if not properly evaluated, tend to come back to haunt the authors, and experience in other states and in federal programs such as the Longshore Act clearly demonstrates the danger in this type of maneuver.

The final act in this drama was played out between July 1982, the end of the legislative session, and January 1983, when a special session was called by the Governor to deal with workers' compensation and unemployment compensation. During that period, pressure on the legislature for enactment of the bill became almost overwhelming, and it became clear that the LABI proposal, or something very similar, was going to pass or some legislators would not be returning for a new term. In addition, the research and educational efforts which had been undertaken began to pay off to an even greater extent, with several key legislators who normally might have opposed a management position becoming active supporters. This included a Senator whose opposition had caused much difficulty in the past and whose eventual support did much to influence others, given the fact that he was a trial lawyer and well-respected in such matters. The bill was passed on January 14, 1983, and signed into law a short time later.

The new Louisiana workers' compensation law is substantially different from the old. For the first time there is an administration, with reporting of accidents and benefits payments, an enforceable penalty structure, and an informal litigation reduction system which in effect requires mediation prior to entering the court system. The maximum weekly benefit was increased, permanent total disability redefined and limited to avoid the payment of such benefits to those actually working or able to work, and a restructuring of the permanent partial disability system to rely primarily on income replacement benefits, with significant impairment benefits payable in the absence of income loss for those with schedule injuries in excess of 50 percent loss of use of the member, and a meaningful vocational rehabilitation program, mandatory for all parties.

## New Mexico

New Mexico is perhaps the best example of a state in which reform has stalled, despite the best of intentions on the part of the participants. Unlike the discussions of the other four states in this paper, much of what I will say concerning New Mexico is based upon hearsay, inference and after-the-fact talks with those involved from the very beginning of the process, since I was only involved for the final two months in early 1983. The effort began with the deliberations of an official study commission of several years duration. It appears that some of the first problems arose during those deliberations and may have sealed the fate of the legislation which was eventually introduced. It has been stated that there has never been an effective study commission. I must take issue with that statement, since I served with two which led to the enactment of major legislation, but I can sympathize with the feelings expressed. New Mexico's experience may show why. Please keep in mind that this portion of the evaluation is based in part on the recollections and perceptions of some of the parties, some of which are totally at odds with others. It appears that representatives of the two interest groups directly involved in the workers' compensation system—management and labor—were not well versed in the operation and structure of the compensation system. This is *not* a criticism. In fact it is to be expected in most instances since the leaders of business and labor organization usually have backgrounds and responsibilities which make it extremely unlikely that they will be able to come into a study commission with the requisite knowledge to make major decisions concerning the system. In the past this problem has often been "solved" by each side using their lawyers as representatives. Once again without necessarily implying criticism, it is a fact that the interests of employers and defense lawyers in the compensation system are not necessarily the same, nor are the interests of employees and their lawyers. Because of this, much of the early work of a study group should focus on educating those of its members without workers' compensation expertise. This was not done in New Mexico, nor does it appear to be the case in most other states. As a result, it is my belief that the labor representatives were left in the position of having to accept either what was being told to them by the other side (particularly the insurance industry, where the employer expertise eventually came from) or what they were told by representatives of the claimants' bar. The reasonable insecurity brought about by this situation was probably heightened by an interesting phenomenon which occurs during the work of most study groups—the impact of "observers." Although there is usually an effort made for study commissions to be balanced in their representation of interest groups, their meetings are often attended by large numbers of association representatives from business and the insurance industry. This can give, and in New Mexico did give, the impression of labor being outnumbered. In addition, large numbers of people make it very difficult to have frank discussions, and often lead to more public posturing than meaningful discussions of real problems.

From the management standpoint, it appears that there was somewhat of an educational effort through the insurance industry and their attorneys. As an aside I might mention, in all fairness, that there did appear to be a legitimate effort made by the representatives of the insurance industry to be candid and fair in their dealings with management, without any of the conflicts of interest of which the industry is often accused. However, it seems that the real educational effort was to a great extent limited to selling a rather narrow legislative program, which left management locked in to a somewhat inflexible program. Since any major change in the proposed bill would have required a time-consuming educational effort, it became virtually impossible for the employer/insurance representatives to seriously consider proposals made after the legislative session began, even though some of them may have been acceptable and might have led to passage of a reform package.

Another factor which eventually led to defeat was a perhaps inadvertent politicizing of a major issue, the permanent partial disability benefit package. Once again, an income replacement system was being considered. Such proposals are automatically tagged as "Florida wage loss," which is a distinct negative to most trial lawyers, and some labor leaders, and immediately puts proponents on the defensive. Unfortunately, some in the business community talked about the proposal in terms which could lead one to believe that it was punitive and antilabor, when in fact there was *no* reduction in the total amount of benefits to be paid to injured workers, but rather a redistribution. This put the leadership of organized labor in an extremely difficult position, since accepting an otherwise favorable package could lead to charges of having given in to management interests. Like politicians, labor leaders are elected and cannot afford to be put in such positions if they wish to remain as leaders. This result might have been avoided if more of the local leadership had been brought into the process at an earlier date, had the benefit of a short course in workers' compensation and the effect of the proposed legislation, and been given an opportunity to have any and all questions answered. I do not know if this was possible from a political standpoint, but it would seem that more input from the rank and file in all states might give the leadership broader support for meaningful change.

As can be seen, the education process, or the lack of it, has significance throughout the reform effort. Once again, it appears that the New Mexico proposal was hampered by lack of education on another level—that of the legislature. As I mentioned previously, it is my belief that a major legislative effort requires the informed backing of several members of each house. Not only does this help to sway votes and avoid debate over nonissues, it also provides a mechanism for resolving conflict, since both sides are often better able to accept a compromise if it originates, or at least seems to originate, from a member of the legislature rather than from a spokesman for an interest group. This cannot be accomplished unless the legislative advocate knows what he or she is talking about. It appears that for a number of reasons, the legislation in New Mexico did not have the benefit of this type of assistance.

The final missing ingredient was research. It is amazing how little is known about the operation of most workers' compensation systems, particularly the important items such as who is getting the benefits and what it takes from a procedural standpoint to get them. In the absence of factual information, what one tends to get from the experts testifying at legislative hearings is myth rather than reality. What is even more disconcerting is the fact that the same myths are heard in every state, which makes for a lot of boredom for those of us who do business in more than one state and must attend what amounts to the same hearings, with what appear to be the same witnesses, in a number of states. When you have heard the same misstatements of fact in two different states five thousand miles apart in the course of two days, you tend to lose faith in the legislative process, or at least in those who should know better than to say the things they do. Neither side has a monopoly in this area, but in New Mexico it was the opponents of the reform proposal who dominated the arena, with the usual tales of how the only thing wrong with the system was insurance company profits, how it was humanly impossible for an administrative structure to handle minor problems more efficiently than the courts, and how an income replacement system, no matter how it was structured, was not only unworkable but virtually guaranteed an 80 percent reduction in benefits paid to injured workers. None of these arguments was new, at least not in other states, and with a year of preparation could have easily been answered. It is possible that the fight was already over by the time these arguments were raised in legislative hearings (where the bill was killed), but had that not been the case a factual defense would have been extremely helpful.

### Conclusion

There should be a point to all this narrative and there is. In fact, there may be several. I would like to start with mention of the comment made earlier by Alan Tebb, that he would be willing to pay in order to have someone from the labor side to talk with. I believe that as that statement was intended—as an attempt to change an unfortunate but not unexpected reality, rather than a criticism—it is true, but does not go far enough. It is good to have someone to talk to on the labor side, but it is better to have an educated public, business community and legislature, also. It goes without saying that this means that the subject of discussion is fact, rather than fancy, and that the necessary research is included as part of the education, negotiation and compromise process. It also assumes a good faith effort by the parties, excluding, to the greatest extent possible, controversies and maneuvering unrelated to the merits of the workers' compensation program. As history now shows us, it is virtually impossible to pass decent legislation without most of these factors being present, particularly research and education, and the more of these elements that come together, the better the changes for real success.

This brings us to Alaska. Several years ago I had the good fortune to come in second or third, I don't know which, in the competition for a contract to investigate the ramifications of open competition in the workers' compensation insurance market. This loss enabled me to enter into a contract with the State of Alaska to study and report on all aspects of its workers' compensation system, including what happens to injured workers after they receive permanent partial disability benefits. Alaska is an excellent research subject in that it has all the potential for real problems, due to extremely high benefits (now approximately $1,000.00 for income benefits), highly seasonal employment and a relatively transitory workforce. At the same time, the state has a very small population, around 400,000, so that it is possible to look at the universe of workers' compensation cases rather than a small sample. And it has a compensation community which, for the most part, is willing to listen and learn. I am quite proud of the resulting report and would like to take a minute to quote a small, highly relevant portion of it.

As can readily be seen, workers' compensation is a complex subject and not an easy one for employers, labor representatives, and an otherwise burdened legislature to deal with in an intelligent manner. Typically, matters are made worse by virtue of the fact that no matter how good their intentions, many interest group representatives do not have a working knowledge of the compensation system, and are familiar primarily with the 'horror stories' that can be developed about any system. The nature of the political process, in which legislative hearings seem to demand highly emotional testimony, results in hearings which offer legislators and the public little in the way of education, but instead rather extreme and emotional arguments having little to do with the normal operation of the compensation system, and having even less to do with the real problems and issues at hand. During the 1982 legislation session, a coalition of employer and labor representatives developed a workers' compensation package which was in part enacted into law. The package was developed not as the result of confrontation politics or the exercise of countervailing political forces, but rather was the result of many hours of education, discussion and debate away from the legislative forum. Hopefully this initial success will be expanded into a commitment by the members of this group to continue their efforts for an extended period of time, using the freedom offered by the private sector to discuss and investigate what might initially be impossible to deal with in the legislature, and to continue the education and legislative process.

If the legislature is to maintain its constitutional responsibilities with regard to the legislative process, it cannot stay involved with the compensation system simply through intermittent contact. Obviously, the entire membership of the legislature cannot devote its time to learning how the workers' compensation system operates and what changes may be needed. However, if there is one common thread running among the states which have had success in controlling their workers' compensation systems, it is the existence of a long-term commitment, not only by labor and management, but also by a small number of legislators, all of whom have taken the trouble to learn enough about the realities of the system to make intelligent decisions which benefit the system as a whole. While politics cannot be totally taken out of a political issue such as workers' compensation, the kind of cooperation which leads to success minimizes totally partisan posturing, and encourages well thought out compromise. This is not the type of compromise which is often found at the last minute on the floor of the Senate or the House, of uncertain outcome. It is compromise that recognizes that neither side can for long totally dominate the compensation program, and that in fact the social and economic impact of the compensation system may make it desirable for both parties to accept something less than what might be in their short-run financial best interests.[1]

I am not a particularly naive person, at least not since 1979 when I quit the practice of law because of the lying, cheating and stealing that one sees when involved in trial practice and instead moved on to the pristine field of legislative work. I know it is naive to assume that in every state we can educate, cooperate and get the legislature to look at the real problems of the workers' compensation system. In some states this is impossible, and power politics will continue to control the fate of the compensation system. In the final analysis, it is up to legislators and representatives of the business and labor communities to learn, perhaps for the first time, what workers' compensation is all about. States such as Florida, Louisiana and Alaska can be copied, *not* as to their laws, but instead with regard to the ways in which they went about obtaining meaningful change. Their similarities can be summarized as follows:

1. Extensive basic research as to how the current system is operating and where the benefits are going.

2. Continuous dialogue between labor and management, with minimal interference by lawyers, doctors, surance carriers and others with only a secondary interest in the system.

3. Education of the public and the legislature, with facts rather than opinion and hyperbole.

4. Decisions on philosophy made before legislative drafting begins and before public positions are taken by the major parties.

These states are good examples of this process, of how to structure a bill and how to get it enacted into law. They are examples of how to really reform rather than patch and how to handle defeat and pressures for immediate action. Workers' compensation is simply too important to be left to any other course.

# NOTE

1. John H. Lewis, *An Analysis of the Alaska Workers' Compensation System*. Report to the State of Alaska, Juneau, Alaska, June 1982.

# 6

# Discussion of Papers
# on Recent State Reforms

Michael Staten
Department of Economics
University of Delaware

The papers in this session offer an interesting geographical and topical cross section of recent legislative efforts. Even this small sample of the 50 states considered most of the major areas of reform, from wage loss to rate-making to revamping the exclusive remedy doctrine. However, it seems to me that the session's most significant message transcends the specifics of any of the proposed changes. I think a crucial lesson resides in the collection of legislative stories related, that is, in the descriptions of the reform process itself.

One can hardly read the four papers together without imagining the legislative halls around the country as so many war zones. This impression is not much affected by the ultimate outcome—even successful efforts come with a struggle. I suppose that is the nature of our democratic process. Much as we may wish it were otherwise, it remains true that our system of collective rule-making is far from costless. But the production of legislation is subject to the same principles that apply to production of all goods we value. That includes the principle that a variety of recipes exist for producing any given final product. For any desired piece of legislation there exist a variety of strategies for transforming the basic idea to a final statute.

An economist would view the problem as one of finding the path of least resistance, the least-cost way of shepherding the proposed bill through the production process in state legislatures. Thus, *how* a bill is sold becomes nearly as important as *what* is being sold. The experience of recent years suggests that students and proponents of workers' compensation reform have paid too little heed to this proposition. I find this all the more curious since workers' compensation has been a statutory creature since its inception in the early 1900s. Participants in this area should be no strangers to political haggling and regulatory tinkering. Yet as Alan Tebb suggested of California, rather than master the vehicle which affects them, the real parties involved—employers and employees—"continue to abrogate their responsibility to participate in the establishment of public policy in the workers' compensation area." The events described in Michigan and Minnesota confirm this observation.

How can we minimize the confrontation politics that have plagued past efforts? Steve Keefe suggests that the usual political warfare over proposed reforms exaggerates the perception of an adversarial, employer versus employee relationship. Too often the image has been that one party gains from reform only at the other's expense. Labor interests have opposed reforms geared to reduce system costs because they expect the price tag will ultimately be a reduction in benefits. Of course, "reform" does not have to be a zero-sum game which precludes everyone from gaining. The practical problem in Minnesota (as everywhere else) was one of demonstrating that premiums could be lowered without cutting benefits. Certainly, premium reduction requires cost reduction, but *cost* is not synonymous with *benefits.* A major point of Keefe's paper is that proposed legislation was supported by studies that demonstrated just that. He suggests that the crucial key to successful reform effort is a thorough, objective examination of prior and existing systems that illustrate how both business *and* labor interests can get a fair shake from reorganization.

The natural confrontational atmosphere that surrounds compensation bills is compounded when only anecdotal evidence can be offered in support. I think this session suggests that the prescription for defusing this confrontation in any given state is (1) to carefully research the state's existing administration to clearly define the problems, and (2) armed with these statistics, to educate the political participants. The experiences related by the participants reveal that without a concerted effort to research and educate, the initial perceptions of a zero-sum game are difficult to dispel, with political warfare as a result.

A related point deserves mention. The suggestions above primarily address a strategy for smoothing the process of getting legislation passed. It should go without saying that the proposed reform itself should be based on research into the state's own experience. Nevertheless, a major trend in compensation reform, the wage loss movement, has exhibited a remarkable propensity for generating a bandwagon effect. The approach has picked up national support among business leaders as the ultimate solution to the problems with permanent partial awards. Delaware's recent bout with the fever of reform provides an example.

Delaware has a full slate of scheduled awards as well as permanent partial awards for percentage loss of use *and* disfigurement. Benefits are paid through an agreement system, whereby both employer and employee must agree to the offered settlement before payment is made. An employee deals with the state's administrative personnel only in the event of a contested claim. One problem that has evolved is a relatively high incidence of contested cases and an average six-to-eight-month delay before initial administrative review. Of course, the greater the delay, or *threat* of delay, the greater the incentive for the injured worker to settle for a smaller amount.

As seems to be the case everywhere, a special commission was appointed in 1979 to bring together labor, business and insurance interests in an effort to reach a compromise reform package. Its report revealed that labor representatives were concerned primarily with delays in benefit payments, the prolonged hearing process and the agreement system of payment. The level of benefits was not a major concern. The reform effort of 1982 grew out of the commission's recommendations. The thrust of the proposed legislation was to streamline the claim procedure in order to (1) speed payment, (2) reduce the potential for disagreement over awards and consequently the incentive to contest awards and (3) increase the predictability of the size of award and when the issue would be resolved. Of course, the hope was that in doing so premiums would fall.

I believe it is fair to say that the impetus for reform was the concern over the cumbersome administrative process and backlog of contested claims (with consequent higher costs). Change in the benefit structure was an issue only because of the presumption that the *type* of benefits (not the level) contributed greatly to the probability of contesting a claim. Although it is never clearly stated, I suspect the rationale behind the proposed solutions was the belief that abolition of permanent partial awards was a necessary sacrifice for streamlining the system, that effective administrative reform was operationally impossible under the existing benefit statutes. When framers of the proposed legislation were briefed on Florida's new "wage loss" bill, they enthusiastically seized the approach as the solution to Delaware's problems. Nevertheless, the rationale for the tradeoff was not effectively conveyed nor backed with statistical evidence from Delaware, or anywhere else. Instead, throughout the debate the image was that business was extracting a price (in the form of reduced benefits) for reform.

Labor representatives had expressed dissatisfaction with the old administrative framework, but once the proposed legislation started moving toward a vote, this interest in streamlining the program took a back seat to the perceived benefit reduction. Opponents of the legislation were careful to construct numerical examples showing injured workers losing thousands of dollars in compensation under the wage loss approach. The distrust over the permanent partial removal overshadowed other dramatic changes, including a proposed increase in the cap on benefits to 125 percent SAWW.

The proposed changes failed to pass, due in no small way to lack of the research and education effort advocated above. But I also wonder if a careful examination of Delaware's claim experience would yield the same recommendations that were proposed? Such a study was never made. My point is that proponents of the move to wage loss in Delaware were easily convinced of the validity of Florida's legislation, without statistical support.

It has been suggested to me by several researchers that the gain from a shift to a wage loss approach varies depending upon prior state statutes, state workforce composition, and the accompanying administrative framework. Moreover (John Lewis' optimism notwithstanding), the papers in this session clearly demonstrate that the political road to a wage loss system is fraught with pitfalls and is potentially very costly. With the experience of several states unfolding, I would like to see a specific discussion of the feasibility of the approach relative to less politically volatile alternatives. I know of no published discussion at this time. Recognizing the constraints imposed by the political process of reform, I am wondering when the wage loss approach is the prescription for states grappling with their permanent partial statutes, and when is it not.

# 7

# Interstate Variations in the Employers' Costs of Workers' Compensation, with Particular Reference to Connecticut, New Jersey, and New York*

John F. Burton, Jr.
New York State School of Industrial and Labor Relations
Cornell University
and
Alan B. Krueger
Economics Department
Harvard University

## Introduction

State-by-state information on the employers' costs of workers' compensation insurance has several uses. The interstate variations in costs can be examined to determine if the magnitude is sufficient to influence plant location decisions. Also, insurance cost differences among states can be compared to differences in benefit levels and other factors to isolate the causes of the cost variations. These two topics were examined in earlier studies we will identify for convenience as the *Dissertation*[1] and the *Upjohn Study*.[2] One conclusion of these studies was that the interstate differences in workers' compensation costs are unlikely to be a significant factor in employer location decisions. Another conclusion was that benefit levels are the major determinant of the costs of workers' compensation insurance in a jurisdiction.

The method developed in these earlier studies was utilized with minor modifications in connection with another use of

111

state-specific data on the employers' costs of workers' compensation, namely, as one factor in estimating the cost of adopting the recommendations contained in *The Report of the National Commission on State Workmen's Compensation Laws.*[3] This topic was examined in a paper that will be identified as the *Supplemental Study.*[4]

Another use of data on workers' compensation costs in various states is to examine the changes through time in the costs and to consider the significance of the changes for the efforts to reform the program. This topic was examined in two studies. The first, *Workers' Compensation Costs for Employers,* provided data through July 1, 1975, and was published by the Interdepartmental Workers' Compensation Task Force; we will identify this as the *Task Force Study.*[5] The second was published in the *Monthly Labor Review* and will be referred to as the *MLR article.*[6] It provided workers' compensation cost information as of July 1, 1978. Both the *Task Force Study* and the *MLR article* found that the interstate differences in the employers' costs of workers' compensation had widened after 1972, when the *Report* of the National Commission had been submitted. Both studies concluded this provided support for the Commission's case for federal minimum standards for workers' compensation.

We recently prepared a report (which will be referred to as the *Ohio-Pennsylvania Study*[7]) that represents still another variation on the use of data on the interstate differences in workers' compensation costs. As a result of the increased costs of workers' compensation in the last decade, employers, legislators, and other interested parties have become more interested in the costs of the delivery system for the program.[8] In some states this concern has translated into changes in the insurance arrangements used to provide workers' compensation benefits. In most states, private insurance carriers traditionally have paid the bulk of the workers' compensation benefits, and have relied on a pricing mechanism that limited the amount of price competition among carriers. Recently, several states have changed their laws or regulations to permit more competition in rates.[9] Some of these changes are examined in this report because of their effect on interstate cost comparisons.

Another manifestation of the concern over costs of the delivery system has been the proposal to reduce the role of private carriers in favor of greater reliance on state insurance funds because of a belief that state funds can deliver benefits with lower administrative costs. This belief was a factor in the recent establishment of a new competitive state fund in Minnesota, which means that for the first time the private carriers in the state will have to compete with a state fund. The argument that state funds are more efficient also underlies the proposal to convert certain competitive state funds into exclusive state funds. That is, rather than the state fund competing with private carriers, as is now the case in 13 states including Minnesota, the state fund would be the sole carrier providing insurance in the jurisdiction, as is now the case in six states. The *Ohio-Pennsylvania Study* examined the possible transmutation of a competitive state fund into an exclusive state fund by focusing on a specific case, Pennsylvania, where such a proposal is extant. The study chose Ohio as a reference point for Pennsylvania because the states are contiguous, have similar benefit levels, and Ohio has the largest exclusive state fund.

The present study reexamines some of the conclusions from these earlier studies. Data are presented on the employers' costs of workers' compensation insurance as of January 1, 1983, which permits an examination of whether the widening of interstate cost differences between 1972 and 1978 has continued into more recent years. In addition, the study examines whether the different rates of increase in workers' compensation costs in Connecticut, New Jersey, and New York between 1972 and 1983 are related to changes in the three states' levels of benefits.

Examination of these topics first requires the development of accurate measures of the employers' costs of workers' compensation. These costs will be measured at several stages of refinement. The first comparison will involve the manual rates in effect on January 1, 1983, which are presented in table 3 and discussed in section IV. The second level of comparison will rely on adjusted manual rates, which are more accurate measures of employers' insurance costs than are manual rates since the adjusted rates reflect factors such as experience rating and premium discounts. The adjusted manual rates are provided in tables 10 and 11 and are examined in section IX. Finally, comparisons will be made using the employers' net costs of insurance, which represent the weekly premiums per worker paid by employers. These net costs, presented in tables 13 and 14 and discussed in section X, are less convenient measures of employers' costs than are the adjusted manual rates since the adjusted manual rates can be viewed as the percentage of payroll devoted to workers' compensation insurance, and therefore most of the emphasis on the costs comparisons will involve the adjusted manual rates. Because of the particular focus of this report on Connecticut, New Jersey, and New York, section XII will extensively examine the cost differences among these jurisdictions. The final section then considers the significance of the changes since 1972 in the interstate differences in workers' compensation costs in all states covered by this study.

## I. Alternative Methods for Providing Workers' Compensation Benefits to Employees

For the employer who has elected or has been required to provide workers' compensation benefits to his employees, three methods are possible. In most states if the employer has a sufficient payroll and a satisfactory record of paying past claims, it may self-insure the risks of industrial accidents. Alternatively, in most states the employer may purchase insurance from a private insurance company. In some states, the employer may purchase insurance from a fund operated by the state.

Costs of self-insurance receive little attention in this study, as self-insurers represent a small percentage of benefit payments; in 1980, self-insurance benefit payment represented 17.5 percent of the total benefit payments.[10] An even more compelling reason, however, is the lack of data. Except for the figures cited above on aggregate benefit payments, only limited data are available on self-insurers and these are virtually useless for the present study.[11]

Most employers purchase their insurance from private companies or from state insurance funds. The determination of the insurance costs begins by assigning the employer to one or more industrial or occupational categories. In about 40 states where private insurance is available, these categories are prescribed by the classifications published by the National Council on Compensation Insurance.[12] Active classifications range from 0005 Nursery Employees to 9620 Funeral Directors. Between these two are several thousand other classifications, at least 500 of which are in common use. Deviations from the National Council's system range from New Jersey, with a few variations, to five states with substantially different classification systems. Three of the states (California, Delaware, and Pennsylvania) have private insurance carriers, while two (Ohio and West Virginia) are exclusive fund states.

After each of the employer's operations has been assigned to a particular insurance classification, an appropriate initial insurance rate, the manual rate, can be located in the state's current schedule. Manual rates are stated as a certain number of dollars per $100 of weekly earnings for each employee. Thus, if an employee earns $200 per week and the appropriate manual rate is $3.50, the week's insurance premium for this employee is $7.00. Unfortunately, this example ignores a number of complications that are relevant for this study.

## II. Impact of Payroll Limitations On Interstate Comparisons

One of the factors that used to be a major obstacle to comparisons of workers' compenation costs was that many states had different payroll limitations. A payroll limitation is a figure that determines the maximum amount of an employee's weekly earnings that will be used in the calculation of insurance premiums. For many years, the normal payroll limitation was $100, which meant that the manual rate would be multiplied by an employee's weekly earnings or $100, whichever was less, to determine the weekly premium. Thus, if the manual rate were $3.00, the employee's weekly earnings $150, and the payroll limitation $100, the employer's weekly insurance premium would be $3.00.

Most states affiliated with the National Council on Compensation Insurance converted from a $100 payroll limitation to a $300 limitation around 1957, and to no limit (which means the manual rates are charged against the whole payroll) during 1974-75. However, four states (Missouri, Texas, Florida, and Louisiana) still had weekly payroll limitations of $200 or less as of July 1, 1975 and they were eliminated from the *Task Force Study*. By July 1, 1978, these four states had payroll limitations of $300 or had eliminated their payroll limitations, and so the *MLR article* included these states. By January 1, 1983, the comparison date for the current study, only Texas had a payroll limitation ($300), which means the data on Texas must be used with caution. Because the manual rates are only applied to the first $300 of payroll, the apparent cost of workers' compensation insurance in Texas as shown in this report is artificially high.[13]

Table 1 provides a catalog of all states, indicating those included in this study because as of January 1, 1983, they have appropriate manual rate data available and either a $300 weekly payroll limit or no limit. The table also provides the reasons that four states with exclusive state funds are omitted. Comparable data are available for 46 states and the District of Columbia. These 47 jurisdictions are divided into three groups in the final column of table 1: two jurisdictions with exclusive state funds; 31 jurisdictions in which the National Council on Compensation Insurance is the designated rating organization; and 14 states with independent local rating organizations. As will be detailed later in this report, the 47 jurisdictions differ in important aspects that must be considered before valid comparisons can be made, including differences in classification systems, experience rating, dividend policies, and the degree of competition among private carriers that is permitted or encouraged.

## III. Inappropriate Methods of Comparing Workers' Compensation Costs

One admittedly crude method of comparing employers' costs of workers' compensation is to ascertain the ratio of earned premium to payroll for each state. Recent figures from the National Council on Compensation Insurance show a range from 0.99 percent in Indiana to 3.73 percent in Arizona, with a national average of 2.46 percent.[14]

For the primary purpose of the *Dissertation* and the *Upjohn Study* (i.e., the significance of the interstate variations in employers' costs of workers' compensation for plant location decisions), such information is irrelevant. Employers

## Table 1
### Catalog of States Showing Reason for Elimination of Certain States From Comparison of Manual Rates and Status of Payroll Limitation Rule

| State | Reason for elimination | Status of payroll limitation rule | Organization that prepares insurance rates |
|---|---|---|---|
| Alabama | | No limit | N |
| Alaska | (Caution: high average wage level may make results misleading.) | No limit | N |
| Arizona | | No limit | N |
| Arkansas | | No limit | N |
| California | | No limit | I |
| Colorado | | No limit | N |
| Connecticut | | No limit | N |
| Delaware | | No limit | I |
| District of Columbia | | No limit | N |
| Florida | | No limit | N |
| Georgia | | No limit | N |
| Hawaii | | No limit | I |
| Idaho | | No limit | N |
| Illinois | | No limit | N |
| Indiana | | No limit | I |
| Iowa | | No limit | N |
| Kansas | | No limit | N |
| Kentucky | | No limit | N |
| Louisiana | | No limit (in transition) | N |
| Maine | | No limit | N |
| Maryland | | No limit | N |
| Massachusetts | | No limit | I |
| Michigan | | No limit | I |
| Minnesota | | No limit | I |
| Mississippi | | No limit | N |
| Missouri | | No limit | N |
| Montana | | No limit | N |
| Nebraska | | No limit | N |
| Nevada | Exclusive state fund; insurance classification not comparable. | _____ | ____ |
| New Hampshire | | No limit | N |
| New Jersey | | No limit | I |
| New Mexico | | No limit | N |
| New York | | No limit | I |

## Table 1 (continued)

| State | Reason for elimination | Status of payroll limitation rule | Organization that prepares insurance rates |
|---|---|---|---|
| North Carolina | | No limit | I |
| North Dakota | Exclusive state fund; insurance classification not comparable. | ———— | —— |
| Ohio | | No limit | E |
| Oklahoma | | No limit | N |
| Oregon | | No limit | N |
| Pennsylvania | | No limit | I |
| Rhode Island | | No limit | N |
| South Carolina | | No limit | N |
| South Dakota | | No limit | N |
| Tennessee | | No limit | N |
| Texas | | $300 per week | I |
| Utah | | No limit | N |
| Vermont | | No limit | N |
| Virginia | | No limit | I |
| Washington | Exclusive state fund; insurance rate based on hours of exposure; not payroll. | ———— | —— |
| West Virginia | | No limit | E |
| Wisconsin | | No limit | I |
| Wyoming | Exclusive state fund; does not use insurance classification system. | ———— | —— |

SOURCE: NCCI, *Workers' Compensation Rating Laws - A Digest of Changes* (1982, with August 15, 1983 quarterly update).

Payroll limitation rules are those in effect January 1, 1983.

Code or organization that prepares insurance rates: E is exclusive fund state; I is independent local rating organization; N is National Council on Compensation Insurance.

who move from state to state are going to be concerned with their own particular insurance rates, not with those of the average employer in each state. Assume that there are only two insurance classifications in states A and B—class 1 and class 2—and that employer would fall into class 1 in both states. Assume that the manual rates for each classification are identical in both states; e.g., class 1 is $0.10 in both states and class 2 is $1.00. Also, assume that all employers pay their employees $300 per week and that there is no payroll limit.

Obviously, there is no incentive for an employer to move from state A to state B because its insurance costs will be unaffected by the move. Yet, if in state A 90 percent of the payroll of all employers is in class 2 and 10 percent in class 1, while in state B 90 percent is in class 1 and 10 percent in class 2, the average earned premium as a percentage of payroll will vary considerably between the states. Specifically, the average earned premium will be 0.91 percent of payroll in state A and 0.19 percent in state B, despite the critical fact that there is no incentive for an interstate movement of the particular employer in question or of any employer, as long as its classification does not change as a result of an interstate move.

To a large extent, the National Council data on standard earned premium are subject to the same limitations found in the hypothetical example. Some industries, such as steel or auto production, are important in some states and nonexistent in others. Even for industries found in all states, the proportion of covered payroll accounted for by the classification varies widely. Because of the influence of such varying payroll distribution on the data, this approach to interstate cost comparisons is not considered further here. The National Council cautions that conclusions drawn from comparisons of such data "have no validity"[15] because of payroll distribution variations and other reasons and will no longer publish this data in its statistical bulletins due to the concerns about validity.

An even more questionable approach to comparing workers' compensation costs among jurisdictions by use of insurance industry data was utilized in a recent article in *Best's Insurance Management Reports.*[16] Average premiums per state were presented for 1981, and showed a range from $63.77 per worker in Indiana to $594.98 in Alaska, with a national average of $189.57. As noted in the article, no effort was made to correct for different industry mixes in the various jurisdictions. A more serious problem is that the insurance premiums are direct premiums written by private carriers and state insurance funds, with state information on self-insurers omitted because such data are unavailable. The data on premiums written "were then divided by the number of wage earners in each state."[17] Although the article does not identify the source of the employment data, presumably the number of wage earners includes workers employed by firms that self-insure. The result is that states with a high proportion of benefits provided by self-insurers will have their cost figures artificially lowered since premiums written exclude the experience of self-insurers but the employment figures do not.[18]

## IV. The Appropriate Method of Comparing Workers' Compensation Costs

The previous section discussed two methods of comparing interstate differences in workers' compensation costs, each with a degree of invalidity. Fortunately, a more valid method for comparing employers' workers' compensation costs in different states is available. To return to the example involving states A and B presented in the previous section, the degree of incentive for employers to move from state A to state B can be shown by using the same distribution of payroll among classes for both states. For example, the distribution of payroll among classes in state A can be used with the state B manual rates to generate a new average earned premium as a percentage of payroll for the state A employers on the assumption they move to state B. Obviously, the state A employers would pay 0.91 percent of their payroll as premium in either state, and the lack of incentive to move is apparent.

This more valid method of interstate comparison using a constant distribution of payroll for all states is the basis for analysis in this study. However, the method has to be refined, and the first step is to increase the number of classifications used beyond two. There are more than 500 active classifications in National Council states, but many of these are generally unsubstantial, or are important only in a few states. Seventy-one classifications were selected for the current study on the basis of their common use, their relative importance as measured by the percentage of total payroll for which they account, and their representative character in three divisions of workers' compensation classifications: Manufacturing, Contracting, and All Other. Table 2 includes a brief description of each of the 71 classifications and shows the percentage of total payroll accounted for by each classification in the aggregate of the 36 National Council states for which payroll information in available.[19]

In categorizing data in table 2, the starting point was the National Council's *Classification Codes* used in 42 of the states included in this study.[20] States using other classification systems were "converted" by selecting the classification which appeared most nearly analogous to each of the 71 National Council classes.[21] However, since the non-Council states often use classifications which are broader than those in National Council states, no attempt was made to incorporate the payroll distribution among classes of these states into the aggregates of table 2.

## Table 2
## Insurance Classifications and Distribution of Payroll*

| Code number | Classification description | Percentage of covered payroll in 36 selected states |
|---|---|---|
| | **Division A - classes substantial in all states, 1950-83** | |
| | **Manufacturing classes** | |
| 2003 | Bakeries | .335 |
| 2070 | Creameries | .189 |
| 4299 | Printing | .668 |
| 4304 | Newspaper publishing | .121 |
| | Total 4 manufacturing classes | 1.313 |
| | **Contracting classes** | |
| 5022 | Masonry N.O.C. | .349 |
| 5183 | Plumbing N.O.C. | .879 |
| 5190 | Electrical wiring-within building | .742 |
| 5213 | Concrete construction N.O.C. | .457 |
| 5215 | Concrete work | .049 |
| | Total 5 contracting classes | 2.476 |
| | **All other classes** | |
| 7219 | Truckmen N.O.C. | 1.278 |
| 7380 | Chauffeurs, drivers, helpers N.O.C. | .910 |
| 7539 | Electric light or power companies-N.O.C.-all operations | .158 |
| 8017 | Retail stores N.O.C. | 1.402 |
| 8018 | Wholesale or combined wholesale-retail N.O.C. | .631 |
| 8033 | Meat, grocery, and provision stores-retail | 1.236 |
| 8232 | Lumber yards | .444 |
| 8293 | Furniture storage warehouses | .073 |
| 8350 | Gasoline or oil dealers | .217 |
| 8387 | Gasoline stations; accessories stations | .677 |
| 8391 | Automobile garages | 1.194 |
| 8742 | Salesmen, collectors, or messengers-outside | 6.418 |
| 8810 | Clerical office employees N.O.C. | 25.425 |
| 9052 | Hotels | .468 |
| 9079 | Restaurant N.O.C. | 2.566 |
| | Total 15 all other classes | 43.097 |
| | Total 24 classes | 46.886 |

## Table 2 (continued)

| Code number | Classification description | Percentage of covered payroll in 36 selected states |
|---|---|---|
| | **Division B-classes with payroll in all states, 1950-83** | |
| | **Manufacturing classes** | |
| | Four classes from division A | 1.313 |
| 2039 | Ice cream | .026 |
| 2157 | Bottling N.O.C. | .186 |
| 2585 | Laundries N.O.C. | .122 |
| 2586 | Cleaning or dyeing | .072 |
| 2802 | Carpentry-shop only | .195 |
| 3081 | Foundries-iron N.O.C. | .116 |
| 3085 | Foundries-nonferrous metals N.O.C. | .055 |
| 4034 | Concrete products | .117 |
| | Total 12 manufacturing classes | 2.202 |
| | **Contracting classes** | |
| | Five classes from division A | 2.476 |
| 5221 | Concrete work: floors, sidewalks, etc. | .289 |
| 5538 | Sheet metal work erection N.O.C. | .429 |
| | Total 7 contracting classes | 3.194 |
| | **All other classes** | |
| | Fifteen classes from division A | 43.097 |
| 8006 | Retail grocery stores-no fresh meats | .240 |
| 8008 | Retail clothing or dry goods stores | .790 |
| 8044 | Wholesale or retail furniture stores | .329 |
| 8292 | General merchandise warehouses N.O.C. | .104 |
| 8748 | Automobile sales or service agencies | .534 |
| 8833 | Hospitals: professional employees | 2.765 |
| 8868 | Colleges or schools: professional employees | 6.361 |
| 9015 | Buildings operation N.O.C. | .544 |
| 9040 | Hospitals: all other employees | .565 |
| 9101 | Colleges or schools: all other employees | .901 |
| | Total 25 all other classes | 56.230 |
| | Total 44 classes | 61.626 |

## Table 2 (continued)

| Code number | Classification description | Percentage of covered payroll in 36 selected states |
|---|---|---|
| | **Division C-all classes with manual rates available, 1958-83** | |
| | **Manufacturing classes** | |
| | Twelve classes from divisions A and B | 2.202 |
| 2501 | Clothing | 1.097 |
| 2883 | Wood furniture N.O.C. | .280 |
| 3066 | Sheet metal work-shop | .196 |
| 3076 | Fireproof equipment | .319 |
| 3082 | Foundries-steel castings | .037 |
| 3113 | Tool N.O.C. | .282 |
| 3179 | Electrical apparatus N.O.C. | .460 |
| 3400 | Metal goods N.O.C. | .228 |
| 3507 | Agricultural machinery | .394 |
| 3612 | Pump and engine N.O.C. | .159 |
| 3643 | Electrical power equipment | .401 |
| 3681 | Telephone apparatus | .549 |
| | Total 24 manufacturing classes | 6.604 |
| | **Contracting classes** | |
| | Seven classes from divisions A and B | 3.194 |
| | Total 7 contracting classes | 3.194 |
| | **All other classes** | |
| | Twenty-five classes from divisions A and B | |
| | Total 25 all other classes | 56.230 |
| | Total 56 classes | 66.028 |
| | **Division D-all classes with manual rates available, 1972-83** | |
| | **Manufacturing classes** | |
| | Twenty-four classes from divisions A, B, and C | 6.604 |
| 2220 | Yarn or thread-cotton | .395 |
| 2361 | Hosiery manufacturing | .115 |
| 2660 | Boot or shoe manufacturing N.O.C. | .159 |
| 3632 | Machine shops N.O.C. | .981 |
| 4484 | Plastics-molded products manufacturing N.O.C. | .358 |
| | Total 29 manufacturing classes | 8.612 |

## Table 2 (continued)

| Code number | Classification description | Percentage of covered payroll in 36 selected states |
|---|---|---|
| | **Contracting classes** | |
| | Seven classes from divisions A and B | 3.194 |
| 3724 | Millwright work N.O.C. | .427 |
| 5403 | Carpentry N.O.C. | .500 |
| 5506 | Street or road construction | .389 |
| 5606 | Contractors-executive supervisors | .433 |
| 5645 | Carpentry-detached private residences | .547 |
| 6217 | Excavation N.O.C. | .330 |
| | Total 13 contracting classes | 5.820 |
| | **All other classes** | |
| | Twenty-five classes from divisions A, B, and C | 56.230 |
| 7720 | Policemen | .615 |
| 8010 | Hardware stores-wholesale or retail | .515 |
| 8039 | Retail department stores | .710 |
| 8829 | Convalescent or nursing homes | .849 |
| | Total 29 all other classes | 58.919 |
| | Total 71 classes | 73.351 |

NOTE: N.O.C. means "not otherwise classified."

*Code number and classification description taken from Classification Code of National Council on Compensation Insurance. The payroll distribution is based on 1978-79, 1979-80, or 1980-81 policy year data for 36 states.

Even though the 71 classifications were chosen deliberately to maximize covered payroll, these classes are not of equal importance. The classes are grouped into divisions A, B, C, and D using criteria that are detailed in the *Ohio-Pennsylvania Study*.[22] Briefly, division A includes 24 classes that had sufficient payroll to warrant the use of special actuarial practices during the rate-making procedures. A second measure of importance is whether the manual rates for the class have been published in the rate pages of a state. The normal criterion for publication is that there must have been some payroll exposure for the class in the state within the previous five years. As division B of table 4 indicates, there were 44 classes that met this requirement or the more stringent requirements of division A for all states included in the *Upjohn Study*.[23]

Division C of table 3 includes 56 classifications for which manual rates could be obtained in any manner for the 29 states for 1958-65 and for which data were available for all 42 jurisdictions included in the *Supplemental Study*.[24] Finally, division D includes 71 classes in use in most jurisdictions in 1983, and was added in the *Supplemental Study* to provide an even broader sample of insurance classification. However, some states for which division C data are available cannot be shown for division D.[25]

The results for the 44 classes in division B are given the strongest emphasis in section XI because division B contains the largest number of classes for which an historically comparable series is available (in the *Dissertation, Upjohn Study, Supplemental Study, Task Force Report,* and *MLR article*) and because some of the classes included in divisions C and D have little or no payroll experience in some states, which means that the averages for these divisions are less reliable than the division B averages.

Table 3

Interstate Variations in Average Costs of Manual Rates for Classes
in Each Division, Weighted by National Payroll Distributions

| Jurisdiction | 24 classes in division A | 44 classes in divisions A and B | 24 manufacturing classes in divisions A, B, and C | 56 classes in divisions A, B, and C | 71 classes in divisions A,B,C, and D |
|---|---|---|---|---|---|
| Alabama | 1.059 | 1.057 | 2.429 | 1.136 | 1.330 |
| Alaska | 2.644 | 2.525 | 4.606 | 2.636 | 2.947 |
| Arizona | 1.565 | 1.704 | 3.890 | 1.816 | 2.094 |
| Arkansas | 1.345 | 1.422 | 3.425 | 1.541 | 1.809 |
| California | 2.297 | 2.519 | 5.844 | 2.708 | 3.216 |
| Colorado | 1.493 | 1.560 | 3.587 | 1.667 | 1.886 |
| Connecticut | 2.005 | 2.086 | 4.558 | 2.199 | 2.654 |
| Delaware | 1.315 | 1.416 | 4.847 | 1.633 | --- |
| District of Columbia | 2.575 | 2.592 | 6.147 | 2.798 | 3.209 |
| Florida | 1.637 | 1.728 | 3.628 | 1.803 | 2.067 |
| Georgia | 1.039 | 1.071 | 2.850 | 1.177 | 1.351 |
| Hawaii | 4.112 | 4.429 | 9.098 | 4.668 | 5.357 |
| Idaho | 1.500 | 1.508 | 3.309 | 1.619 | 1.881 |
| Illinois | 1.431 | 1.426 | 3.416 | 1.541 | 1.800 |
| Indiana | 0.379 | 0.394 | 0.847 | 0.420 | 0.483 |
| Iowa | 1.120 | 1.119 | 1.995 | 1.163 | 1.339 |
| Kansas | 0.941 | 0.975 | 2.238 | 1.052 | 1.253 |
| Kentucky | 1.315 | 1.371 | 3.570 | 1.510 | 1.827 |
| Louisiana | 1.515 | 1.572 | 3.769 | 1.706 | 2.027 |
| Maine | 1.866 | 1.954 | 4.262 | 2.065 | --- |
| Maryland | 2.277 | 2.274 | 4.467 | 2.365 | 2.729 |

| | | | | | |
|---|---|---|---|---|---|
| Massachusetts | 1.686 | 1.782 | 4.249 | 1.915 | 2.294 |
| Michigan | 2.203 | 2.327 | 7.038 | 2.602 | 3.045 |
| Minnesota | 1.603 | 1.685 | 4.855 | 1.886 | 2.191 |
| Mississippi | 0.975 | 0.973 | 2.018 | 1.032 | 1.214 |
| Missouri | 0.671 | 0.703 | 1.622 | 0.760 | 0.904 |
| Montana | 1.819 | 1.856 | 4.167 | 1.998 | — |
| Nebraska | 0.906 | 0.933 | 1.994 | 0.978 | 1.142 |
| New Hampshire | 1.536 | 1.598 | 3.338 | 1.681 | 2.073 |
| New Jersey | 1.564 | 1.683 | 3.976 | 1.807 | 2.067 |
| New Mexico | 2.263 | 2.297 | 4.511 | 2.424 | 2.713 |
| New York | 1.372 | 1.391 | 3.504 | 1.510 | 1.716 |
| North Carolina | 0.837 | 0.856 | 1.618 | 0.893 | 1.059 |
| Ohio | 1.393 | 1.439 | 2.750 | 1.488 | 1.680 |
| Oklahoma | 1.573 | 1.627 | 3.959 | 1.773 | 2.101 |
| Oregon | 2.058 | 2.161 | 5.181 | 2.342 | — |
| Pennsylvania | 1.728 | 1.786 | 3.811 | 1.877 | — |
| Rhode Island | 1.564 | 1.708 | 5.155 | 1.909 | 2.181 |
| South Carolina | 1.092 | 1.105 | 1.993 | 1.145 | 1.372 |
| South Dakota | 0.839 | 0.859 | 1.582 | 0.900 | 1.073 |
| Tennessee | 0.883 | 0.926 | 2.210 | 1.001 | 1.219 |
| Texas | 1.844 | 1.929 | 5.076 | 2.130 | 2.495 |
| Utah | 0.885 | 0.929 | 2.416 | 1.020 | 1.185 |
| Vermont | 0.839 | 0.856 | 1.819 | 0.904 | 1.040 |
| Virginia | 1.201 | 1.225 | 2.235 | 1.268 | 1.500 |
| West Virginia | 1.104 | 1.063 | 2.044 | 1.130 | 1.253 |
| Wisconsin | 0.868 | 0.928 | 2.215 | 0.999 | 1.186 |

## Table 4
### Premium Discount Schedule for Annual Premium in States Affiliated with the National Council on Compensation Insurance

| Standard earned premium | Stock carriers (percentage) | Non-stock carriers (percentage) |
|---|---|---|
| First $5,000 | 0.0 | 0.0 |
| Next $95,000 | 9.5 | 2.0 |
| Next $400,000 | 11.9 | 4.0 |
| Over $500,000 | 12.4 | 6.0 |

SOURCE: National Council on Compensation Insurance.

Using the national payroll distribution by classifications from table 2 and the manual rates from each state, we present average manual rates for various combinations of classifications in table 3. Column 1 uses the national payroll distribution for the classes in division A of table 2 and shows the average manual rates for 24 classes. Column 2 presents averages using the 44 classes in divisions A and B of table 2. Averages for the 24 manufacturing classes in divisions A, B, and C are shown in column 3; for all 56 classes in divisions A, B, and C in column 4; and for all 71 classes in divisions A to D in column 5, where averages for some states are unavailable.

The average manual rates shown in table 3 have been adjusted for Minnesota and Oregon for reasons related to the factors that complicate interstate comparisons when different states use different payroll limitations.[26] In five states—Delaware, Pennsylvania, Ohio, Utah, and West Virginia—premiums are assessed against the full overtime premium, while in the other 42 jurisdictions examined by this study, hours of overtime work are considered at the regular hourly wage.[27] Since the overtime premium does not appear to represent a significant portion of payroll,[28] manual rates in the five states were not adjusted to reflect interstate differences in payroll bases.

In three states—Kentucky, Michigan, and Oregon—the published rates do not include expense loadings and therefore the rates used to prepare the average in table 3 were calculated for this study. The procedure used to make the calculations are explained in section VII in conjunction with the discussion of open competition.

## V. Modifications of Manual Rates in National Council States: Phase 1

The averages of various combinations of manual rates provide only a beginning toward accurate comparisons of workers' compensation costs. Even assuming that the various states are using the same payroll limitations, other problems arise because the published manual rates are only a starting point for the computation of the employer's insurance premiums. The employer does not simply pay as a premium the product of the manual rate and his covered payroll; its insurance costs are influenced by premium discounts for quantity purchases, dividends received from mutual companies and participating stock companies, and the modification of the manual rate caused by the employer's own compensable accident experience. The effects of these factors are calculated for the 31 jurisdictions that use the National Council on Compensation Insurance as the rating organization in this section. In the next section, the influence of these factors (premium discounts, dividends, and experience rating) in the 14 jurisdictions with independent rating organizations is examined. Insurance costs are also affected by open competition, deviations, and schedule rating, and the impact of these factors in all 45 states with private carriers included in this study is discussed in section VII. Section VIII then reviews the impact of factors such as experience rating in the states with exclusive state funds.

## A. A Catalog of the Modifying Factors on Manual Rates in National Council States

The terminology in workers' compensation is not "standard, descriptive, and orderly."[29] Therefore, the terms as defined in the following discussion must be used with caution since they sometimes are defined differently in other publications or exhibits.

If the employer's total payroll falling within the payroll limit is multiplied by the appropriate manual rate published in the state's rate pages, the result is the *manual premium*. In practice, few employers pay such an amount.

The first modification is caused by experience rating for larger companies. In simple terms, experience rating uses the employer's own past record of benefit payments to modify the published manual rates. If the employer's record is worse than the experience of the average employer in its classification, then its actual premium for the current policy period is larger than its manual premium. Basically, the same experience rating formula is used in all the National Council states and therefore comparisons among these states are not complicated by use of this modification. Thus, if an employer whose accident experience is 20 percent better than its classification in state A has its premium reduced accordingly, it will find the premium similarly modified in state B if its own relative accident rate remains the same.[30]

Although experience rating does not complicate comparisons among National Council states, it is necessary to determine the general effects of experience rating in these states in order to compare them with other states that have their own experience rating plans. The product of the experience rating factor and the manual premium is termed the *standard earned premium excluding constants*.[31]

The standard earned premium excluding constants also is modified for most employers, although there are divergent paths depending on the size of the premium. In order to cover minimum costs of issuing and servicing a policy, in almost all states employers are assessed a flat charge termed an *expense constant.*[32] In addition, employers in most states previously were assessed a flat charge, a *loss constant,* designed to compensate for the generally inferior safety record of small businesses. The loss constant program is in the process of being eliminated on a state-by-state basis. If the expense and loss constants are added to the standard earned premium excluding constants, the result is termed the *standard earned premium including constants.*

Employers with annual premiums in excess of $5,000 are entitled to reductions in their standard earned premiums because of economies of scale. *Premium discounts* based on the schedule in table 4 are compulsory in the National Council states, unless both the insurance carriers and the employer agree to substitute *retrospective rating* for the premium discounts. Despite varieties of retrospective rating plans in National Council states, basically all are similar in that they allow the employer to increase the effect of its own experience on the published manual rates. The main difference between experience rating and retrospective rating is that the former uses the employer's experience from previous periods to modify the current policy period rate, whereas the retrospective plan uses experience from the current policy period to determine the current premium, on an *ex post facto* basis. The same expense reductions provided by the premium discounts are built into the retrospective rating plans.

The use of premium discounts or retrospective rating should not complicate comparisons among the National Council states. The same discount schedule and the same retrospective plans are available in virtually all these states; the few deviations are unsubstantial.

The result of starting with the standard earned premium including constants and subtracting any amounts saved by employers because of premium discounts or retrospective rating is to arrive at *net earned premium.*[33]

There is a further "wedge" in National Council states between the published manual rates and the rates actually paid by employers. A substantial proportion of the workers' compensation insurance is written by mutual companies or stock companies with participating policies. While these companies normally use a quantity discount schedule less steeply graded than the nonparticipating stock companies, they pay dividends which usually cut the net cost to policyholders to less than that charged by nonparticipating stock companies, especially for large employers.

Participation is not a crucial detriment to comparisons among National Council states. Most workers' compensation insurance is sold by companies operating in more than one state; in fact typically the employer with operations in more than one state buys its insurance from the same or a similar participating company in state A and B is not likely to have the relative interstate differences in insurance costs altered because of the dividends received; a 10 percent dividend on premiums paid in either state will not influence interstate relativity.

This final modification of subtracting dividends paid by mutuals and participating stocks from the net earned premium results in the *net cost to policyholders.* This exercise thus began with manual premium and then, because of a series of additions and subtractions, moved to standard earned premium excluding constants, then to standard earned premiums including constants, then to net earned premium, and finally arrived at net cost to policyholders.

The manual premium divided by the appropriate payroll equals the manual rate. In this study the net cost to policyholders divided by the payroll is defined as the *high adjusted manual rate*. An attempt to quantify these concepts is presented below.

## B. Estimates of Influence of Modifying Factors on Manual Rates in National Council States

There are no data that can be used to calculate directly the total differential between manual premium and the net cost to policyholders. Instead, it is necessary to determine initially the difference between manual premium and standard earned premium excluding constants, then to measure the amount of the constants, and finally to measure the difference between standard earned premium including constants and the net cost to policyholders. The combining of the smaller differentials into the total differential is complicated because data on differences between the manual premium and standard earned premium excluding constants are available only on a policy year basis,[34] whereas data on the differences between standard earned premium and net cost to policyholders are available only on a calendar year basis.

Table 5 includes information on the differential between manual premium and standard earned premium excluding constants. The data as provided by the National Council on Compensation Insurance actually included the expense and loss constant amounts in the premiums and therefore were adjusted for this study.[35] This study will assume that 1.000 is the relevant ratio of standard earned premium excluding constants-to-manual premium for the National Council states. Historically, standard earned premium has been lower than manual premium, but the recent data show the two are essentially identical.[36]

## Table 5
### Ratio of Standard Earned Premium to Manual Premium in 38 States with Private Insurance Carriers
(all amounts in thousands)

| Policy period | Standard earned premium including expense and loss constants (1) | Standard earned premium excluding expense and loss constants (2) | Manual premium including expense and loss constants (3) | Manual premium excluding expense and loss constants (4) | Ratio of standard earned premium (2) to manual premium (4) (both exclude constants) (5) |
|---|---|---|---|---|---|
| 1979-80 | $ 9,264,520 | $ 9,232,094 | $ 9,325,231 | $ 9,292,593 | .993 |
| 1978-79 | 8,147,740 | 8,123,297 | 8,061,167 | 8,036,983 | 1.011 |
| 1977-78 | 6,620,118 | 6,600,257 | 6,640,834 | 6,620,912 | .997 |
| Total | $24,032,377 | $23,955,648 | $24,027,232 | $23,950,488 | 1.000 |

SOURCES: Data in columns 1 and 3 from National Council on Compensation Insurance, based on Unit Statistical Plan dates for 38 states (the 31 National Council states enumerated in table 1 plus Hawaii, Indiana, Michigan, Minnesota, North Carolina, Virginia, and Wisconsin). The figures in columns 2 and 4 are estimates prepared by John F. Burton, Jr. based on information provided by the National Council on Compensation Insurance.

NOTE: Figures may not add to totals because of rounding.

The most recent data on standard earned premium in table 5 are from policy period 1979-80. Loss constants were of miniscule importance as of then, and are even less significant now since they are being eliminated on a state-by-state basis. For this study the loss constants are therefore assumed to be nil.[37] In contrast, expense constants have become more significant in recent years as a program has been introduced in most states to increase the annual amounts per policy to $35, then $60, and currently $75. The National Council on Compensation Insurance estimates that the impact of these various levels of expense constants is to increase standard earned premium by approximately 1.2 percent, 2.0 percent, and 2.6 percent respectively. The National Council also provided information on the amount of the expense constant in effect in each state as of January 1, 1983 (which is the date of rate comparisons for this study). For each state, the difference between standard earned premium excluding constants and standard earned premium including constants was calculated using this information.[38]

Table 6, also provided by the National Council, presents data on the differential between standard earned premium including constants and the net cost to policyholders.[39] The figure of .835 as the ratio of net cost to policyholders-to-standard earned premium including constants will be used in subsequent calculations in this study.

If the ratio of 1.000 between standard earned premium excluding constants and manual premium is multiplied by the state's appropriate ratio between standard earned premium including constants and standard earned premium excluding constants (which will be 1.012, 1.020, or 1.026 depending on the state), and the product in turn is multiplied by 0.835, which is the ratio between the net cost to policyholders and standard earned premium including constants, then the overall ratio between the net cost to policyholders and

## Table 6

## Ratio of Net Cost to Policyholders to Standard Earned Premium, Including Constants, All Carriers

(all amounts in thousands)

| | 1977 | 1978 | 1979 | 1980 | 1981 | Five year total | |
| --- | --- | --- | --- | --- | --- | --- | --- |
| | | | | | | Dollar amount | Percentage of standard earned premium |
| 1. Standard earned premium including constants | $9,527,172 | $11,153,598 | $13,585,611 | $15,476,268 | $15,752,452 | $65,495,101 | 100.0 |
| 2. Return to policyholders through premium discounts and retrospective rating plans | 724,284 | 938,047 | 1,303,078 | 1,893,233 | 1,761,765 | 6,620,407 | 10.1 |
| 3. Dividends to policyholders | 456,607 | 597,519 | 816,761 | 1,091,992 | 1,205,039 | 4,167,918 | 6.4 |
| 4. Net cost to policyholders (1)-(2)-(3) | 8,346,281 | 9,618,032 | 11,465,772 | 12,491,043 | 12,785,648 | 54,706,776 | 83.5 |

SOURCE: National Council on Compensation Insurance, Compilations of Insurance Expense Exhibits, 1977-1981. These figures exclude state fund experience and are based on data from the 45 jurisdictions with private insurance carriers.

manual premium is 0.845, 0.852, or 0.857, depending on the state. These figures purport to say that the average employer in the states that use the National Council on Compensation Insurance as the rating organization does not pay insurance premiums equal to the published manual rates times his payroll, but pays an amount from 14.3 to 15.5 percent less than this because of such factors as premium discounts. In order words, including the expense constant adjustment, there is a 14.3 to 15.5 percent differential between manual rates and high adjusted manual rates as defined above. Obviously, these percentages are only an approximation and clearly would vary from employer to employer and from state to state for reasons other than different expense constants. Nonetheless, as the best available estimates of the difference between manual premiums and net costs, they are used in this study. The average manual rates in table 3 were reduced by the appropriate percentage for each of the 31 National Council states to produce the high adjusted manual rates in table 10.

## VI. Modification of Manual Rates in States with Independent Rating Organizations: Phase 1

The previous section examined the influence of factors such as premium discounts, dividends, and experience rating on the employers' costs of workers' compensation insurance in the 31 jurisdictions that use the National Council on Compensation Insurance as the rating organization. In this section we examine the influence of these factors in the 14 jurisdictions listed in table 1 that rely on local independent rating organizations to help determine workers' compensation insurance rates.

There are significant differences among these 14 jurisdictions. In six (Hawaii, Indiana, North Carolina, Texas, Virginia and Wisconsin) the National Council rate-making,

rating plans, and classification systems are used, and
therefore any differences between these states and the 31 National Council jurisdictions can be safely ignored.[40]
Michigan and Minnesota also utilize National Council services and have a classification system that is closely patterned after the NCCI classification codes, and for purposes of
this study will be treated as close enough to the National
Council states to justify using the figures developed in the
previous section as applicable to the two states. High adjusted manual rates are 14.3 to 15.5 percent less than manual
rates in these eight states, depending on the size of the expense constant in effect on January 1, 1983.[41]

The remaining six local rating organizations are completely independent of the National Council on Compensation Insurance. They are found in California, Delaware,
Massachusetts, New Jersey, New York, and Pennsylvania.
Three of these jurisdictions (California, Delaware, and
Pennsylvania) use classification systems that are significantly
different from the NCCI classification system; the other
three states use systems patterned on the NCCI codes.
California does not allow any form of premium discount,
while New Jersey allows the same discount schedule as in the
31 NCCI states but limited solely to premiums written in
New Jersey. The other five states provide for premium discounts based on the interstate premium amount. As to experience rating, California, Delaware, New Jersey, and
Pennsylvania operate intrastate plans in which the experience from other states is not considered in modifying the
manual rates in the state, nor is the state's experience included in the interstate experience rating calculations. In
Massachusetts and New York, the experience in the state is
combined with experience from other states to determine the
experience rating modifications.

This review indicates that two of the states with completely independent rating bureaus, Massachusetts and New York, are very similar to the 31 states that use the National Council on Compensation Insurance as the rating organization. In both states, the classification system closely parallels the NCCI codes, the NCCI premium discount schedule is used in conjunction with the entire interstate premium, and the experience rating formula also considers interstate experience. For these two states, the figures developed in the previous section that relate net cost to policyholders to manual premiums can be used without major qualms.

In contrast, California differs substantially from the National Council states in the methods used to modify manual premiums in order to arrive at the net cost paid by the employer, as it has no premium discount schedule, nor has it used the flat loss and expense constant charges in recent years. California does use experience rating, retrospective rating, and dividend payments; these to some extent probably reflect the absence of the premium discounts.

The relation between New Jersey and the NCCI jurisdictions is also attenuated compared to the relationship between the NCCI jurisdictions and Massachusetts and New York. New Jersey only applies the premium discount to intrastate business, and the experience rating modification only considers New Jersey experience.[42] It is likely that the retrospective rating and dividend payment plans in New Jersey to some extent compensate for the limited scope of the premium discounts and experience rating plans.

These features of California and New Jersey suggest that the figures developed in the previous section for the difference between manual rates and net costs to policyholders in NCCI states are only rough approximations of the differences in these two states. Unfortunately, these are the only estimates reasonably available for this study, and thus will be used. With this caveat, we proceed as if California, Massachusetts, New Jersey, and New York were directly comparable with the 31 National Council jurisdictions. Specifically, we assume that high adjusted manual rates for these four jurisdictions are 83.5 percent of manual rates (with the percentage modified to reflect each state's expense constant as of January 1, 1983), the same relationship developed for the NCCI jurisdictions in the last section.[43]

The two remaining jurisdictions with independent local rating bureaus are Delaware and Pennsylvania, for which data were developed in the *Ohio-Pennsylvania Study* to allow manual rates to be adjusted to determine net cost to policyholders.

While the ratio of standard earned premium without constants to manual premium is 1.000 in the NCCI jurisdictions (see table 5), it is .966 in Delaware, indicating a larger impact of experience rating in the state.[44] The expense constant in effect in Delaware on January 1, 1983 was $75, which means that standard earned premium with constants was estimated as 1.026 of standard earned premium without constants. In Delaware, the ratio of net cost to policyholders to standard earned premium with constants is .848, which is comparable to the .835 ratio in table 6 for the NCCI jurisdictions.[45] The larger ratio in Delaware indicates a somewhat smaller impact of premium discounts and dividends there than in the NCCI jurisdictions. In order to develop the overall differences between manual rates and net cost to policyholders in Delaware, the three ratios (.966, 1.026, and .848) were multiplied together. The result is a figure of .840, which means that the high adjusted manual rates in Delaware are 84.0 percent of manual rates.

The ratio of standard earned premium without constants to manual premium is .947 in Pennsylvania,[46] which is smaller than the similar ratio for the NCCI jurisdictions included in table 5. The smaller ratio in Pennsylvania indicates that the experience rating plan in the state produces a larger reduction than in the NCCI jurisdictions. The Pennsylvania expense constant in effect on January 1, 1983 was $60, which means that standard earned premium with constants was estimated as 1.020 of standard earned premium without constants. The ratio of net cost to policyholders to standard earned premium with constants in Pennsylvania is .835,[47] which by coincidence is the same figure for the NCCI jurisdictions found in table 6. In order to develop the overall difference between manual rates and net cost to policyholders in Pennsylvania, the three ratios (.947, 1.020, and .835) were multiplied together. The result is a figure of .807, which means that high adjusted manual rates in Pennsylvania are 80.7 percent of manual rates.

To recapitulate this section, state-specific data have been used to determine the relationship between manual rates and high adjusted manual rates for Delaware and Pennsylvania. For the other 12 jurisdictions with independent local rating organizations, the data from the NCCI jurisdictions have been used to make the adjustments. For some of these jurisdictions, the use of NCCI data is clearly appropriate because the NCCI procedures and rating plans are used in the states. For other jurisdictions, most notably California and New Jersey, the NCCI data must be viewed as rough approximations. For each of the 14 states with independent rating organizations, the average manual rates in table 3 were reduced by the appropriate percentage to produce the high adjusted manual rates in table 10.

## VII. Modifications of Manual Rates in All States with Private Carriers: Phase 2

The previous two sections reviewed a number of modifications that are made to manual rates before the employer's insurance premium is determined. There are two important characteristics of these modifications. First, they involve either (1) formulas that all carriers must adhere to that modify the manual rates at the beginning of the policy period, such as experience rating, loss constants, and premium discounts for quantity purchases, or (2) dividends that are paid only after the policy year is over. In short, there is virtually no chance for carriers to compete in terms of price at the beginning of the policy period with any of these types of modifications. Second, these modifications have been in use for many years and previously were the only modifications necessary to consider in determining the difference between manual premiums and net costs to policyholders. From the *Dissertation* through to the *Task Force Study* and the *MLR article,* estimates were made of the modifying influence of just these factors.[48] The comparable figures produced by this procedure for this study are termed high adjusted manual rates.

This report is forced to widen the scope of inquiry for modifying factors because of the significant changes in the pricing mechanism for workers' compensation insurance that have occurred in the past few years. In many jurisdictions it is now possible for private carriers to compete for business by varying the insurance rates at the beginning of the policy period. The variations in some instances are made for groups of employers and sometimes are even made for individual employers.

The desirability and causes for this increased ability of carriers to compete on an *ex ante* basis have been widely discussed and will not be repeated here.[49] Suffice it to say that the increased competition means the determination of the interstate differences in the employers' costs of workers' compensation has been considerably complicated. Indeed, because the movement towards competition has been so recent, only limited information is available about the extent of the competition and the impact of the various competitive devices on workers' compensation costs. This section relies on the information that is available, which was provided by the National Council on Compensation Insurance[50] and the chapter of this volume by C. Arthur Williams.[51] The data pertain to January 1, 1983, in order to be comparable with the manual rates used to produce table 3. Since that date, the use of the various competitive devices has continued to spread.[52]

Table 7 provides information on three types of competitive devices that have been adopted in those states with private insurance carriers. The most drastic change in the pricing mechanism has occurred in those states with open competition. In such states, carriers may charge whatever insurance rates they feel are appropriate. Carriers are required to file their rates with the state insurance department but do not require approval before using these rates. There are differences among the open competition states, including whether a rating bureau (renamed data service organization) can publish advisory rates, and, if so, what those rates can include. As shown in table 7, there were six states with open competition laws in effect as of January 1, 1983, the date of comparisons for this report. In Arkansas, Illinois, and Rhode Island the advisory rates contain both pure premium (covering expected losses) and an expense loading; these rates are comparable to manual rates in states without open competition and therefore were used without modification in table 3.

In Kentucky, the advisory rates contain only pure premium, and to place them on a comparable basis to manual rates in other states, the expense loading of 36.2 percent formerly used in Kentucky was used to inflate the advisory rates. In Michigan, the advisory rates include loss adjustment expenses but exclude other components of the expense loading and also exclude the trend factor, so a loading of 53.9 percent was used to simulate manual premiums com-

Table 7
**Ability of Private Carriers to Modify Insurance Rates on an Ex Ante Basis as of January 1, 1983**

| | Open competition | | Stating of rate adherence agreements and deviations | | Impact on rate level | Schedule rating |
| | Status | Effective date | Status | Number of companies | | Type |
|---|---|---|---|---|---|---|
| Alabama | | | 5 | N.A. | U | I |
| Alaska (1) | | | X | 2 | 0.03 | U |
| Arizona | | | X | 52 | 12.3 | |
| Arkansas | O | 6/17/81 | No | | | |
| California | | | NP | | | |
| Colorado | | | NP | 33 | 18.1 | I |
| Connecticut | | | NP | | | |
| Delaware | | | X | 9 | 0.5 | |
| District of Columbia | | | X | 4 | N.A. | I |
| Florida | | | X | 93 | 4.4 | |
| Georgia | (O) | 1/1/84 | NP | 33 | 0.6 | I |
| Hawaii | | | X | N.A. | N.A. | |
| Idaho | | | X | 2 | N.A. | |
| Illinois | O | 8/18/82 | X | N.A. | N.A. | |
| Indiana | | | X | 42 | 1.2 | |
| Iowa | | | X | 22 | 1.3 | |
| Kansas | | | | | | |
| Kentucky | O | 7/15/82 | X | 4 | N.A. | |
| Louisiana | | | X | 0 | 0 | |
| Maine | | | X | 30 | 2.0 | |
| Maryland | | | No | | | |
| Massachusetts | | | | | | |
| Michigan | O | 1/1/83 | | | | |
| Minnesota | (O) | 1/1/84 | | | | |
| Mississippi | | | X | 5 | 0.5 | |
| Missouri | | | X | 17 | 0.6 | |

| State | | | | | |
|---|---|---|---|---|---|
| Montana | | NP | 11 | N.A. | I |
| Nebraska | | X | 12 | 0.7 | |
| New Hampshire | | No | 0 | 0 | |
| New Jersey | | No | | | |
| New Mexico | | X | 2 | N.A. | U |
| New York | | X | 15 | 0.1 | |
| North Carolina | | No | | | |
| Oklahoma | | X | 3 | N.A. | |
| Oregon | O | 7/1/82 | | | |
| Pennsylvania (2) | O | X | 55 | 3.2 | |
| Rhode Island | O | 9/1/82 | X | | U |
| South Carolina | | X | 3 | N.A. | |
| South Dakota | | X | 3 | N.A. | |
| Tennessee | | X | 43 | 2.8 | U |
| Texas | | No | | | |
| Utah | | X | 20 | 9.0 | I,U |
| Vermont | | X | 5 | N.A. | |
| Virginia | | X | 38 | N.A. | |
| Wisconsin | | No | | N.A. | |

SOURCES: Derived from *Workers' Compensation Rating Laws - A Digest of Changes*, NCCI, 1982, with quarterly updates thru November 1983; C. Arthur Williams, Jr., "Workers' Compensation Insurance Rates: Their Determination and Regulation, A Regional Perspective," manuscript presented at the First Annual Conference on Workers' Compensation, Rutgers University, May 9-10, 1983; correspondence from Barry I. Llewellyn, Assistant Secretary, NCCI, letters, June 24, 1983 and February 7, 1984.

O denotes presence of open competition.

(O) denotes that open competition will be effective in the near future.

X denotes deviations permitted.

NP denotes rate adherence agreements not permitted.

I denotes individual schedule rating.

U denotes uniform schedule rating.

(1) Three additional companies in Alaska write deviations only for selected class codes. The total market share of these companies is 11.9 percent.

(2) The Pennsylvania data were provided in correspondence from Stephen S. Makgill, President, Pennsylvania Compensation Rating Bureau, letter, September 7, 1984.

parable to those in other jurisdictions. Finally, in Oregon, the advisory rates only contain pure premium, and were increased by the expense loading of 38.7 percent previously used in the jurisdiction.[53]

These adjustments to the published rates in the states with open competition in order to make them comparable to manual rates in other jurisdictions seem reasonable, since in all jurisdictions the manual rates are only the starting point and have to be adjusted before meaningful comparisons can be made. The difficult task is to make the adjustments in the manual rates in states with open competition in order to arrive at adjusted manual rates comparable to those in other jurisdictions. Unfortunately, as of the date of the *Ohio-Pennsylvania Study* (from which the information in the present study is derived) there were no data showing the actual impact of open competition on the employers' costs of workers' compensation. This is not surprising, since the earliest open competition law only went into effect in Arkansas in June of 1981, and the other five states with open competition laws in effect as of January 1, 1983—the date for comparisons in this study—had laws that had been in effect for six months or less as of that date.

If another study of insurance costs is made in four or five years, sufficient information may be available to estimate with reasonable precision the impact of open competition on insurance costs. For this study, two estimates are used. First, one view of workers' compensation is that prior to open competition, the use of dividends, retrospective rating, etc. had squeezed all excess profits out of workers' compensation insurance. If this is true, then arguably the only result of open competition will be to reduce insurance rates at the beginning of the policy period with a corresponding reduction in dividends at the end of the policy period. This view amounts to saying that open competition has no impact on the employers' costs of workers' compensation, and therefore the procedure that was developed in sections V and VI to determine the difference between manual rates and adjusted manual rates requires no further adjustment. In other words, the "high adjusted manual rates" shown in table 10 for the six states with open competition correspond to the view that open competition does not reduce the costs of workers' compensation insurance.

The other view of workers' compensation insurance is that prior to open competition and other competitive devices discussed in this section, excess profits or unnecessary administrative expenses existed in the insurance industry, and that open competition eliminates or reduces these expenses, thereby reducing the costs of workers' compensation to employers. This view is equivalent to saying that the difference between manual rates and adjusted manual rates is greater than the percentages developed in sections V and VI indicate. Even if this view is correct, there are no data available to permit a precise estimate of the impact of open competition as of January 1, 1983. Arbitrarily, a 10 percent adjustment factor has been used to produce the "low adjusted manual rates" shown in table 11 for the states with open competition. That is, for the six states with open competition as of January 1, 1983 (Arkansas, Illinois, Kentucky, Michigan, Oregon, and Rhode Island), the "low adjusted manual rates" shown in table 11 are 10 percent less than the "high adjusted manual rates" shown in table 10.

The second type of competitive device included in table 7 is deviations. (A similar device—a prohibition of rate adherence agreements—is also shown in table 7.) In some of the states in which rating organizations publish manual rates, individual carriers are permitted to deviate from the bureau rates after securing the insurance commissioner's approval. The crucial differences from open competition are that prior approval of the deviations is required, while in open competition no such approval is required, and the deviations offered by a particular carrier are uniform for all policyholders in the state, while in open competition, no such uniformity is necessary. As an example of deviations, the Zenith Insurance Company offers a 12 percent deviation on all policies in Arizona.[54]

The information on deviations in table 7 is incomplete because most of the data were provided by the National Council on Compensation Insurance, and the National Council has only limited information of deviations in states with independent local rating organizations. There are National Council data available for a few of these jurisdictions, and additional information derived from the paper by C. Arthur Williams has been added to the table. For 16 states the National Council has provided information on the impact of deviations on the insurance rates, and these figures are included in table 7.

As with open competition, there are two possible views of the impact of deviations on the employers' costs of workers' compenstion. If there are no excess profits or unnecessary administrative expenses in the workers' compensation insurance industry, then reductions in premiums due to deviations will result in offsetting reductions in dividends and in adjustments through the retrospective rating plans. This view is equivalent to saying that deviations have no impact on the employers' costs of workers' compensation, and therefore for all states with deviations, the "high adjusted manual rates" shown in table 10 require no further adjustments.

The other view of workers' compensation is that excess profits or excessive administrative expenses exist in the insurance industry, and therefore deviations reduce the actual costs of insurance to employers. The view means that the difference between manual rates and adjusted manual rates is greater than the percentages developed in sections V and VI.

For the 16 states, the "high adjusted manual rates" in table 10 were reduced by the percentages shown in the "Impact on Rate Level" column of table 7 to produce the "low adjusted manual rates" shown in table 11. To the extent that deviations are only partially used to reduce dividends and retrospective rating adjustments, the actual costs of workers' compensation will fall between the "high adjusted manual rates" in table 10 and the "low adjusted manual rates" in table 11. In those states with deviations for which the National Council was unable to provide information on the impact of the deviations on the rate level, there is no difference between the low and high adjusted manual rates shown in tables 10 and 11.

The third type of competitive device catalogued in table 7 is schedule rating. Schedule rating plans have been introduced in many jurisdictions in recent years. Under these plans, insurers can change (usually decrease) the insurance rate the employer would otherwise pay through debits or credits based on a subjective evaluation of factors such as the employer's loss control program. There are two types of schedule rating. In states with uniform schedule rating plans, the regulators have decided that it is permissible for all carriers to use the proposed schedule rating plan. If all carriers are not given this permission, then individual carriers can apply for approval of their schedule rating plans. Unfortunately, only limited data are available about the overall impact of schedule rating plans of the employers' costs of workers' compensation, and therefore states with such plans do not have their insurance rates further adjusted in this study.

## VIII. Modifications of Published Manual Rates by Exclusive Fund States

Included in this study are Ohio and West Virginia, which have exclusive state funds. These states publish manual rates and then modify them to the detriment of easy interstate comparisons. Unlike the National Council states, the exclusive fund states do not use premium discounts for quantity purchasers, nor do they use retrospective rating plans, nor do they pay dividends as do the mutual and participating stock companies. However, Ohio, and West Virginia use experience rating plans that are similar to each other and to the National Council experience rating plan because they cause the rates paid by some employers to be different from the published manual rates. We shall see how experience rating affects their costs relative to other states.

## A. Ohio

The experience rating plan in Ohio is complex and similar in sophistication to the method used in National Council states. The influence of experience rating can be determined with a reasonable degree of precision. Manual rates are promulgated yearly on July 1. For each calendar year, data are available by insurance classification showing payroll and the premium actually collected after the application of any experience rating modification.[55] The main problem is that the calendar year includes manual rates promulgated in two years. In order to match collected premiums with manual rates, the average manual rates in effect during a particular calendar year were calculated. Thus for Ohio classification 2000 (equivalent to NCCI Class 2003) the manual rate effective July 1, 1980 was $3.68 and the manual rate effective July 1, 1981 was $3.50; assuming an equal payroll distribution in the first and second half of 1981, this means the average manual rate in effect in calendar year 1981 was $3.59. The 1981 total payroll for classification 2000 was $92,967,000 and with the average manual premium of $3.59 (per $100 of payroll), this produces a simulated manual premium of $3,338,000. The actual premium collected during 1981, however, was $3,487,000, indicating that experience rating produced actual premiums 4.5 percent higher than simulated manual premiums.

The effect of experience rating for a sample of 58 Ohio insurance classifications that are comparable to the 71 insurance classifications used in the National Council states is shown in table 8. In both 1980 and 1981, the actual collected premiums were less than the simulated manual premiums, indicating that, in general, experience rating reduces the costs of workers' compensation in Ohio. For the combined 1980-81 experience, actual collected premiums were .946 of simulated manual premiums, indicating that the influence of experience rating for this combination of classifications was to reduce manual premium by 5.4 percent. For the remainder of this report, it is assumed that the 5.4 percent influence of experience rating for 1980-81 is relevant also for the rates in effect on January 1, 1983. All subsequent calculations are based on adjusted manual rates that are 5.4 percent lower than the manual rates shown in table 3.

The Ohio workers' compensation program has separate assessments for Administrative Costs and for the Disabled Workers' Relief Fund. As of January 1, 1983, the assessments for private employers were $0.15 and $0.10 per $100 of payroll, for a total assessment of $0.25 per $100 of payroll. The handling of these assessments in our study can be illustrated with data for Ohio classification 2000. As of January 1, 1983, the published manual rate for classification 2000 was $3.84 per $100 of payroll; with the assessment added, the total is $4.09 per $100 of payroll. This $4.09 figure was one of the rates used to calculate the average manual rates for Ohio shown in table 3. The experience rating factor does not affect the assessments. Thus, the experience rating adjustment of 5.4 percent was used to reduce the published manual rate (for classification 2000) from $3.84 to $3.63 per $100 of payroll; with the assessment of $0.25 added the total is $3.88 per $100 of payroll. This $3.88 is one of the rates used to calculate the adjusted manual rates for Ohio shown in tables 10 and 11.

Table 8
**Ratio of Collected Premiums to Manual Premiums in Ohio**
(Based on Data for a Sample of 58 Insurance Classifications)

| Year | Collected premiums | Manual premiums (simulated) | Ratio of collected premiums to manual premiums |
|------|------|------|------|
| 1980 | $339,266,000 | $365,999,328 | .927 |
| 1981 | 348,596,000 | 361,368,092 | .965 |
| Total | $687,862,000 | $727,367,420 | .946 |

SOURCES: Data provided with July 8, 1983 correspondence from Paul C. Whitacre, Jr., Director, Actuarial Section, Ohio Bureau of Workers' Compensation; simulated manual premiums calculated by John Burton and Alan Krueger, July 1983.

### B. West Virginia

In recent years, West Virginia has used an experience rating plan that is similar in sophistication to the plan used in National Council states. It is described in detail in two publications issued by the West Virginia Workmen's Compensation Fund,[56] and therefore the method will not be discussed here, only the quantitative impact is estimated.

The influence of experience rating can be determined with precision, using a variation of the method used for Ohio.[57] Manual rates are promulgated yearly on July 1 and are in effect until the following June 30. For the same 12-month period, data are available by insurance classification showing payroll and the premiums actually collected after the application of any experience rating modification. Thus, for West Virginia classification D-7, the manual rate effective July 1, 1980 was $4.32 per $100 of payroll. Since the payroll between July 1980 and June 1981 for this class was $9,112,681.90, the simulated manual premium was $393,667.85. The gross premium actually collected for the corresponding period was $413,693.57, indicating that experience rating produced actual premiums 5.1 percent higher than simulated manual premiums.

The effect of experience rating for a sample of 24 West Virginia classifications that are comparable to the 71 insurance classifications used in the National Council states is shown in table 9. In both July-June periods for 1979-80 and 1980-81, the actual collected premiums were greater than the simulated manual premiums, indicating that in general experience rating increases the employers' costs of workers' compensation in West Virginia. For the combined 1979-81 experience, actual collected premiums were 9.3 percent greater than simulated manual premiums, indicating that the influence of experience rating for this combination of classifications increased manual premiums by 9.3 percent. For the remainder of this report, it is assumed that the 9.3 percent influence of experience rating for 1971-81 is also relevant for the rates in effect on January 1, 1983 for West Virginia.[58] All subsequent calculations are based on adjusted manual rates that are 9.3 percent higher than the manual rates shown in table 3.

**Table 9**

**Ratio of Collected Premiums to Manual Premiums in West Virginia**

(Based on Data for a Sample of 24 Insurance Classifications)

| Year | Collected premiums | Manual premiums (simulated) | Ratio of collected premiums to manual premiums |
|------|--------------------|------------------------------|------------------------------------------------|
| 1980 | $ 63,626,663 | $ 59,242,978 | 1.074 |
| 1981 | 73,861,833 | 66,506,269 | 1.111 |
| Total | $137,488,496 | $125,749,249 | 1.093 |

SOURCES: Data from West Virginia Workmen's Compensation Fund, *Annual Report and Financial Statement,* Year Ending June 30, 1980 and Year Ending June 30, 1981, table 15; simulated manual premium calculated by Alan Krueger and John Burton, July 1983.

The West Virginia workers' compensation program has the assessments for administrative expenses and for the catastrophe and second injury accounts included in the base or manual rates, and therefore the rates as published were used to calculate the average manual rates for West Virginia shown in table 3. Likewise, the gross premiums shown in table 9 include the charges for these accounts and for administrative expenses. Thus the experience rating adjustment of 9.3 percent was used with the data in table 3 to calculate the adjusted manual rates for West Virginia shown in tables 10 and 11.

## IX. Interstate Variations in Adjusted Manual Rates

The previous three sections have attempted to ascertain systematically the influence of experience rating, premium discounts, retrospective rating, policyholders' dividends, open competition, and deviations on the costs of workers' compensation. In table 3, data were presented on the averages of published manual rates for various combinations of insurance classifications. Table 10 was developed from the earlier table by decreasing these averages for manual rates by the appropriate percentages for the 31 National Council states that were developed in section V, by the appropriate percentages for the 14 states with independent rating organizations that were developed in section VI, and by the appropriate percentages for Ohio and West Virginia developed in section VIII. Table 10 is based on the view that open competition, deviations, and schedule rating do not have a net impact on workers' compensation costs (once the offsetting changes in dividends, etc. are considered), and produces what are termed "high adjusted manual rates." Table 11 was developed from table 10 by decreasing the high adjusted manual rates in those states with open competition or with data available on the impact of deviations, using the percentage adjustments developed in section VII. Table 11 is based on the view that open competition and deviations do have a net impact on workers' compensation costs, producing what are termed "low adjusted manual rates."

Columns 1 and 2 of tables 10 and 11 present the average costs of adjusted manual rates on January 1, 1983 for 24 and 44 classifications using national payroll distributions. Column 3 presents the averages for 24 manufacturing classes using national payroll distribution. Column 4 presents the average adjusted manual rates based on the 56 classifications in divisions A, B, and C of table 3, and column 5 shows the rates based on the 71 classes in divisions A to D.

The results in tables 10 and 11 can be interpreted as the percentage of payroll expended on workers' compensation insurance by employers in 47 jurisdictions (including the District of Columbia) as of January 1, 1983. The results in column 2 of tables 10 and 11 are the most reliable and useful for reasons explained above. The results indicate, for example, that as of January 1, 1983, the 44 types of employers in divisions A and B, would, on average, expend 0.905 percent of payroll on workers' compensation premiums in Alabama. (The "high" and "low" adjusted manual rates for Alabama are identical.)

## X. Further Adjustment to Interstate Cost Variations Necessitated by Interstate Variations in Employee Earnings

Even the adjustments in the preceding section to published manual rates do not complete the modifications necessary for comparisons of the interstate differences in the dollar costs of workers' compensation premiums per employee. Assume that the adjusted manual rates for an employer's classification in states A and B were an identical $1.00 of payroll, with no payroll limit in each state. Further assume that A is northern, industrialized, unionized, etc., and the average weekly earnings of employees are $500, while B lacks these attributes and the average weekly earnings of employees are $250. The result is that equal manual rates in A and B lead to dissimilar insurance premiums, since the

### Table 10
### Interstate Variations in Average Costs of High Adjusted Manual Rates for Classes in Each Division of Table 3, Weighted by National Payroll Distributions

| Jurisdiction | 24 classes in division A | 44 classes in divisions A and B | 24 manufacturing classes in divisions A, B, and C | 56 classes in divisions A, B, and C | 71 classes in divisions A,B,C, and D |
|---|---|---|---|---|---|
| Alabama | 0.907 | 0.905 | 2.080 | 0.973 | 1.139 |
| Alaska | 2.264 | 2.162 | 3.945 | 2.257 | 2.524 |
| Arizona | 1.333 | 1.452 | 3.314 | 1.547 | 1.784 |
| Arkansas | 1.146 | 1.212 | 2.918 | 1.313 | 1.541 |
| California | 1.918 | 2.103 | 4.880 | 2.261 | 2.685 |
| Colorado | 1.279 | 1.336 | 3.072 | 1.428 | 1.615 |
| Connecticut | 1.717 | 1.786 | 3.904 | 1.883 | 2.273 |
| Delaware | 1.105 | 1.190 | 4.072 | 1.372 | --- |
| District of Columbia | 2.194 | 2.208 | 5.237 | 2.384 | 2.734 |
| Florida | 1.383 | 1.460 | 3.066 | 1.524 | 1.747 |
| Georgia | 0.885 | 0.913 | 2.428 | 1.003 | 1.151 |
| Hawaii | 3.522 | 3.793 | 7.792 | 3.998 | 4.588 |
| Idaho | 1.285 | 1.291 | 2.834 | 1.387 | 1.611 |
| Illinois | 1.198 | 1.194 | 2.861 | 1.291 | 1.508 |
| Indiana | 0.325 | 0.337 | 0.725 | 0.360 | 0.414 |
| Iowa | 0.959 | 0.958 | 1.709 | 0.996 | 1.147 |
| Kansas | 0.795 | 0.824 | 1.891 | 0.889 | 1.059 |
| Kentucky | 1.101 | 1.148 | 2.990 | 1.265 | 1.530 |
| Louisiana | 1.291 | 1.339 | 3.211 | 1.454 | 1.727 |
| Maine | 1.563 | 1.636 | 3.569 | 1.729 | --- |
| Maryland | 1.950 | 1.947 | 3.826 | 2.025 | 2.337 |

| | | | | | |
|---|---|---|---|---|---|
| Massachusetts | 1.444 | 1.526 | 3.639 | 1.640 | 1.965 |
| Michigan | 1.862 | 1.967 | 5.947 | 2.199 | 2.574 |
| Minnesota | 1.343 | 1.411 | 4.066 | 1.580 | 1.835 |
| Mississippi | 0.831 | 0.829 | 1.719 | 0.879 | 1.034 |
| Missouri | 0.575 | 0.602 | 1.389 | 0.651 | 0.774 |
| Montana | 1.558 | 1.589 | 3.569 | 1.711 | --- |
| Nebraska | 0.776 | 0.799 | 1.708 | 0.838 | 0.978 |
| New Hampshire | 1.298 | 1.351 | 2.821 | 1.421 | 1.752 |
| New Jersey | 1.322 | 1.422 | 3.360 | 1.527 | 1.747 |
| New Mexico | 1.938 | 1.967 | 3.863 | 2.076 | 2.323 |
| New York | 1.169 | 1.185 | 2.986 | 1.287 | 1.462 |
| North Carolina | 0.717 | 0.733 | 1.386 | 0.765 | 0.907 |
| Ohio | 1.331 | 1.375 | 2.614 | 1.421 | 1.602 |
| Oklahoma | 1.340 | 1.386 | 3.373 | 1.511 | 1.790 |
| Oregon | 1.754 | 1.841 | 4.414 | 1.995 | --- |
| Pennsylvania | 1.394 | 1.441 | 3.075 | 1.515 | --- |
| Rhode Island | 1.322 | 1.444 | 4.357 | 1.613 | 1.843 |
| South Carolina | 0.930 | 0.942 | 1.698 | 0.976 | 1.169 |
| South Dakota | 0.719 | 0.736 | 1.355 | 0.771 | 0.919 |
| Tennessee | 0.752 | 0.789 | 1.883 | 0.853 | 1.039 |
| Texas | 1.571 | 1.644 | 4.325 | 1.815 | 2.126 |
| Utah | 0.758 | 0.796 | 2.069 | 0.874 | 1.015 |
| Vermont | 0.715 | 0.729 | 1.550 | 0.770 | 0.886 |
| Virginia | 1.023 | 1.044 | 1.904 | 1.080 | 1.278 |
| West Virginia | 1.206 | 1.162 | 2.234 | 1.235 | 1.369 |
| Wisconsin | 0.740 | 0.791 | 1.887 | 0.851 | 1.011 |

Table 11

Interstate Variations in Average Costs of Low Adjusted Manual Rates for Classes
in Each Division of Table 3, Weighted by National Payroll Distributions

| Jurisdiction | 24 classes in division A | 44 classes in divisions A and B | 24 manufacturing classes in divisions A, B, and C | 56 classes in divisions A, B, and C | 71 classes in divisions A,B,C, and D |
|---|---|---|---|---|---|
| Alabama | 0.907 | 0.905 | 2.080 | 0.973 | 1.139 |
| Alaska | 2.264 | 2.162 | 3.943 | 2.257 | 2.523 |
| Arizona | 1.169 | 1.273 | 2.907 | 1.357 | 1.565 |
| Arkansas | 1.031 | 1.090 | 2.626 | 1.182 | 1.387 |
| California | 1.918 | 2.103 | 4.880 | 2.261 | 2.685 |
| Colorado | 1.047 | 1.094 | 2.516 | 1.169 | 1.323 |
| Connecticut | 1.717 | 1.786 | 3.904 | 1.883 | 2.273 |
| Delaware | 1.099 | 1.184 | 4.052 | 1.365 | --- |
| District of Columbia | 2.194 | 2.208 | 5.237 | 2.384 | 2.734 |
| Florida | 1.323 | 1.396 | 2.931 | 1.457 | 1.670 |
| Georgia | 0.880 | 0.907 | 2.414 | 0.997 | 1.144 |
| Hawaii | 3.522 | 3.793 | 7.792 | 3.998 | 4.588 |
| Idaho | 1.285 | 1.291 | 2.834 | 1.387 | 1.611 |
| Illinois | 1.079 | 1.075 | 2.575 | 1.162 | 1.357 |
| Indiana | 0.325 | 0.337 | 0.725 | 0.360 | 0.414 |
| Iowa | 0.948 | 0.947 | 1.688 | 0.984 | 1.133 |
| Kansas | 0.785 | 0.813 | 1.867 | 0.878 | 1.045 |
| Kentucky | 0.991 | 1.033 | 2.691 | 1.138 | 1.377 |
| Louisiana | 1.291 | 1.339 | 3.211 | 1.454 | 1.727 |
| Maine | 1.563 | 1.636 | 3.569 | 1.729 | --- |
| Maryland | 1.911 | 1.909 | 3.749 | 1.985 | 2.290 |

| | | | | | |
|---|---|---|---|---|---|
| Massachusetts | 1.444 | 1.526 | 3.639 | 1.640 | 1.965 |
| Michigan | 1.676 | 1.770 | 5.352 | 1.979 | 2.317 |
| Minnesota | 1.343 | 1.411 | 4.066 | 1.580 | 1.835 |
| Mississippi | 0.827 | 0.825 | 1.711 | 0.875 | 1.029 |
| Missouri | 0.571 | 0.598 | 1.381 | 0.647 | 0.770 |
| Montana | 1.558 | 1.589 | 3.569 | 1.711 | -- |
| Nebraska | 0.770 | 0.793 | 1.696 | 0.832 | 0.971 |
| New Hampshire | 1.298 | 1.351 | 2.821 | 1.421 | 1.752 |
| New Jersey | 1.322 | 1.422 | 3.360 | 1.527 | 1.747 |
| New Mexico | 1.938 | 1.967 | 3.863 | 2.076 | 2.323 |
| New York | 1.168 | 1.184 | 2.983 | 1.285 | 1.461 |
| North Carolina | 0.717 | 0.733 | 1.386 | 0.765 | 0.907 |
| Ohio | 1.331 | 1.375 | 2.614 | 1.421 | 1.602 |
| Oklahoma | 1.340 | 1.386 | 3.373 | 1.511 | 1.790 |
| Oregon | 1.578 | 1.657 | 3.973 | 1.796 | -- |
| Pennsylvania | 1.350 | 1.395 | 2.977 | 1.466 | -- |
| Rhode Island | 1.190 | 1.299 | 3.921 | 1.452 | 1.659 |
| South Carolina | 0.930 | 0.942 | 1.698 | 0.976 | 1.169 |
| South Dakota | 0.719 | 0.736 | 1.355 | 0.771 | 0.919 |
| Tennessee | 0.731 | 0.767 | 1.830 | 0.829 | 1.010 |
| Texas | 1.571 | 1.644 | 4.325 | 1.815 | 2.126 |
| Utah | 0.690 | 0.724 | 1.883 | 0.795 | 0.924 |
| Vermont | 0.715 | 0.729 | 1.550 | 0.770 | 0.886 |
| Virginia | 1.023 | 1.044 | 1.904 | 1.080 | 1.278 |
| West Virginia | 1.206 | 1.162 | 2.234 | 1.235 | 1.369 |
| Wisconsin | 0.740 | 0.791 | 1.887 | 0.851 | 1.011 |

workers' compensation bill is a product of the manual rate and the weekly earnings. In this example the employers' insurance cost is $5.00 per employee per week in A and $2.50 in B.

In reality, interstate variations in employee earnings can influence the relative costs of workers' compensation. Unfortunately, there is a paucity of weekly earnings differential information relevant for this study.[59] Information is needed that shows the interstate variations in the weekly earnings of workers employed in the same industries, not information that reflects interstate differences in the industry mix, which is characteristic of most published data. A method developed in the *Dissertation* to derive the appropriate information[60] used earnings data broken down by the Standard Industrial Classification (SIC) system. The results are presented in table 12.

The meaning of the earnings index as used in this study is the following: since the index for Michigan is 1.1315, it is assumed that, for every industry, workers in Michigan earn 13.15 percent more per week than the average worker in the United States. Because of the varying quantity of information available from the states, the index numbers should be viewed as approximations. Unfortunately we have no more precise measure of interstate earnings variations readily available.

The ultimate goal of this study is to quantify the interstate variations in the net cost to employers of workers' compensation. This necessitates not only the use of the adjusted manual rates from the previous section but also the use of an appropriate earnings figure adjusted for the interstate earnings variations. The weekly earnings figure which is used is the national average of earnings of workers covered by the unemployment insurance program, which for 1980 (the latest data available) was $297.09.

## Table 12
## 1980 Weekly Earnings Indexes

| | | | |
|---|---|---|---|
| Alabama | .9537 | Mississippi | .8147 |
| Alaska | 1.5665 | Missouri | .9916 |
| Arizona | .9867 | Montana | 1.0574 |
| Arkansas | .8172 | Nebraska | .9772 |
| California | 1.0923 | New Hampshire | .8759 |
| Colorado | 1.0360 | New Jersey | 1.0310 |
| Connecticut | .9723 | New Mexico | .9032 |
| Delaware | .9538 | New York | 1.0460 |
| District of Columbia | 1.1761 | North Carolina | .8370 |
| Florida | .8693 | Ohio | 1.0661 |
| Georgia | .8756 | Oklahoma | .9509 |
| Hawaii | .9809 | Oregon | 1.0463 |
| Idaho | .9089 | Pennsylvania | 1.0003 |
| Illinois | 1.0667 | Rhode Island | .8506 |
| Indiana | 1.0591 | South Carolina | .8296 |
| Iowa | 1.0543 | South Dakota | 1.0040 |
| Kansas | .9532 | Tennessee | .9265 |
| Kentucky | 1.0339 | Texas | .9721 |
| Louisiana | .9961 | Utah | .9838 |
| Maine | .9246 | Vermont | .9115 |
| Maryland | .9735 | Virginia | .8790 |
| Massachusetts | .9418 | West Virginia | 1.0160 |
| Michigan | 1.1315 | Wisconsin | 1.0558 |
| Minnesota | .9901 | | |

SOURCE: Data for most states are from U.S. Bureau of Labor Statistics, *Supplement to Employment and Earnings, States and Areas, Data for 1977-81,* Bulletin 1370-16 (September 1982).

NOTES: Indexes are based on data for individual 2-digit industries except in Alaska, Arizona, Hawaii, Idaho, Nebraska, New Mexico, South Dakota, and Utah. In these states, because of a paucity of such data, wage data for combined 2-digit SIC industries were used.

Colorado wage index pertains to 1970 because 1980 data are unavailable.

Finally, we can compute the interstate variations in the net cost to policyholders. Table 13 presents the "high" weekly net costs per workers, which are the products of the "high" adjusted manual rates found in table 10, the interstate earnings index numbers from table 12, and the national average

Table 13

Interstate Variations in Average Costs of High Adjusted Net Costs for Classes
in Each Division of Table 3, Weighted by National Payroll Distributions

| Jurisdiction | 24 classes in division A | 44 classes in divisions A and B | 24 manufacturing classes in divisions A, B, and C | 56 classes in divisions A, B, and C | 71 classes in divisions A, B, C, and D |
|---|---|---|---|---|---|
| Alabama | 2.570 | 2.565 | 5.894 | 2.757 | 3.227 |
| Alaska | 10.538 | 10.064 | 18.358 | 10.506 | 11.746 |
| Arizona | 3.909 | 4.256 | 9.716 | 4.536 | 5.230 |
| Arkansas | 2.782 | 2.942 | 7.085 | 3.188 | 3.742 |
| California | 6.224 | 6.826 | 15.835 | 7.338 | 8.714 |
| Colorado | 3.935 | 4.112 | 9.455 | 4.394 | 4.971 |
| Connecticut | 4.960 | 5.160 | 11.276 | 5.440 | 6.566 |
| Delaware | 3.131 | 3.371 | 11.539 | 3.888 | --- |
| District of Columbia | 7.666 | 7.717 | 18.300 | 8.330 | 9.553 |
| Florida | 3.573 | 3.772 | 7.919 | 3.935 | 4.512 |
| Georgia | 2.303 | 2.374 | 6.317 | 2.609 | 2.994 |
| Hawaii | 10.358 | 11.156 | 22.917 | 11.758 | 13.494 |
| Idaho | 3.707 | 3.727 | 8.178 | 4.001 | 4.649 |
| Illinois | 3.798 | 3.785 | 9.066 | 4.090 | 4.777 |
| Indiana | 1.021 | 1.062 | 2.282 | 1.132 | 1.302 |
| Iowa | 3.004 | 3.002 | 5.352 | 3.120 | 3.592 |
| Kansas | 2.252 | 2.333 | 5.356 | 2.518 | 2.999 |
| Kentucky | 3.383 | 3.527 | 9.184 | 3.884 | 4.700 |
| Louisiana | 3.820 | 3.964 | 9.503 | 4.302 | 5.112 |
| Maine | 4.293 | 4.495 | 9.805 | 4.751 | --- |
| Maryland | 5.640 | 5.632 | 11.064 | 5.858 | 6.759 |

| | | | | |
|---|---|---|---|---|
| Massachusetts | 4.040 | 4.270 | 10.182 | 4.589 | 5.497 |
| Michigan | 6.620 | 6.611 | 19.991 | 7.391 | 8.653 |
| Minnesota | 3.949 | 4.151 | 11.960 | 4.646 | 5.398 |
| Mississippi | 2.011 | 2.007 | 4.162 | 2.128 | 2.504 |
| Missouri | 1.693 | 1.774 | 4.092 | 1.917 | 2.281 |
| Montana | 4.894 | 4.993 | 11.211 | 5.375 | — |
| Nebraska | 2.253 | 2.320 | 4.958 | 2.432 | 2.839 |
| New Hampshire | 3.378 | 3.514 | 7.341 | 3.697 | 4.559 |
| New Jersey | 4.049 | 4.357 | 10.293 | 4.678 | 5.351 |
| New Mexico | 5.200 | 5.279 | 10.366 | 5.570 | 6.235 |
| New York | 3.633 | 3.683 | 9.278 | 3.998 | 4.544 |
| North Carolina | 1.782 | 1.823 | 3.446 | 1.902 | 2.255 |
| Ohio | 4.216 | 4.355 | 8.281 | 4.500 | 5.074 |
| Oklahoma | 3.786 | 3.916 | 9.529 | 4.268 | 5.057 |
| Oregon | 5.451 | 5.723 | 13.722 | 6.203 | — |
| Pennsylvania | 4.144 | 4.283 | 9.138 | 4.501 | — |
| Rhode Island | 3.340 | 3.648 | 11.010 | 4.077 | 4.658 |
| South Carolina | 2.293 | 2.320 | 4.185 | 2.404 | 2.881 |
| South Dakota | 2.143 | 2.194 | 4.041 | 2.299 | 2.741 |
| Tennessee | 2.071 | 2.172 | 5.183 | 2.348 | 2.859 |
| Texas | 4.538 | 4.747 | 12.491 | 5.241 | 6.139 |
| Utah | 2.215 | 2.325 | 6.047 | 2.553 | 2.966 |
| Vermont | 1.936 | 1.975 | 4.197 | 2.086 | 2.400 |
| Virginia | 2.672 | 2.726 | 4.973 | 2.821 | 3.338 |
| West Virginia | 3.640 | 3.507 | 6.743 | 3.728 | 4.132 |
| Wisconsin | 2.320 | 2.480 | 5.920 | 2.670 | 3.170 |

Table 14

Interstate Variations in Average Costs of Low Net Costs for Classes
in Each Division of Table 3, Weighted by National Payroll Distributions

| Jurisdiction | 24 classes in division A | 44 classes in divisions A and B | 24 manufacturing classes in divisions A, B, and C | 56 classes in divisions A, B, and C | 71 classes in divisions A,B,C, and D |
|---|---|---|---|---|---|
| Alabama | 2.570 | 2.565 | 5.894 | 2.757 | 3.227 |
| Alaska | 10.535 | 10.061 | 18.352 | 10.503 | 11.742 |
| Arizona | 3.428 | 3.733 | 8.521 | 3.978 | 4.587 |
| Arkansas | 2.504 | 2.647 | 6.376 | 2.869 | 3.368 |
| California | 6.224 | 6.826 | 15.835 | 7.338 | 8.714 |
| Colorado | 3.223 | 3.368 | 7.744 | 3.599 | 4.072 |
| Connecticut | 4.960 | 5.160 | 11.276 | 5.440 | 6.566 |
| Delaware | 3.115 | 3.354 | 11.482 | 3.868 | --- |
| District of Columbia | 7.666 | 7.717 | 18.300 | 8.330 | 9.553 |
| Florida | 3.416 | 3.606 | 7.570 | 3.762 | 4.313 |
| Georgia | 2.289 | 2.360 | 6.279 | 2.593 | 2.976 |
| Hawaii | 10.358 | 11.156 | 22.917 | 11.758 | 13.494 |
| Idaho | 3.707 | 3.727 | 8.178 | 4.001 | 4.649 |
| Illinois | 3.418 | 3.406 | 8.160 | 3.681 | 4.300 |
| Indiana | 1.021 | 1.062 | 2.282 | 1.132 | 1.302 |
| Iowa | 2.968 | 2.966 | 5.287 | 3.082 | 3.549 |
| Kansas | 2.223 | 2.303 | 5.287 | 2.485 | 2.960 |
| Kentucky | 3.045 | 3.174 | 8.265 | 3.496 | 4.230 |
| Louisiana | 3.820 | 3.964 | 9.503 | 4.302 | 5.111 |
| Maine | 4.293 | 4.495 | 9.805 | 4.751 | --- |

| State | | | | | |
|---|---|---|---|---|---|
| Maryland | 5.527 | 5.520 | 10.843 | 5.741 | 6.624 |
| Massachusetts | 4.040 | 4.270 | 10.182 | 4.589 | 5.497 |
| Michigan | 5.634 | 5.950 | 17.992 | 6.652 | 7.789 |
| Minnesota | 3.949 | 4.151 | 11.960 | 4.646 | 5.398 |
| Mississippi | 2.001 | 1.997 | 4.141 | 2.117 | 2.491 |
| Missouri | 1.683 | 1.763 | 4.067 | 1.906 | 2.267 |
| Montana | 4.894 | 4.993 | 11.211 | 5.375 | --- |
| Nebraska | 2.237 | 2.303 | 4.923 | 2.415 | 2.819 |
| New Hampshire | 3.378 | 3.514 | 7.341 | 3.697 | 4.559 |
| New Jersey | 4.049 | 4.357 | 10.293 | 4.678 | 5.351 |
| New Mexico | 5.200 | 5.279 | 10.366 | 5.570 | 6.235 |
| New York | 3.629 | 3.679 | 9.269 | 3.994 | 4.539 |
| North Carolina | 1.782 | 1.823 | 3.446 | 1.902 | 2.255 |
| Ohio | 4.216 | 4.355 | 8.281 | 4.500 | 5.074 |
| Oklahoma | 3.786 | 3.916 | 9.529 | 4.268 | 5.057 |
| Oregon | 4.906 | 5.151 | 12.350 | 5.583 | --- |
| Pennsylvania | 4.011 | 4.146 | 8.846 | 4.357 | 4.192 |
| Rhode Island | 3.006 | 3.283 | 9.909 | 3.670 | 2.881 |
| South Carolina | 2.293 | 2.320 | 4.185 | 2.404 | 2.741 |
| South Dakota | 2.143 | 2.194 | 4.041 | 2.299 | 2.779 |
| Tennessee | 2.013 | 2.111 | 5.038 | 2.282 | |
| Texas | 4.538 | 4.747 | 12.491 | 5.241 | 6.139 |
| Utah | 2.016 | 2.116 | 5.503 | 2.323 | 2.699 |
| Vermont | 1.936 | 1.975 | 4.197 | 2.086 | 2.400 |
| Virginia | 2.672 | 2.726 | 4.973 | 2.821 | 3.338 |
| West Virginia | 3.640 | 3.507 | 6.743 | 3.728 | 4.132 |
| Wisconsin | 2.320 | 2.480 | 5.920 | 2.670 | 3.170 |

weekly earnings figure of $297.09; the product must be divided by 100 since the manual rates are per $100 of payroll. Table 14 presents the "low" weekly costs per worker which are the products of the "low" adjusted manual rates found in table 11, the interstate earnings index numbers from table 12, and the national average weekly earnings figure of $297.09, again divided by 100. The results indicate, for example, that the 44 types of employers in divisions A and B of table 4 would, on average, spent $2.565 per week per worker on workers' compensation premiums in Alabama as of January 1, 1983. (The "high" and "low" net costs for Alabama are identical.)

## XI. Historical Data

Information on the employers' costs of workers' compensation is available for the 44 types of employers included in divisions A and B of table 2 for selected years since 1950. (Prior to 1983, these divisions contained 45 classes, as was explained in section IV.) Data for 20 states are available for nine years between 1950 and 1983; data for eight more states are available for seven years between 1958 and 1983; 42 jurisdictions have data for 1972, 1975, 1978, and 1983; and for 1978 and 1983, there are 47 jurisdictions that may be compared.

The average adjusted manual rates for the 44-employer group are shown in table 15. For example, Illinois employers expended, on average, the equivalent of 0.437 percent of payroll on workers' compensation premiums in 1950, compared with 1.194 percent (high adjusted rates) or 1.075 percent (low adjusted rates) in 1983. Table 16 presents the approximate net cost to the same group of policyholders for several years between 1950 and 1983. These results show, for example, that the employers in Illinois expended a weekly average of $0.261 per worker on premiums in 1950, and $3.785 (high net costs) or $3.406 (low net costs) in 1983.

The data in tables 15 and 16 are valuable for tracing changes in workers' compensation costs over time in a particular state, but the volume of information makes it difficult to comprehend general developments. Tables 17 and 18 provide a compact summary of these data, permitting evaluations of interstate trends.

Table 17, for example, illustrates the changes over time in the average adjusted manual rates for the various combinations of states. Columns 1 and 2 pertain to 20 states for which data are available from 1950 to 1983; columns 3 and 4 relate to 28 states for which data are available from 1958 to 1983; columns 5 and 6 present data for 42 states that are available from 1972 to 1983; and columns 7 and 8 present data on the 47 states for 1978 and 1983. Panel A relies on unweighted observations, while panel B weights each states' observation by the size of the state's nonagricultural labor force.[61] The text will refer to the weighted data from panel B because they are more representative of national experience.

The mean adjusted manual rate in the 20 states was the equivalent of 0.470 percent of payroll in 1950, 0.678 percent in 1972, and 1.227 percent in 1978. In 1983, the mean for high adjusted manual rates was 1.393 and the mean for low adjusted manual rates was 1.343. Of particular interest is the rapid rise in costs between 1972 and 1978, which was more than double the 1950-72 increase. Between 1978 and 1983 the employers' costs of workers' compensation insurance continued to increase for this combination of 20 states, but at a less torrid pace than during the earlier portion of the 1970s. The data in table 17 also indicate that the average adjusted manual rates increased between 1978 and 1983 for the 28 jurisdictions for which data are available since 1958. However, for the averages of adjusted manual rates for the 42 and 47 jurisdictions, the data indicate that the employers' costs of workers' compensation (measured as premiums as a percentage of payroll) actually declined between 1978 and

## Table 15
### Interstate Variations in Average Costs of Adjusted Manual Rates for 44 Classes in Divisions A and B of Table 3
#### Weighted by National Payroll Distribution Insurance Rates in Effect 1950-83

| Jurisdiction | 1950 | 1954 | 1958 | 1962 | 1965 | 1972 | 1975 | 1978 | High 1983 | Low 1983 |
|---|---|---|---|---|---|---|---|---|---|---|
| Alabama | .282 | .310 | .348 | .364 | .437 | .479 | .599 | .855 | .905 | .905 |
| Alaska | | | | | | .832 | 1.721 | 1.762 | 2.162 | 2.162 |
| Arizona | | | | | | 1.385 | 2.178 | 2.505 | 1.452 | 1.273 |
| Arkansas | | | | | | .915 | 1.038 | 1.292 | 1.212 | 1.090 |
| California | | | .707 | .858 | 1.183 | 1.102 | 1.406 | 2.135 | 2.103 | 2.103 |
| Colorado | | | | | | .649 | .654 | 1.210 | 1.336 | 1.094 |
| Connecticut | .660 | .838 | .812 | .762 | .689 | .697 | .827 | 1.353 | 1.786 | 1.786 |
| Delaware | | | | | | .578 | .736 | 1.428 | 1.190 | 1.184 |
| District of Columbia | | | | | | .737 | 1.404 | 3.502 | 2.208 | 2.208 |
| Florida | | | | | | | .760 | 2.641 | 1.460 | 1.396 |
| Georgia | | | | | | .501 | | 1.077 | .913 | .907 |
| Hawaii | | | | | | .960 | 1.335 | 2.057 | 3.793 | 3.793 |
| Idaho | .519 | .664 | .581 | .582 | .667 | .865 | 1.283 | 1.287 | 1.291 | 1.291 |
| Illinois | .437 | .497 | .514 | .609 | .624 | .657 | 1.002 | 1.382 | 1.194 | 1.075 |
| Indiana | .358 | .363 | .410 | .398 | .430 | .385 | .417 | .480 | .337 | .337 |
| Iowa | | | | | | .451 | .662 | 1.084 | .958 | .947 |
| Kansas | | | | | | .575 | .766 | .879 | .824 | .813 |
| Kentucky | .390 | .369 | .394 | .448 | .558 | .668 | 1.065 | 1.382 | 1.148 | 1.033 |
| Louisiana | | | | | | | | 1.512 | 1.339 | 1.339 |
| Maine | .415 | .398 | .340 | .370 | .337 | .520 | .981 | 1.380 | 1.636 | 1.636 |
| Maryland | .501 | .600 | .661 | .747 | .854 | .816 | 1.009 | 1.262 | 1.947 | 1.909 |

| | | | | | | | | | | |
|---|---|---|---|---|---|---|---|---|---|---|
| Massachusetts | .476 | | .859 | 1.034 | 1.141 | 1.106 | 1.171 | 1.373 | 1.526 | 1.526 |
| Michigan | | .416 | .450 | .694 | .715 | .914 | 1.238 | 1.890 | 1.967 | 1.770 |
| Minnesota | | .727 | .653 | .692 | .738 | .854 | 1.240 | 1.821 | 1.411 | 1.411 |
| Mississippi | .638 | | .758 | .988 | .980 | .751 | .902 | .902 | .829 | .825 |
| Missouri | | | | | | | | .740 | .602 | .598 |
| Montana | .590 | .644 | .792 | .721 | .845 | .948 | 1.565 | 1.404 | 1.589 | 1.589 |
| Nebraska | .572 | .474 | .437 | .527 | .447 | .529 | .789 | .710 | .799 | .793 |
| New Hampshire | .528 | .586 | .531 | .495 | .560 | .534 | .746 | 1.166 | 1.351 | 1.351 |
| New Jersey | | | | | | | | 1.687 | 1.422 | 1.422 |
| New Mexico | .463 | .858 | .911 | 1.054 | 1.039 | 1.224 | 1.233 | 1.441 | 1.967 | 1.967 |
| New York | | | .838 | .863 | .945 | .787 | 1.069 | 1.770 | 1.185 | 1.184 |
| North Carolina | .392 | .512 | .473 | .492 | .474 | .420 | .433 | .532 | .733 | .733 |
| Ohio | | | .627 | .813 | .820 | .885 | 1.109 | 1.550 | 1.375 | 1.375 |
| Oklahoma | | | | | | | 1.052 | 1.446 | 1.386 | 1.386 |
| Oregon | | | .630 | 1.007 | | 1.491 | 2.074 | 2.918 | 1.841 | 1.657 |
| Pennsylvania | .829 | | .355 | .396 | .386 | .387 | .776 | 1.173 | 1.441 | 1.395 |
| Rhode Island | .658 | .930 | .831 | .834 | .842 | .767 | .899 | 1.303 | 1.444 | 1.299 |
| South Carolina | .537 | .607 | .567 | .690 | .696 | .609 | .590 | .836 | .942 | .942 |
| South Dakota | | .400 | .315 | .392 | .389 | .511 | .635 | .842 | .736 | .736 |
| Tennessee | | | | | | .664 | .710 | .903 | .789 | .767 |
| Texas | | | | | | | | 1.753 | 1.644 | 1.644 |
| Utah | .524 | .545 | .502 | .422 | .531 | .503 | .766 | .892 | .796 | .724 |
| Vermont | .398 | .457 | .524 | .505 | .595 | .514 | .588 | .875 | .729 | .729 |
| Virginia | | | | | | .391 | .539 | .880 | 1.044 | 1.044 |
| West Virginia | | | .268 | .345 | .404 | .428 | .671 | .660 | 1.162 | 1.162 |
| Wisconsin | | | .523 | .556 | .603 | .505 | .581 | .752 | .791 | .791 |

## Table 16
### Interstate Variations in Net Costs of Insurance for 44 Classes in Divisions A and B of Table 3 Weighted by National Payroll Distribution Insurance Rates in Effect 1950 - 83

| Jurisdiction | 1950 | 1954 | 1958 | 1962 | 1965 | 1972 | 1975 | 1978 | High 1983 | Low 1983 |
|---|---|---|---|---|---|---|---|---|---|---|
| Alabama | .136 | .183 | .242 | .281 | .369 | .611 | .938 | 1.544 | 2.565 | 2.565 |
| Alaska | | | | | | 1.627 | 4.127 | 4.879 | 10.064 | 10.061 |
| Arizona | | | | | | 2.066 | 3.985 | 5.293 | 4.256 | 3.733 |
| Arkansas | | | | | | 1.040 | 1.447 | 2.078 | 2.942 | 2.647 |
| California | | | .631 | .858 | 1.296 | 1.755 | 2.746 | 4.816 | 6.826 | 6.826 |
| Colorado | | | | | | .968 | 1.196 | 2.554 | 4.112 | 3.368 |
| Connecticut | .353 | .548 | .627 | .669 | .663 | 1.008 | 1.467 | 2.768 | 5.160 | 5.160 |
| Delaware | | | | | | .835 | 1.304 | 2.922 | 3.371 | 3.354 |
| District of Columbia | | | | | | 1.219 | 2.847 | 8.199 | 7.717 | 7.717 |
| Florida | | | | | | | | 4.793 | 3.772 | 3.606 |
| Georgia | | | | | | .629 | 1.169 | 1.912 | 2.374 | 2.360 |
| Hawaii | | | | | | 1.306 | 2.229 | 3.964 | 11.156 | 11.156 |
| Idaho | .253 | .396 | .409 | .447 | .561 | 1.063 | 1.933 | 2.238 | 3.727 | 3.727 |
| Illinois | .261 | .363 | .443 | .588 | .660 | 1.029 | 1.925 | 3.063 | 3.785 | 3.406 |
| Indiana | .197 | .245 | .326 | .357 | .422 | .576 | .766 | 1.016 | 1.062 | 1.062 |
| Iowa | | | | | | .644 | 1.159 | 2.190 | 3.002 | 2.966 |
| Kansas | | | | | | .767 | 1.253 | 1.659 | 2.333 | 2.303 |
| Kentucky | .205 | .237 | .299 | .380 | .518 | .949 | 1.856 | 2.781 | 3.527 | 3.174 |
| Louisiana | | | | | | | | 2.909 | 3.964 | 3.964 |
| Maine | .195 | .229 | .230 | .286 | .286 | .687 | 1.588 | 2.581 | 4.495 | 4.495 |
| Maryland | .266 | .390 | .507 | .639 | .800 | 1.154 | 1.750 | 2.526 | 5.632 | 5.520 |

| | | | | | | | | | | |
|---|---|---|---|---|---|---|---|---|---|---|
| Massachusetts | .271 | | .660 | .888 | 1.073 | 1.569 | 2.037 | 2.757 | 4.270 | 4.270 |
| Michigan | | .290 | .370 | .655 | .740 | 1.493 | 2.480 | 4.372 | 6.611 | 5.950 |
| Minnesota | .273 | | .519 | .620 | .724 | 1.237 | 2.203 | 3.733 | 4.151 | 4.151 |
| Mississippi | | .382 | .469 | .671 | .729 | .856 | 1.261 | 1.457 | 2.007 | 1.097 |
| Missouri | | | | | | | | 1.196 | 1.774 | 1.763 |
| Montana | .310 | .414 | .600 | .584 | .750 | 1.330 | 2.695 | 2.795 | 4.993 | 4.993 |
| Nebraska | .303 | .308 | .335 | .468 | .435 | .782 | 1.430 | 1.484 | 2.320 | 2.303 |
| New Hampshire | .250 | .339 | .363 | .385 | .477 | .689 | 1.179 | 2.128 | 3.514 | 3.514 |
| New Jersey | | | .759 | .993 | 1.072 | 1.872 | 2.312 | 3.651 | 4.357 | 4.357 |
| New Mexico | .249 | .565 | .650 | .722 | .866 | .957 | 1.594 | 2.479 | 5.279 | 5.279 |
| New York | | | | | | 1.326 | 1.830 | 3.844 | 3.683 | 3.679 |
| North Carolina | .167 | .267 | .291 | .335 | .354 | .501 | .634 | .899 | 1.823 | 1.823 |
| Ohio | | | .509 | .755 | .834 | 1.352 | 2.077 | 3.352 | 4.355 | 4.355 |
| Oklahoma | | | | | | | 1.673 | 2.654 | 3.916 | 3.916 |
| Oregon | | | .541 | .949 | | 2.269 | 3.872 | 6.288 | 5.723 | 5.151 |
| Pennsylvania | .404 | | .280 | .346 | .369 | .554 | 1.365 | 2.382 | 4.283 | 4.146 |
| Rhode Island | .284 | .555 | .586 | .656 | .726 | .993 | 1.427 | 2.387 | 3.648 | 3.283 |
| South Carolina | .274 | .321 | .353 | .500 | .553 | .700 | .832 | 1.360 | 2.320 | 2.320 |
| South Dakota | | .250 | .233 | .330 | .358 | .706 | 1.077 | 1.649 | 2.194 | 2.194 |
| Tennessee | | | | | | .866 | 1.134 | 1.666 | 2.172 | 2.111 |
| Texas | | | | | | | | 3.293 | 4.747 | 4.747 |
| Utah | .283 | .361 | .392 | .365 | .504 | .678 | 1.267 | 1.701 | 2.325 | 2.116 |
| Vermont | .192 | .270 | .365 | .396 | .511 | .684 | .963 | 1.646 | 1.975 | 1.975 |
| Virginia | | | | | | .478 | .808 | 1.525 | 2.726 | 2.726 |
| West Virginia | | | .200 | .279 | .358 | .563 | 1.069 | 1.229 | 3.507 | 3.507 |
| Wisconsin | | | .412 | .494 | .587 | .751 | 1.060 | 1.582 | 2.480 | 2.480 |

Table 17
Adjusted Manual Rates for 44 Types of Employers
Means and Standard Deviations for Various Combinations of States, 1950-1983

Panel A: Unweighted observations

| Year | 20 states Mean (1) | 20 states Std. Dev. (2) | 28 states Mean (3) | 28 states Std. Dev. (4) | 42 states Mean (5) | 42 states Std. Dev. (6) | 47 states Mean (7) | 47 states Std. Dev. (8) |
|---|---|---|---|---|---|---|---|---|
| 1950 | .508 | .127 | | | | | | |
| 1954 | .560 | .176 | | | | | | |
| 1958 | .554 | .172 | .571 | .186 | | | | |
| 1962 | .600 | .183 | .630 | .214 | | | | |
| 1965 | .631 | .189 | .676 | .237 | | | | |
| 1972 | .644 | .168 | .692 | .233 | .723 | .267 | | |
| 1975 | .870 | .293 | .914 | .299 | .980 | .403 | | |
| 1978 | 1.109 | .357 | 1.190 | .419 | 1.348 | .616 | 1.376 | .621 |
| H 1983 | 1.206 | .488 | 1.263 | .459 | 1.340 | .597 | 1.334 | .576 |
| L 1983 | 1.172 | .473 | 1.236 | .451 | 1.303 | .594 | 1.300 | .573 |

## Panel B: Weighted observations

| | 1 | 2 | 3 | 4 | 5 | 6 | 7 | 8 |
|---|---|---|---|---|---|---|---|---|
| 1950 | .470 | .097 | | | | | | |
| 1954 | .590 | .192 | | | | | | |
| 1958 | .592 | .176 | .618 | .178 | | | | |
| 1962 | .656 | .174 | .711 | .205 | | | | |
| 1965 | .694 | .190 | .791 | .270 | | | | |
| 1972 | .678 | .162 | .783 | .260 | .779 | .266 | | |
| 1975 | .908 | .266 | 1.019 | .291 | 1.008 | .334 | | |
| 1978 | 1.227 | .405 | 1.420 | .472 | 1.454 | .526 | 1.503 | .550 |
| H 1983 | 1.393 | .550 | 1.498 | .491 | 1.428 | .502 | 1.423 | .481 |
| L 1983 | 1.343 | .539 | 1.468 | .492 | 1.395 | .501 | 1.393 | .480 |

H High

L Low

SOURCES: Weights are each state's total nonagricultural employment in 1980 from U.S. Bureau of Labor Statistics, *Supplement to Employment and Earnings, States and Areas, Data for 1977-81*, Bulletin 1370-16 (September 1982). The weighted standard deviations were calculated using a formula provided by Cornell University Professors Paul F. Belleman and Philip J. McCarthy, to whom we express our appreciation.

The 20 states in columns 1 and 2 are: Alabama, Connecticut, Idaho, Illinois, Indiana, Kentucky, Maine, Maryland, Michigan, Mississippi, Montana, Nebraska, New Hampshire, New Mexico, North Carolina, Rhode Island, South Carolina, South Dakota, Utah, and Vermont.

The 28 states in columns 3 and 4 are the 20 states listed above plus: California, Massachusetts, Minnesota, New Jersey, Ohio, Pennsylvania, West Virginia, and Wisconsin.

The 42 states in columns 5 and 6 are the 28 states listed above plus: Alaska, Arizona, Arkansas, Colorado, Delaware, District of Columbia, Georgia, Hawaii, Iowa, Kansas, New York, Oregon, Tennessee, and Virginia.

The 47 states in columns 7 and 8 are the 42 states listed above plus: Florida, Louisiana, Missouri, Oklahoma, and Texas.

Table 18
Net Costs of Insurance for 44 Types of Employers
Means and Standard Deviations for Various Combinations of States, 1950-1983

| Year | 20 states Mean (1) | 20 states Std. Dev. (2) | 28 states Mean (3) | 28 states Std. Dev. (4) | 42 states Mean (5) | 42 states Std. Dev. (6) | 47 states Mean (7) | 47 states Std. Dev. (8) |
|---|---|---|---|---|---|---|---|---|
| | | | Panel A: Unweighted observations | | | | | |
| 1950 | .256 | .063 | | | | | | |
| 1954 | .346 | .111 | | | | | | |
| 1958 | .405 | .131 | .431 | .153 | | | | |
| 1962 | .486 | .148 | .534 | .198 | | | | |
| 1965 | .564 | .169 | .628 | .248 | | | | |
| 1972 | .872 | .260 | .968 | .378 | 1.027 | .439 | | |
| 1975 | 1.453 | .546 | 1.569 | .587 | 1.721 | .849 | | |
| 1978 | 2.144 | .825 | 2.370 | .990 | 2.746 | 1.496 | 2.770 | 1.465 |
| H 1983 | 3.448 | 1.513 | 3.685 | 1.463 | 4.020 | 2.086 | 3.979 | 2.000 |
| L 1983 | 3.343 | 1.444 | 3.605 | 1.425 | 3.911 | 2.075 | 3.878 | 1.989 |

## Panel B: Weighted observations

|      |       |       |       |       |       |       |       |       |
|------|-------|-------|-------|-------|-------|-------|-------|-------|
| 1950 | .248  | .050  |       |       |       |       |       |       |
| 1954 | .381  | .127  |       |       |       |       |       |       |
| 1958 | .452  | .140  | .495  | .154  |       |       |       |       |
| 1962 | .558  | .151  | .638  | .205  |       |       |       |       |
| 1965 | .647  | .180  | .782  | .307  |       |       |       |       |
| 1972 | .938  | .273  | 1.145 | .443  | 1.136 | .450  |       |       |
| 1975 | 1.549 | .538  | 1.827 | .627  | 1.805 | .701  |       |       |
| 1978 | 2.426 | .974  | 2.956 | 1.173 | 3.022 | 1.2966 | 3.061 | 1.273 |
| H 1983 | 4.040 | 1.668 | 4.511 | 1.609 | 4.294 | 1.662 | 4.240 | 1.583 |
| L 1983 | 3.879 | 1.583 | 4.417 | 1.592 | 4.193 | 1.645 | 4.148 | 1.568 |

H High

L Low

See notes for table 17 for other information pertaining to table 18.

1983. Data for the largest combination of jurisdictions (46 states plus the District of Columbia) indicate that employers on average spent 1.503 percent of payroll on workers' compensation insurance in 1978, and 1.423 percent (high adjusted manual rates) or 1.393 percent (low) in 1983.

The average (mean) adjusted manual rate for a particular year obviously reflects data from some states that are more expensive than the mean and some that are less expensive. For example, the average adjusted rate for the 20 states was 0.470 percent of payroll in 1950 (table 17, panel B, column 1), but the average employer in Alabama paid only 0.282 percent while the average employer in Rhode Island paid 0.829 percent of payroll for workers' compensation insurance (table 15, column 1). A statistic that provides a convenient summary of the extent of variations among the states around the average (mean) cost is the standard deviation.[62] The larger the standard deviation, the greater is the variation among the states in the percentage of payroll expended on workers' compensation insurance. The data indicate that from 1950 through 1978, there was an increase in the amount of variation among the states in the percentages of payroll expended on insurance. However, between 1978 and 1983, the variations increased for the combinations of 20 and 28 states, but decreased for the combinations of 42 and 47 states.

Table 18 presents information on the changes through time in the net costs to policyholders for various combinations of states. The layout is similar to table 17, and again the text will use the weighted observations data from panel B. The net costs are measured as the weekly premiums per worker, and in all instances show an increase through time. For example, the weighted mean for the 20 jurisdictions (table 18, panel B, column 1) indicates that employers paid $2.426 weekly in 1978, while in 1983 the cost was $4.040

(high net costs) or $3.879 (low net costs). Data for the largest combination of jurisdictions (47) indicate that in 1978, employers on average paid $3.061 weekly on workers' compensation premiums, while in 1983 they paid $4.240 (high net costs) or $4.148 (low net costs).

Table 18 also provides information on the extent of variation among the states around the average (mean) net costs to policyholders. In 1950, when the average cost was $.248 per worker per week in the 20 states, the standard deviation among the states was $.050. The data indicate that through time there have been continuing increases in the amount of variation among the states in the cost in dollars of workers' compensation insurance (table 18, panel B, columns 2, 4, 6, and 8).

## XII. Comparisons of Connecticut, New Jersey, and New York

This section provides a closer examination of Connecticut, New Jersey, and New York, the three states of particular interest to the conference for which this paper was prepared. We examine the changes in the employers' costs of workers' compensation since 1972, the earliest date when data are available for all three states. We also attempt to explain these cost developments in terms of changes in benefit levels and other relevant factors.

Table 19 presents data on the percent of payroll devoted to workers' compensation insurance by a sample of employers. These data correspond to the adjusted manual rates shown in tables 15 and 17. For 1983, only high adjusted manual rates are shown since as of January 1983, Connecticut and New Jersey did not permit private carriers to modify insurance rates on an *ex ante* basis, and New York had only a very limited use of deviations (table 7). The result is that for Connecticut and New Jersey, low and high adjusted manual rates are identical, while for New York the impact of deviations is so slight that the two variants of adjusted manual rates are virtually the same.

The data in table 19 present an interesting history of workers' compensation costs (measured as a percentage of payroll) both nationally and in the three states. From 1972 to 1978, the 42-jurisdiction average of employers' costs almost doubled (from 0.779 percent to 1.454 percent), and then from 1978 to 1983 there was a slight decline. In Connecticut, the employers' costs of workers' compensation relative to the national average (column 3 of table 19) were roughly 80-90 percent of the national figure from 1972 to 1978. Then Connecticut costs increased rapidly so that by 1983 Connecticut employers were paying insurance premiums some 25 percent above the national average. In New Jersey, the employers' costs relative to the national average (as shown in column 5) began about 60 percent higher in 1972, dropped to about 20 percent above that average in 1975 and 1978, and almost exactly matched the national average in 1983. The New York record is more erratic, since costs began some 10 percent above the national average in 1972 (column 7), dropped slightly below the national average in 1975, increased to about 20 percent above the national average in 1978, and then fell to about 20 percent below the national figure in 1983.

The patterns just described involving workers' compensation cost measured as a percent of payroll are paralleled by the behavior of costs measured by the weekly insurance premium per worker. Table 20 indicates that in 1972 Connecticut employers' costs were about 10 percent below the national average, while in 1983 the costs were some 20 percent above the national average. In contrast, New Jersey employers began with costs almost 65 percent above the national average, but found their costs almost exactly equal to the 42-jurisdiction average in 1983. In New York, costs were

Table 19
Percent of Payroll Devoted to Workers' Compensation Insurance
By a Sample of Employers

| Year | Average cost in 42 jurisdictions (1) | Connecticut | | New Jersey | | New York | |
|---|---|---|---|---|---|---|---|
| | | Cost (2) | Cost relative to 42 jurisdictions average (3) | Cost (4) | Cost relative to 42 jurisdictions average (5) | Cost (6) | Cost relative to 42 jurisdictions average (7) |
| 1972 | 0.779 | 0.697 | 87.2 | 1.224 | 157.1 | 0.864 | 110.9 |
| 1975 | 1.008 | 0.827 | 82.0 | 1.233 | 122.3 | 0.973 | 96.5 |
| 1978 | 1.454 | 1.353 | 93.1 | 1.687 | 116.0 | 1.770 | 121.7 |
| 1983 (high) | 1.428 | 1.786 | 125.1 | 1.422 | 99.6 | 1.185 | 83.0 |

SOURCE: Data in tables 15 and 17 (panel B).

Table 20

Weekly Insurance Premiums for Workers' Compensation Insurance (Net Costs of Insurance)
Expended by a Sample of Employers

| Year | Average cost in 42 jurisdictions (1) | Connecticut | | New Jersey | | New York | |
|---|---|---|---|---|---|---|---|
| | | Cost (2) | Cost relative to 42 jurisdictions average (3) | Cost (4) | Cost relative to 42 jurisdictions average (5) | Cost (6) | Cost relative to 42 jurisdictions average (7) |
| 1972 | $1.136 | $1.008 | 88.7 | $1.872 | 164.8 | $1.326 | 116.7 |
| 1975 | $1.805 | $1.467 | 81.3 | $2.312 | 128.1 | $1.830 | 101.4 |
| 1978 | $3.022 | $2.768 | 91.6 | $3.651 | 120.8 | $3.844 | 127.2 |
| 1983 (high) | $4.294 | $5.160 | 120.2 | $4.357 | 101.5 | $3.683 | 85.8 |

SOURCE: Data in tables 16 and 18 (panel B).

about 20 percent above the national average from 1972 until 1978, and then fell to 15 percent below in 1983.

Both measures of workers' compensation costs thus show a considerable movement in the relative costs among Connecticut, New Jersey, and New York over the last decade. Connecticut began as the low cost state and ended as the most expensive. New Jersey began as much more expensive than the others and ended up in the middle, while New York moved from the middle to the least expensive. These rankings are based on comparisons among the employers' costs of workers' compensation for a representative sample of 44 types of employers (or 45 types before 1983). However, the rankings are not particularly sensitive to the types of employers that are compared. There are, for example, five different combinations of employers for whom the adjusted manual rates as of January 1, 1983, are presented in table 10. For all combinations, New York insurance rates are lowest, New Jersey are the next most expensive (ranging from 13 to 20 percent more expensive than New York rates), and Connecticut rates are the most expensive (ranging from 31 to 56 percent more expensive than New York rates).

A statistical or quantitative explanation of the cost differences among the three jurisdictions is not possible, given the limited number of observations.[63] What we will therefore present is a largely qualitative explanation of the factors that appear to explain the cost developments shown in tables 19 and 20.

An obvious candidate for a variable that explains the costs of workers' compensation insurance in a jurisdiction is the generosity of benefits provided by the state's workers' compensation program. Table 21 presents information on several important aspects of the workers' compensation statutes in Connecticut, New Jersey, and New York as of January 1, 1983, the date for the costs of the program as measured in this study.

**Table 21**
**Selected Comparisons of Temporary Disability,**
**Permanent Disability, and Fatal Benefits**
**in Connecticut, New Jersey, and New York**
**as of January 1, 1983**

| Temporary total disability | CT | NJ | NY |
|---|---|---|---|
| Nominal rate of compensation | 66 2/3% | 70% | 66 2/3% |
| Minimum weekly benefit | $65.20 | $62.81 | $30.00 |
| Maximum weekly benefit | $326.00 | $236.00 | $215.00 |
| Waiting period | 3 days | 7 days | 7 days |
| Retroactive after | 7 days | 7 days | 14 days |
| Dependency allowance per child | $10.00 | -- | -- |
| Cost-of-living adjustment for outstanding cases | Yes | No | No |
| **Permanent total disability** | **CT** | **NJ** | **NY** |
| Nominal rate of compensation | | | |
| 1st 450 weeks | -- | 70% | -- |
| after 450 weeks | -- | 70% minus wages earned | -- |
| all cases | 66 2/3% | -- | 66 2/3% |
| Minimum weekly benefit | | | |
| 1st 450 weeks | -- | $62.81 | -- |
| after 450 weeks | -- | $5.00 | -- |
| all cases | $65.20 | -- | $20.00 |
| Maximum weekly benefit | $326.00 | $236.00 | $215.00 |
| Maximum duration | life | life | life |
| Benefit subject to Social Security offset | no | yes | no |
| Dependency allowance per child | $10.00 | -- | -- |
| Cost-of-living adjustment for outstanding cases | yes | no | no |
| **Permanent partial disability benefits** | **CT** | **NJ** | **NY** |
| Scheduled benefits | | | |
| Nominal rate of compensation | 66 2/3% | 70% | 66 2/3% |
| Minimum weekly benefit | $20.00 | $35.00 | $20.00 |
| Maximum weekly benefit | | | |
| 1st 96 weeks | -- | $49.00 | -- |
| 97-420 varies from | -- | $51.00-219.84 | -- |
| 421-600 weeks | -- | $236.00 | -- |
| All cases | $326.00 | -- | $105.00 |
| Duration varies by impairment, examples: | | | |
| Total loss of arm | 312 weeks | 330 weeks | 312 weeks |
| Total loss of leg | 238 weeks | 315 weeks | 288 weeks |
| Total loss of hand | 252 weeks | 245 weeks | 244 weeks |

## Table 21 (continued)

|  | CT | NJ | NY |
|---|---|---|---|
| Total loss of foot | 188 weeks | 230 weeks | 205 weeks |
| Amputation cases | -- | award increased by 30% | -- |
| **Nonscheduled benefits** |  |  |  |
| Nominal rate of compensation |  |  |  |
| Percent of preinjury wage | -- | 70% | -- |
| Percent of (preinjury wage-postinjury earning capacity) | -- | -- | 66 2/3% |
| Percent of wage loss | 66 2/3% | -- | -- |
| Minimum weekly benefit | none | $35.00 | none |
| Maximum weekly benefit |  |  |  |
| 1st 96 weeks | -- | $49.00 | -- |
| 97-420 varies from | -- | $51.00-219.84 | -- |
| 421-600 weeks | -- | $236.00 | -- |
| All cases | $326.00 | -- | $105.00 |
| Maximum duration | 780 weeks | 600 weeks x % of disability | length of disability |
| **Fatal benefits** | **CT** | **NJ** | **NY** |
| Nominal rate of compensation-widow only | 66 2/3% | 50% | 66 2/3% |
| Minimum weekly benefit-widow | $20.00 | $62.81 | $45.00 |
| Maximum weekly benefit-widow | $326.00 | $236.00 | $322.50 |
| Maximum duration-widow | life or remarriage | life or remarriage | life or remarriage |
| Widow's benefit reduced by wages earned after 450 weeks | no | yes | no |
| Widow's benefit subject to Social Security offset | no | no | yes |
| Cost-of-living adjustment for outstanding cases | yes | no | no |

SOURCES: National Council on Compensation Insurance, *Legislative Update Service* (1983 with supplements); data on duration of scheduled benefits from U.S. Department of Labor, Employment Standards Administration, Office of State Liaison and Legislative Analysis, Division of State Workers' Compensation Programs, *State Workers' Compensation Laws* (January 1983), table 8.

Temporary total disability benefits are the most common type of cash benefits in the workers' compensation program. The data in table 21 indicate that for most aspects of this type of benefit, Connecticut had the most generous provisions. Connecticut had the highest minimum and maximum benefits, the shortest waiting period before benefits began, and was the only state that provided cost-of-living adjustments for outstanding cases. New Jersey had a slightly higher nominal rate of compensation that Connecticut, but to some extent this advantage was overcome by Connecticut's payment of a dependency allowance for children.

The benefits for permanent total disability were also generally more adequate in Connecticut than in the other two jurisdictions. Connecticut had higher minimum and maximum benefits, had a dependency allowance, and was the only jurisdiction that provided a cost-of-living adjustment for outstanding cases.

Scheduled permanent partial disability benefits are difficult to compare among jurisdictions because of the complexity of the statutory provisions for such benefits. Those aspects summarized in table 21 suggest that Connecticut is perhaps somewhat less generous in terms of the number of weeks of benefits paid for particular types of injuries (such as the loss of a leg), but considerable more generous in terms of the weekly benefit. In New Jersey, the maximum weekly benefit started at $49 and did not reach $236 until there were 421 weeks of benefits; in New York, the weekly maximum was $105 for all durations; in Connecticut, the maximum for all durations as $326.

Statutory provisions for nonscheduled permanent partial disability benefits are also difficult to compare because of the different approaches used to provide the benefits. New Jersey determines the duration by evaluating the extent of the worker's impairment and multiplying the rating percentage times 600 weeks; the maximum weekly benefit ranges from $49 to $236. New York has a maximum weekly benefit of $105, which is relatively low, but the payments can continue for the length of disability, which can be for life. Connecticut pays benefits that are related to the percent of wage loss, with a maximum duration of 780 weeks and a maximum weekly benefit of $326. It is not evident which jurisdiction's provisions for nonscheduled benefits are more generous, but Connecticut does not appear to be deficient.

The final type of benefit included in table 21 is fatal benefits, where Connecticut generally has the most liberal provisions. The nominal percentage of 63 2/3 percent found in Connecticut is matched in New York, but in the latter case the benefits are subject to an offset provision that reduces workers' compensation benefits when social security benefits are received by the widow or widower. The minimum weekly benefit is lower in Connecticut, but the levels are so low in all three jurisdictions that few cases are likely to be affected. More significant is the maximum weekly benefit, highest in Connecticut, and the cost of living adjustment for outstanding cases, a provision found only in Connecticut.

This qualitative assessment of the workers' compensation statutes in Connecticut, New Jersey, and New York as of January 1, 1983 suggests that Connecticut has the most generous provisions for most types of benefits. As between New Jersey and New York, the differences are not as pronounced, although for all types of benefits except fatal the New Jersey maximum weekly benefits are higher. Thus, at least in a rough sense, the ranking of workers' compensation costs as of January 1983 as shown in tables 19 and 20 corresponds to the ranking of statutory benefit generosity shown in table 21.

The view that employers' costs of workers' compensation are affected by statutory provisions is reinforced by information on the changes through time in these factors. Tables 19 and 20 demonstrated the changes between 1972 and 1983 in the costs in the three states, with Connecticut moving from least to most expensive, while New York costs were declining to least expensive. Table 22 presents information on the changes between 1972 and 1983 in the extent of compliance with the 19 essential recommendations of The National Commission on State Workmen's Compensation Laws.[64] These essential recommendations primarily pertain to benefit amounts and durations, the types of provisions for which increasing compliance is likely to lead to higher costs. It is instructive that the state with the most dramatic change in compliance scores between 1972 and 1983 is Connecticut. Further, most of the improvements in Connecticut took place between 1978 and 1983, which matches the interval when the employers' costs of workers' compensation increased sharply in the state.

Table 22
State Compliance With the 19 Essential Recommendations
of the National Commission
on State Workmen's Compensation Laws

| Year (as of January 1) | Average of 52 jurisdictions | Connecticut | New Jersey | New York |
|---|---|---|---|---|
| 1972 | 6.9 | 10.5 | 10.5 | 9.0 |
| 1975 | 9.4 | 10.5 | 10.5 | 9.0 |
| 1978 | 11.7 | 10.75 | 10.5 | 10.0 |
| 1980 | 12.1 | 13.75 | 10.5 | 10.0 |
| 1983 | 12.2 | 14.0 | 10.75 | 10.0 |

SOURCE: U.S. Department of Labor, Employment Standards Administration, Office of Workers' Compensation Programs, Division of State Workers' Compensation Standards, *State Compliance with the 19 Essential Recommendations of the National Commission on State Workmen's Compensation Laws, 1972-1980* (January 1981), as supplemented by January 1, 1983 release from the Division (now the Division of State Workers' Compensation Programs).

An even more compelling demonstration of the relationship between changes in statutory provisions and changes in workers' compensation costs is provided by comparing the cost data in tables 19 and 20 with the data in table 23 showing the levels of the maximum weekly benefits for temporary total disability. Both in terms of the dollar amounts of the maximums and in terms of the maximum benefit as a percentage of the state's average weekly wage, Connecticut had the greatest increase between 1972 and 1983, followed by New Jersey, and then by New York. Again of interest is that most of the improvement in Connecticut's maximum for temporary total disability took place after 1978, corresponding to the time when the cost of the program in the state also sharply increased.

While this analysis suggests that changes in benefit levels are an important determinant of changes in the employers' costs of workers' compensation, we do not want to suggest that benefits are the only factor that affects costs. In a separate study, we are examining the influence on costs of variables such as coverage and the type of insurance arrangements (as measured by the importance of state insurance funds and of self-insurance).[65] Another factor that affects costs is the administration of the law, and in particular the application of the statutory provisions for permanent total disability and permanent disability benefits. Tables 24 to 26 present information on the number and costs of these types of benefits in Connecticut, New Jersey, and New York.

The data are based on claims that occurred in the policy years closest to 1958, 1968, 1973, and 1978. Because of the delays between the ends of the policy years and the dates when information on the claims from those years are available, 1978 is the most recent year for which data are available on both the number and costs of permanent

Table 23
Maximum Weekly Benefit for Temporary Total Disability
Connecticut, New Jersey, and New York, 1972-1983

| Year (as of January 1) | Connecticut | | New Jersey | | New York | |
|---|---|---|---|---|---|---|
| | Dollars | As percentage of SAWW | Dollars | As percentage of SAWW | Dollars | As percentage of SAWW |
| 1972 | $ 95.00 | 63.3 | $ 95.00 | 71.5 | $ 95.00 | 63.3 |
| 1975 | 119.00 | 75.2 | 119.00 | 70.2 | 125.00 | 69.6 |
| 1978 | 147.00 | 73.3 | 146.00 | 70.3 | 125.00 | 57.9 |
| 1980 | 261.00 | 114.7 | 185.00 | 78.8 | 215.00 | 88.6 |
| 1983 | 326.00 | 118.5 | 236.00 | 81.9 | 215.00 | 71.6 |

SOURCE: See table 22.

NOTE: SAWW is the state's average weekly wage.

disability claims and the employers' costs of workers' compensation insurance.

The shares of all cases with cash benefits accounted for by permanent disability cases in the three jurisdictions are examined in table 24. The most significant finding is the considerably greater importance of permanent disability cases in New Jersey than in Connecticut or New York. In particular, minor permanent partial disability benefits dominated the New Jersey caseload, accounting for almost half of all cases in 1978.

The average costs of permanent disability cases are presented in table 25. Overall, New Jersey has the lowest average, reflecting in large part the predominance of the minor permanent partial disability cases. As of 1978, Connecticut had the highest average cost per case for each of the three types of permanent disability cases as well as for the overall average.

The shares of all cash benefits accounted for by permanent disability cases are presented in table 26. While Connecticut devoted the highest percentage of all cash benefits to major permanent partial disability benefits in 1978, New Jersey expended the largest percentages on permanent total, minor permanent partial, and all permanent disability cases. Indeed, for each of the four years shown between 1958 and 1978, New Jersey expended the highest percentage of all cash benefits on the total of the three types of permanent disability benefits.

These data confirm what has been widely discussed elsewhere, namely, the unusual emphasis in New Jersey on the compensation of relatively minor permanent impairments.[66] This probably is one reason why the employers' costs of workers' compensation were relatively high in the state, given the level of benefits. For example, in 1978, when

Table 24

**Share of All Cases with Cash Benefits Accounted for by Permanent Disability Cases in Connecticut, New Jersey, and New York, 1958-1978, in percentages**

| | Permanent total | | | Major permanent partial | | | Minor permanent partial | | | All permanent disability cases | | |
|---|---|---|---|---|---|---|---|---|---|---|---|---|
| | CT (1) | NJ (2) | NY (3) | CT (4) | NJ (5) | NY (6) | CT (7) | NJ (8) | NY (9) | CT (10) | NJ (11) | NY (12) |
| 1958 | 0.05 | 0.08 | 0.09 | 1.79 | 1.83 | 2.34 | 22.16 | 67.08 | 30.49 | 24.00 | 68.99 | 32.93 |
| 1968 | 0.04 | 0.05 | 0.03 | 2.24 | 2.77 | 2.17 | 17.00 | 58.48 | 31.73 | 19.28 | 61.30 | 33.93 |
| 1973 | 0.03 | 0.09 | 0.05 | 1.52 | 3.20 | 2.82 | 12.77 | 49.89 | 27.02 | 14.32 | 53.18 | 29.89 |
| 1978 | 0.04 | 0.14 | 0.08 | 3.24 | 4.24 | 4.36 | 11.82 | 49.84 | 24.14 | 15.10 | 54.22 | 28.58 |

SOURCE: National Council on Compensation Insurance, "Countrywide Workers' Compensation Experience Including Certain Competitive State Funds—1st Report Basis," Exhibits dated (no date), March 15, 1972, July 1976, and April 1982.

## Table 25
## Average Cost of Permanent Disability Cases
## in Connecticut, New Jersey, and New York, 1958-1978, in dollars

| | Permanent total | | | Major permanent partial | | | Minor permanent partial | | | All permanent disability cases | | |
|---|---|---|---|---|---|---|---|---|---|---|---|---|
| | CT (1) | NJ (2) | NY (3) | CT (4) | NJ (5) | NY (6) | CT (7) | NJ (8) | NY (9) | CT (10) | NJ (11) | NY (12) |
| 1958 | 34,167 | 32,500 | 19,714 | 7,462 | 8,451 | 8,897 | 1,358 | 904 | 1,044 | 1,875 | 1,141 | 1,616 |
| 1968 | 92,840 | 66,464 | 33,280 | 10,831 | 10,308 | 12,368 | 2,230 | 1,566 | 1,722 | 3,407 | 2,015 | 2,430 |
| 1973 | 120,356 | 63,396 | 42,358 | 17,332 | 11,713 | 14,337 | 3,174 | 1,918 | 1,819 | 4,926 | 2,617 | 3,072 |
| 1978 | 105,208 | 87,944 | 62,925 | 25,450 | 15,344 | 18,534 | 4,446 | 2,482 | 2,351 | 9,204 | 3,711 | 4,997 |

SOURCE: See table 24.

## Table 26
## Share of All Cash Benefits Accounted for by Permanent Disability Cases
## in Connecticut, New Jersey, and New York, 1958-1978, in percentages

| | Permanent total | | | Major permanent partial | | | Minor permanent partial | | | All permanent disability cases | | |
|---|---|---|---|---|---|---|---|---|---|---|---|---|
| | CT (1) | NJ (2) | NY (3) | CT (4) | NJ (5) | NY (6) | CT (7) | NJ (8) | NY (9) | CT (10) | NJ (11) | NY (12) |
| 1958 | 1.86 | 2.74 | 1.84 | 15.99 | 16.45 | 21.73 | 36.09 | 64.55 | 31.92 | 53.94 | 83.74 | 55.50 |
| 1968 | 3.35 | 1.86 | 0.66 | 23.43 | 15.49 | 18.67 | 36.55 | 49.65 | 37.98 | 63.33 | 67.03 | 57.30 |
| 1973 | 3.06 | 2.90 | 1.43 | 21.87 | 18.20 | 25.07 | 33.67 | 46.44 | 30.50 | 58.60 | 67.54 | 56.99 |
| 1978 | 1.68 | 4.61 | 1.99 | 36.11 | 23.99 | 30.97 | 22.98 | 45.65 | 21.72 | 60.77 | 74.25 | 54.67 |

SOURCE: See table 24.

the maximum weekly benefits for temporary total disability in Connecticut and New Jersey were virtually identical (table 23), the costs of workers' compensation insurance were much higher in the latter state.

What the data in tables 24 to 26 cannot reveal because the terminal date in 1978 is the impact of the major reform in 1979 of the permanent partial disability benefits in New Jersey.[67] The law was amended to require objective evidence of permanent impairments, presumably to preclude payment of permanent partial disability benefits for minor injuries. Apparently the reform had the intended effect of reducing the costs of workers' compensation insurance in New Jersey: even though the maximum weekly benefit for temporary total disability increased more rapidly than the state's average weekly wage between 1978 and 1983 (table 23), insurance costs as a percentage of payroll dropped markedly during the same interval (table 19).

The data on permanent disability benefits in tables 24 to 26 have other interesting aspects. In New York, the share of cash benefits accounted for by all types of permanent disability cases fluctuated in a very narrow band over the 1958 to 1978 period (from 55 to 57 percent). However, this represented a significant decline in importance of minor permanent partial cases and an offsetting increase in importance of major permanent partial cases. Additional data on permanent partial disability benefits in New York are presented in table 27. These data are from records kept by the Workers' Compensation Board and pertain to cases closed in a given year, regardless of the year of injury, while the data in tables 24-26, from insurance industry records, pertain to injuries that occurred in a given policy year regardless of when the cases were closed. Another difference is that the insurance industry data divide permanent partial disability cases between major and minor categories depending on the seriousness of the injury (or the amount of benefits paid), while the table 27 data distinguish between scheduled and nonscheduled permanent partial cases. The latter distinction is particularly interesting because New York uses different approaches for the two types of benefits: scheduled benefits are paid on the basis of the extent of physical impairment without regard to the amount of actual wage loss, while the nonscheduled benefits are largely based on the amount of actual earnings losses.

### Table 27
### New York
### Number of Cases and Cost of Compensation
### for Scheduled and Nonscheduled Permanent Partial Disability
### as a Percentage of All Cases, Selected Years, 1960-1982

| Year | Scheduled awards as percentage of | | Nonscheduled awards as percentage of | |
|---|---|---|---|---|
| | Number of cases | Amount of compensation | Number of cases | Amount of compensation |
| 1960 | 34.1 | 35.0 | 3.0 | 32.2 |
| 1965 | 38.9 | 34.8 | 2.6 | 34.8 |
| 1970 | 37.9 | 35.7 | 2.6 | 34.5 |
| 1975 | 37.3 | 30.0 | 3.1 | 44.7 |
| 1980 | 35.6 | 24.0 | 3.8 | 52.2 |
| 1982 | 36.4 | 24.2 | 4.2 | 52.4 |

SOURCE: *Compensated Cases Closed,* Workers' Compensation Board, State of New York, for years shown.

The data in table 27 indicate a rapid increase during the 1970s in the share of cases and cash payments accounted for by nonscheduled awards, with a significant decline in the amount of compensation going to scheduled awards. Burton has examined these patterns in a recent study,[68] and found that a major reason why nonscheduled permanent partial cases have become more expensive during the last decade is the relatively high unemployment rates during the period. Indeed, given the magnitude of the increases shown in table 27 for nonscheduled cases and the high levels of unemployment so far in the 1980s, it is surprising that workers' compensation costs have declined so rapidly in New York since 1978 (table 19).

This analysis of Connecticut, New Jersey, and New York thus provides some interesting findings on the behavior of workers' compensation costs between 1972 and 1983, and some partial explanations of the changes in costs. There were significant changes in the relative costs among the three jurisdictions, with Connecticut having experienced the most rapid increase and New Jersey the largest decline. The explanation of Connecticut's increase appears to be largely due to the jurisdiction's significant improvement in benefits compared to the other states. In New Jersey, the rapid decline in costs compared to the other two jurisdictions between 1972 and 1983 appears to reflect both a deterioration in benefit levels compared to Connecticut and the reduction in the prevalence of minor permanent partial disability benefits. The New York experience of declining costs between 1978 and 1983 reflects in part the slippage of benefits compared to those in Connecticut during this interval; it is not clear why the increasing costs of nonscheduled benefits have not limited the costs declines shown in table 19. Perhaps the best one sentence summary is that over the 1972 to 1983 interval, the changing relative costs in workers' compensation insurance in Connecticut, New Jersey, and New York can be largely but not entirely explained by changing levels of benefits.

## XIII. Significance of the Cost Developments Since 1972

The historical data on the employers' costs of workers' compensation insurance were presented in tables 17 and 18 and described in section XI. The essence is that between 1950 and 1978 there were significant increases both in the percentage of payroll devoted to workers' compensation premiums and in the weekly insurance premium per worker. Also, the variations among the states in these two measures of workers' compensation costs significantly increased through time. The developments between 1978 and 1983 are more complex. For the combinations of states for which the historical record is the longest (20 and 28 states), the adjusted manual rates showed continuing increases in the means and the standard deviations (table 17, columns 1-4). However, for the larger combinations of states (42 and 47 states), there were decreases in the means and standard deviations of adjusted manual rates between 1978 and 1983 (table 17, columns 5-8). The behavior of weekly premiums per worker continued the patterns of earlier years in the 1978 to 1983 interval: for all combinations of states, the means and standard deviations increased between these years (table 18).

Although the patterns of cost changes in the most recent five-year interval are somewhat mixed, a clear picture emerges if we consider developments over the entire period since 1972. That starting point seems appropriate since it is the first year for which data are available for all three states of primary concern to this study (Connecticut, New Jersey, and New York) and because 1972 was the year that the National Commission on State Workmen's Compensation Laws issued its report and called attention to the issue of interstate cost differences.[69] Between 1972 and 1983, every combination of states shown in tables 17 and 18 for which data are available has shown increases both in the average costs and the differences in costs among states.

The determinants of these cost developments are largely beyond the scope of this study. Several findings are relevant, however. In an earlier study, Burton found that the level of workers' compensation benefits were the most significant variable in explaining interstate differences in costs among 25 states.[70] In a current research project, we have confirmed the statistical significance of the level of benefits in explaining workers' compensation cost differences among 31 jurisdictions.[71] Because of data limitations, neither of these studies included New Jersey and New York. However, the qualitative analysis in section XII of this study suggests that changes in benefit levels between 1972 and 1983 were an important factor in explaining changes in workers' compensation costs in these two states relative to the cost changes in Connecticut.

We believe this evidence supports the proposition that interstate differences in the levels of workers' compensation benefits are a major (though not the only) determinant of interstate differences in the employers' costs of workers' compensation. If this proposition is true, then the developments since 1972 in costs are particularly disturbing because they suggest the interstate inequities in benefits that were of major concern to the National Commission have become worse in the last decade. The changes in maximum weekly benefits for temporary total disability between 1972 and 1983 in Connecticut, New Jersey and New York provide a partial validation of the disturbing developments. In January 1972, the dollar amounts were identical in the three states. In January 1983, injured workers qualifying for the maximum weekly benefit received $100 more per week in Connecticut than in New Jersey, while New York workers at the maximum were another $21 below the New Jersey figure.[72] To be sure, New Jersey and New York employers had lower workers' compensation costs than did Connecticut employers, but since the two inexpensive jurisdictions failed to comply with the National Commission's recommendations for maximum weekly benefits for temporary total, permanent total, and death cases, their achievement seems more due to parsimony than prudence.

# NOTES

*The present study is based in large part on a study prepared by Burton with the assistance of Krueger entitled "Interstate Variations in the Employers' Costs of Workers' Compensation, With Particular Reference to Ohio and Pennsylvania." The January 1984 study was prepared through the auspices of Workers' Disability Income Systems, Inc. (202 Blackstone Avenue, Ithaca, NY 14850) with financial support from the Workers' Compensation Coalition. The Coalition consists of CIGNA, Crum & Forster, Harleysville Mutual Insurance Company, Liberty Mutual Insurance Company, and Pennsylvania Manufacturers Association Insurance Company. We appreciate the opportunity to use the material from the study sponsored by the Workers' Compensation Coalition. The views in the present study are not necessarily those of the Coalition.

In preparing the present study, refined estimates were prepared for the costs of workers' compensation in five jurisdictions. The estimated costs were increased significantly for Michigan and decreased slightly for Delaware, New York, Pennsylvania, and West Virginia.

We appreciate the assistance of Dane Partridge, who prepared several of the tables involving comparisons among Connecticut, New Jersey, and New York, and Nancy Voorheis, for typing this article. We assume responsibility for all views and data, no matter how persuasive and accurate.

1. John F. Burton, Jr., *The Significance and Causes of the Interstate Variations in the Employers' Costs of Workmen's Compensation* (Ph.D. dissertation, Department of Economics, The University of Michigan, 1965).

2. John F. Burton, Jr., *Interstate Variations in Employers' Costs of Workmen's Compensation* (Kalamazoo, MI: W. E. Upjohn Institute for Employment Research, 1966).

3. The National Commission on State Workmen's Compensation Laws, *The Report of the National Commission on State Workmen's Compensation Laws* (Washington: U.S. Government Printing Office, 1972).

4. Nancy L. Watkins and John F. Burton, Jr., "Employers' Costs of Workmen's Compensation," in *Supplemental Studies for the National Commission on State Workmen's Compensation Laws,* Vol. II (Washington: U.S. Government Printing Office, 1973), pp. 217-240.

5. John F. Burton, Jr., "Workers' Compensation Costs for Employers," in *Research Report of the Interdepartmental Workers' Compensation Task Force,* Vol. 3 (Washington: U.S. Department of Labor, Employment Standards Administration, Division of State Workers' Compensation Standards, 1979), pp. 9-32.

6. Martin W. Elson and John F. Burton, Jr., "Workers' Compensation Insurance: Recent Trends in Employer Costs," *Monthly Labor Review* (March 1981), pp. 45-50.

7. John F. Burton, Jr. (with the assistance of Alan B. Krueger), "Interstate Variations in the Employers' Costs of Workers' Compensation, With Particular Reference to Ohio and Pennsylvania," Ithaca, NY: Workers' Disability Income Systems, 1984.

8. The delivery system includes all the parties in the public and private sectors who are involved in providing benefits and services to workers injured on the job.

9. These changes are reviewed in a paper by C. Arthur Williams, Jr., included in this volume.

10. The 17.5 percent figure excludes payments for the Federal Black Lung benefits program and was calculated from data in Daniel N. Price, "Workers' Compensation: Coverage, Benefits, and Costs, 1980," *Social Security Bulletin* (May 1983), table 2, p. 17.

11. A serious problem is that most data on self-insurance are not broken down by the insurance classifications used throughout this study.

12. *Classification Codes for Workers' Compensation and Employers' Liability Insurance* (New York: National Council on Compensation Insurance, 1983).

13. An extended discussion of the difficulties of making interstate cost comparisons because of the use of payroll limitations is provided in the *Ohio-Pennsylvania Study,* section II.

14. These data are included in the *Ohio-Pennsylvania Study,* table 2.

15. The Average Earned Rate Exhibit prepared by the National Council on Compensation Insurance contains a two-page supplement (dated May

1983) explaining "why conclusions drawn from the comparison of rates among states have no validity." The methodology explained in section IV of this report is designed to overcome most of the problems caused by comparisons involving average earned rates.

16. "1981 Workers' Compensation Average Premium per Employee," *Best's Insurance Management Reports* (Oldwick, NJ: A.M. Best Company, Property/Casualty Release No. 2, January 31, 1983).

17. Ibid., p. 1.

18. Ohio, for example, has an average premium of $152.10 per worker in the *Best's* table, while Pennsylvania has average premiums of $271.18 per worker. However, as of 1980 (the latest data available) self-insurers accounted for 36.8 percent of benefit payments in Ohio and only 23.2 percent in Pennsylvania; it is hardly surprising that Ohio appears to have lower costs using the *Best's* methodology.

19. The distribution of payroll by classification shown in table 2 is a revised version of the payroll distribution used in the *Supplemental Study,* the *Task Force Study,* and the *MLR article,* which was based on 1966-67, 1967-68, or 1968-69 policy year data for 28 states.

20. Of the 47 jurisdictions included in table 1, two (Ohio and West Virginia) have exclusive state funds and their own classification systems. There are also three states (California, Delaware, and Pennsylvania) that have private insurance carriers, but each uses a classification system with significant deviations from the National Council's scheme.

21. Most of the conversions were fairly obvious from comparing the classification descriptions in the National Council's *Classification Codes* and the "deviant" state's classification manual. Where ambiguity existed, the National Council class descriptions were sent to the appropriate official in the non-Council state and he or she chose the most nearly analogous class in that state, or the staff of the National Council selected the most nearly analogous class. As an example, the Council provided the entire set of substitute classifications for Delaware when the *Supplemental Study* was prepared. Similarly, the Pennsylvania Compensation Rating Bureau provided the entire set of substitute classifications for Pennsylvania for the *Ohio-Pennsylvania Study.*

22. Table 3 was originally developed for the *Dissertation,* and has been modified several times in subsequent studies of interstate differences in workers' compensation costs. The original formulation and modifica-

tions are discussed in the *Ohio-Pennsylvania Study,* section IV, especially footnote 28.

23. Previously, there were 45 classes included in division B, but subsequent to the *MLR article,* which used 1978 data, one of the manufacturing classes in division B was absorbed by another such class.

24. Previously, there were 64 classes in division C, but subsequent to 1978 the seven "All Other Classes" in division C were absorbed by "All Other Classes" in divisions A or B.

25. Prior to 1983, there were 79 classes in division D, but subsequent to 1978—because of the deletions already catalogued—there were 8 classes absorbed by other classes.

26. Manual rates will appear artificially high in a state with a payroll limitation (that is low relative to the average wages paid in the state) compared to the rates in a state with no payroll limitation. The similar factor present in Minnesota is that, unlike other states, Minnesota excludes from the payroll base all payments for vacations, holidays, and sick leave. (This rule has been in effect since January 1, 1982.) Employers are permitted to pay premiums based on the published manual rates times this truncated version of the payroll base, or the employers may pay premiums that are reduced 10 percent if the published manual rates are multiplied times the full payroll base, comparable to that used in other states. In order to place the Minnesota rates on a comparable basis to those elsewhere, all average manual rates for Minnesota have been reduced by 10 percent. Oregon excludes from the payroll base payments for vacations and for bonuses unless part of a contract for hire. In order to make the Oregon rates comparable to those elsewhere, all average manual rates for Oregon have been reduced by 5.1 percent. South Dakota has a payroll limitation similar to Minnesota's that became effective in July 1983. This limitation will not affect the comparisons in this study, which involve rates in effect on January 1, 1983.

27. The rules concerning overtime are presented in the *Ohio-Pennsylvania Study,* footnote 31.

28. Unfortunately, data on overtime pay and hours are limited and are only available for production workers in manufacturing, which are likely to overstate the importance of the weekly overtime premium. Table 5 of the *Ohio-Pennsylvania Study* shows that the weekly overtime premium for production workers involved in manufacturing ranged from 2.9 percent of payroll in 1982 to 4.3 percent of payroll in 1978.

29. C.A. Kulp, "The Rate-Making Process in Property and Casualty Insurance Goals, Techniques, and Limits," *Law and Contemporary Problems* (Autumn 1950), p. 486.

30. For the case where the employer finds identical accident rate is above the classification average in state A and below in state B, see the *Ohio-Pennsylvania Study,* footnote 33.

31. For those employers too small to qualify for experience rating, there is, in effect, no difference between manual premium and standard earned premium excluding constants.

32. Under the old expense constant program in effect in most states until about 1980, the charge was only assessed to employers with standard earned premium of $500 or less. The new program assesses the expense constant for all policies.

33. There are intermediate size employers who are large enough to be experience rated but too small to receive premium discounts or retrospective rating. For these employers, the standard earned premium including constants becomes the net earned premium.

34. Compensation insurance rate calculations are based primarily upon the experience of all policies written within a specified time period known as a policy year. The policy year usually does not coincide with the calendar year.

35. The data in columns 1 and 3 of table 5 were provided by the National Council on Compensation Insurance. The data in columns 2 and 4 were calculated by John Burton using a procedure explained in the *Ohio-Pennsylvania Study,* footnote 39.

36. For policy years 1970-71 and 1971-72, the ratio of standard earned to manual premiums was 0.951. See *Task Force Study,* table 6, p. 23.

37. See footnote 39 of the *Ohio-Pennsylvania Study* for information on the magnitude of the loss constants.

38. The information on each state's expense constant is included in footnote 42 of the *Ohio-Pennsylvania Study.*

39. Table 9 of the *Ohio-Pennsylvania Study* provides data on the relationship between standard earned premium including constants and net cost to policyholders for four types of carriers: nonparticipating stock, participating stock, mutual, and other.

40. Indiana uses the discount schedule presented in table 4, but unlike the National Council states, makes the premium discounts optional. The differences between Indiana and the NCCI states can be ignored because, in practice, apparently all eligible Indiana employers either elect to take the premium discounts or choose retrospective rating.

41. The expense constants used for these states are indicated in footnote 42 of the *Ohio-Pennsylvania Study*.

42. The New Jersey experience rating plan is also different from that used in the NCCI jurisdictions because the New Jersey plan has a 5 percent adjustment built into the rate level in order to compensate for the off-balance of the rating plan.

43. The expense constants used for these states are indicated in footnote 42 of the *Ohio-Pennsylvania Study*.

44. The Delaware data comparable to table 5 of this study are included in table 10 of the *Ohio-Pennsylvania Study*.

45. The Delaware data comparable to table 6 of this study are included in table 11 of the *Ohio-Pennsylvania Study*.

46. The Pennsylvania data comparable to table 5 of this study are included in table 12 of the *Ohio-Pennsylvania Study*.

47. The Pennsylvania data comparable to table 6 of this study are included in tables 13 and 14 of the *Ohio-Pennsylvania Study*.

48. For the *Dissertation*, the National Council data indicated that adjusted manual rates were 86.6 percent of manual rates. For the *Task Force Study*, the data indicated that adjusted manual rates were 82.0 percent of manual rates. For the current report, high adjusted manual rates are 83.5 percent of manual rates, plus the adjustment for the expense constant.

49. Many of the arguments for and against open competition are presented in *Williams,* supra note 9.

50. National Council on Compensation Insurance, *Workers' Compensation Rating Laws - A Digest of Changes* (New York: 1982 with supplements), and exhibits included with June 24, 1983 letter from Barry Llewellyn, Assistant Secretary, National Council on Compensation Insurance.

51. *Williams,* supra note 9.

52. New York provides a good example of the spread of competitive devices. Table 7 indicates 15 insurance companies were deviating from published rates on January 1, 1983. By September 7, 1983 another 47 companies had filed deviations. *Ratings Laws Digest,* quarterly update November 1983.

53. The adjustment figures for all states but Michigan were provided in a September 16, 1983 letter from Barry Llewellyn, Assistant Secretary, National Council on Compensation Insurance. The Michigan adjustment figure was provided by R. Kevin Clinton, Chief Actuary, State of Michigan Insurance Bureau.

54. *Rating Laws Digest.*

55. Data for 1980 and 1981 were provided in an exhibit included with a July 8, 1983 letter from Paul C. Whitacre, Jr., Director, Actuarial Section, Ohio Bureau of Workers' Compensation.

56. *West Virginia 1981 Annual Report;* and West Virginia Workmen's Compensation Fund, *An Employers Guide to the Ratemaking System of the Workmen's Compensation Fund of the State of West Virginia* (preliminary version, 1983).

57. The West Virginia calculations are facilitated since manual rates and premiums actually collected are available for the same 12-month period.

58. This assumption that the influence of experience rating for 1979-81 is also relevant for the rates in effect on January 1, 1983 must be used with caution. Frederick Kilbourse, the consulting actuary for West Virginia, indicated in a phone conversation with John Burton on November 21, 1983, that a new experience rating formula was introduced in West Virginia in 1982. However, there are no data available yet to document the impact of the revised formula, and so the 9.3 percent figure discussed in the text will be used by default.

59. The generally available information on earnings by state is inappropriate. The most common statistics used in connection with earnings on a state level are the average weekly earnings of manufacturing workers for each state compiled by the Bureau of Labor Statistics. (See, e.g., U.S. Bureau of Labor Statistics, *Employment and Earnings Statistics for States and Areas, 1939-70,* bulletin 1370-8 [1971].) Similar statistics collected by the National Council on Compensation Insurance for affiliated states are the average weekly earnings of injured workmen by state. Both sets of statistics suffer from the same limitation as far as the current interest in variations in employers' costs of workers' compen-

sation is concerned: they are influenced both by interstate variations in the earnings received by workers in the same industry and interstate variations in the composition of industries. For a demonstration of the inappropriateness of such data for the present study, see *Dissertation*, note 32, pp. 88-89.

60. *Dissertation*, note 33, pp. 89-90.

61. The size of the state's labor force in 1980 was used for the 1950 to 1983 data. The procedure used in the *Task Force Report* and the *MLR article* relied on the state's labor force size in 1970. This explains why the entries for 1950 to 1978 in tables 17 and 18 differ from the figures shown in the earlier publications.

62. The standard deviation is the square root of the variance, which is found by calculating the deviation of each item from the mean, squaring these deviations, and then calculating the mean square deviation. When there is a "normal" distribution of items, about two-thirds of all items are within the range from one standard deviation below the mean to one standard deviation above the mean. For an elementary discussion of these concepts, see Daniel B. Suits, *Statistics: An Introduction to Quantitative Economic Research* (Chicago: Rand McNally, 1963), pp. 38-51.

63. We are currently preparing a statistical study of the determinants of interstate differences in workers' compensation insurance among 31 jurisdictions, including Connecticut but not New Jersey or New York. See note 65 below.

64. *National Commission Report*, p. 127.

65. Alan B. Krueger and John F. Burton, Jr., "Interstate Differences in the Employers' Costs of Workers' Compensation: Magnitudes, Causes, and Cures," (mimeo: February 1984).

66. Monroe Berkowitz, *Workmen's Compensation* (New Brunswick, NJ: Rutgers University Press, 1960), and Monroe Berkowitz and John F. Burton, Jr., *Permanent Disability Benefits in the Workers' Compensation Program: A Multistate Study of Criteria and Procedures* (Kalamazoo, MI: W. E. Upjohn Institute, forthcoming).

67. These developments are described in *Permanent Disability Benefits*, chapter 7.

68. John F. Burton, Jr., "Compensation for Permanent Partial Disabilities," in John D. Worrall, ed., *Safety and the Work Force* (Ithaca, NY: ILR Press, 1983), esp. pp. 52-58.

69. *National Commission Report,* pp. 124-125.

70. *Dissertation,* chapter VII.

71. Krueger and Burton, *Interstate Differences.*

72. Even with the subsequent amendments to the New York law, the maximum weekly benefit for temporary total disability will not reach $300 until 1985. Because the Connecticut law has an automatic increase in the maximum tied to changes in the state's wages, Connecticut will maintain a higher maximum for the foreseeable future: by late 1983, the figure had already reached $345.

# 8

# Workers' Compensation Insurance Rates
## Their Determination and Regulation
## A Regional Perspective

C. Arthur Williams, Jr.
School of Management
University of Minnesota

One of the most discussed issues of the day is the high cost of workers' compensation insurance. As of September 1, 1982, in the 45 states (including the District of Columbia) with private insurers, workers' compensation standard earned premiums (a term to be defined later) averaged about $2.41 per $100 of payroll. The variation among states was great, however, ranging from $.74 in Indiana to $4.83 in Hawaii.[1] Comparable data are not available for the six states with exclusive state funds (Ohio, Nevada, North Dakota, Washington, West Virginia, and Wyoming). Because this session is directed mainly toward regional experience in Connecticut, New Jersey, and New York, the relative cost in those three states is of special interest. Connecticut ranked 16th highest with a $2.75 rate, New Jersey 22nd with a $2.48 rate, and New York 39th with a $1.55 rate.

Many factors account for the variation in these rates, including differences in the following: (1) the mix of payrolls according to industry and firm size; (2) injury and disease frequency and severity rates; (3) statutory benefits including eligibility requirements; (4) administrative and court interpretations of these benefits; (5) medical expenses for the same treatment; (6) the effectiveness of loss control and claims handling services provided by employers, insurers, and state agencies; (7) insurer expense and profit loadings; and (8) the presence or absence of a competitive state fund.

This paper will concentrate on how the ways in which workers' compensation insurance rates are determined and regulated vary among the states, with special attention to Connecticut, New Jersey, and New York.

## Workers' Compensation Insurance Rate Determination

Insured employers can be classified according to whether they are (1) class-rated, (2) experience rated, (3) schedule-rated, or (4) retrospectively-rated. This section will discuss first how insurers determine the insured's premium, given a set of rates and rating plans. Second, it will describe in general terms how insurers determine the class rates printed in their rating manuals. In addition to these rating methods many insurers return a dividend that reduces the net cost. The dividend may vary among firms depending upon their size and individual loss experience. Because these methods tend to be the same in all jurisdictions, no special attention will be paid to regional practices in this section.

### Class Premiums

Employers who are class-rated pay a rate per $100 of payroll that is based primarily on the industry or industries in which they are engaged. Separate rates have been developed for over 600 industries. However, the payroll assigned to certain employees such as clerical office employees, drivers (usually but not always), and outside salespersons is assigned the same rate regardless of the employer's industry. For example, suppose a small abrasive paper manufacturer has a total payroll of $250,000-$200,000 for plant workers and $50,000 for clerical office employees. Further assume that the class rates per $100 of payroll are $2.50 for the plant workers and $.25 for the clerical employees. The class premium would be 2,000($2.50) + 500($.25) or $5,125.[2] Traditionally all workers' compensation insurers in the state charged the same class rates, but in an increasing number of states some price competition exists with respect to class rates.

For employers whose average class premium is under $2,500 (still $750 in some states), the class premium is the amount charged. Over half the insured employers are class-rated, but because they employ few workers, these class-rated firms pay less than 10 percent of the premiums received by insurers. All other employers are experience rated. An increasing number are both experience rated and schedule-rated. Employers whose premiums exceed $5,000 may be permitted to be retrospectively-rated in addition to being experience rated. Insurers, however, usually limit retrospective rating to firms paying premiums of at least $100,000. Employers whose experience premiums exceed $5,000 (still $1,000 in some states) receive a premium discount because the insurer's expenses (not loss payments) do not increase proportionately with the premium size. Retrospectively-rated employers receive this discount through the retrospective rating formula. Other eligibile employers are rated under a separate premium discount plan.

## Experience Rating

Under experience rating an employer's class premium is modified to reflect two factors.[3] The first factor is how the employer's loss experience during a recent three-year period compares with the amount the insurer would have expected to pay (given current rates except for changes in the workers' compensation law since the experience period) if the employer had been an average employer in the same industry with the same payroll. For example, if the employer's losses were half the insurer's expectation, this factor alone would suggest cutting the rate in half. If the losses were twice the insurer's expectation, this comparison would suggest a doubling of the rate. However, the adjustment also depends on how much credibility or confidence the insurer should assign to this employer's loss experience. The reasoning behind this factor is that chance alone may cause the experience of individual employers to fluctuate greatly from year to year. The smaller the payroll exposure for a given hazard class, the more important this chance factor becomes. For example, a very small employer may have no losses for 10 years followed by a substantial loss the next year. As the employer's payroll increases, his or her experience becomes more predictable because the future tends to resemble the past more and more closely. Of course, no matter how large the employer may be, the future may differ from the past because of such factors as law amendments, inflation, or changes in the work environment. In practice, insurers assign no credibility to the experience of employers with average class premiums of less than $2,500. Above that point the credibility increases gradually from 1 percent to 100 percent. Few employers have enough exposure for their experience to be considered 100 percent credible. If an employer had a credibility factor of 20 percent and experience period losses equal to half the insurer's expectations, instead of cutting the class premium in half the insurer would reduce the class premium (20 percent) (50 percent) or 10 percent. If the experience period losses had been twice the insurer's loss expectation, instead of doubling the premium the insurer would increase the class premium (20 percent) (100 percent) or 20 percent.

The net effect of experience rating is that the employer pays a rate that is in effect a weighted average of two rates. The first of these two rates is one based on his or her own loss experience during the experience period adjusted to reflect what these payments would have been under the current workers' compensation law. The second is the appropriate class rate. The first rate is weighted by the employer's credibility factor, the second by one minus that same factor. For example, if the credibility factor is 20 percent, the rate based on the employer's experience is .50, and the class rate is 1.00, the experience rate will be (20 percent) (.50) + (80 percent) (1.00) = .90. The higher the credibility factor the less the experience rate will depend upon the class rate.

## Schedule Rating

In many states many insurers have in recent years introduced schedule rating plans. Under these plans insurers usually decrease the rate the employer would otherwise pay through credits based on a subjective evaluation of such factors as the employer's loss control program.

## Retrospective Rating

Retrospective rating bases the employer's premium on the employer's loss experience during the policy period, subject to the condition that the premium cannot be less than a stated minimum nor higher than a stated maximum. Between the minimum and maximum limits the retrospective premium is equal to the losses the employer incurs during the policy period plus the expenses that are related to the losses incurred and a basic premium. The basic premium covers the expenses that do not vary with the losses incurred and a net insurance charge. The insurer imposes a net insurance charge because in the aggregate the insurer loses more dollars (because of the maximum premium limitation) than it gains from those who pay the minimum premium. Retrospective rating permits quasi-self-insurance. In most cases the premium depends upon the employer's own loss experience, but the insurer administers the program and the premium is bounded by the minimum and maximum premiums. Because the basic premium is a function of the experience premium, it is affected by any change in the class premium in the same manner as the experience premium. For the most part, however, an employer's retrospective premium does not depend upon its class rates.

A version of retrospective rating that has become popular in many states in recent years is paid-loss retro. Instead of paying a deposit premium in advance, subject to later adjustments as more information on payrolls and losses becomes available, the insured pays the retrospective premium in annual installments. Each year's installment is the benefits and expenses paid that year because of accidents that occurred during the policy period. The insured may prefer this approach because (1) the insured retains the use of the premium dollars longer and (2) the premium paid never depends upon the insurer's estimate of future payments. However, the insurer may increase its charges because it loses some of the investment income it would otherwise make. A related practice that affects more insureds than paid-loss retro plans waives the requirement that employers with a premium of at least $2,500 pay in advance a full deposit premium.

## *Dividends*

Many workers' compensation insurers return dividends to their policyholders. These dividends may vary among firms depending upon their size and their individual loss experience.

## How Insurers Determine Their Class Rates

In order to understand how insurers determine the class rates in the rating manual, one must know the elements of a class rate. A class rate includes allowances for (1) expected losses, (2) the expenses the insurer expects to incur in servicing the insured, and (3) a profit for the insurer or a margin for policyholder dividends.

The *expected loss allowance* is the amount the insurer expects to pay in benefits per $100 of payroll to all insured employees in the same industry during the period the rate is in effect. The principal reasons the insurer may change this allowance are that it expects changes in (1) the frequency and severity of job-related injuries or diseases, (2) the propensity of employees to claim benefits for their injuries or diseases, (3) the workers' compensation law, or (4) the cost of settling claims because of such economic factors as rising or falling wage levels or medical costs. The expected loss allowance, therefore, is based on expectations for the future that are subject to considerable error. In establishing these expectations, the insurer analyzes its experience in the recent past, modified to reflect changes that it expects to occur during the future because of law changes and trends in claim frequency and severity. Even if the law will remain the same and there are no changes in claim frequency or severity, the past experience may suggest that the current rates be increased or decreased. The current rates may be inadequate or excessive because the insurers or the regulators either underestimated or overestimated the insurer's needs when they established those rates, or because the rates have been in effect for some time and conditions have changed.

The *expense allowance* is expressed as a percent of the rate. Some of these expenses, such as commissions, are budgeted and paid as a percent of the rate. Others, such as general administrative expenses, are not budgeted, but on the basis of past experience and future trends the insurer can determine what proportion of the rate it will use for this purpose.

The *profit* or *profit and contingency* allowance is also expressed as a percent of the rate. As will be explained later, the profit allowance in most states is 2.5 percent. Consequently if the insurer's expected loss and expense allowances exactly matched actual losses and expenses, the insurers would have earned an underwriting profit equal to 2.5 percent of the class premiums written. Because these expectations are almost never realized exactly, the actual underwriting profit rate may be more or less than 2.5 percent. Insurers argue that this 2.5 percent profit rate plus the investment income generated by writing workers' compensation insurance would produce a reasonable profit on net worth.

If the expense allowance were set at 32.5 percent of the rate and the profit allowance at 2.5 percent, the remainder of the rate, 65 percent, would be available to pay losses. If the dollar amount required to pay losses was determined to be $1.30 per $100 of payroll, the rate would be $1.30/.65 or $2.00.

## Workers' Compensation
## Insurance Rate Regulation

Workers' compensation rates are regulated in a variety of ways. Except for Texas, where a state board makes the rates, states are commonly grouped into two general categories: (1) rating bureau—prior approval states and (2) open-competition states. In rating bureau—prior approval states, the largest category at the present time, rating bureaus are permitted to develop and file rates in behalf of their members and subscribers. Membership in the rating bureau may be compulsory or optional. Agreements to adhere to these rates may or may not be permitted; where such agreements are permitted, members and subscribers may or may not be permitted to deviate from these rates. All of these states require the insurance commissioner to approve workers' compensation rates before they can be used.

Open-competition states may or may not permit rating bureaus, renamed data service organizations, to publish advisory rates. All, however, make membership in the organization optional, and prohibit agreements to adhere to these rates. All require insurers to file their rates with the state insurance department, but none have a prior approval requirement. Insurers, however, may be unable to use filed rates until after they have been on file for a designated period of time. The six open-competition states at present are Arkansas, Illinois, Kentucky, Michigan, Oregon, and Rhode Island. Georgia and Minnesota have also enacted open-competition laws that soon will become effective.

As this discussion indicates, a two-way classification of states (other than Texas) oversimplifies the situation. Within each of these two categories some significant differences exist. Table 1 shows for each of the 45 states in which private insurers operate (1) the role that rating bureaus are permitted to play in rate determinations and (2) whether the state insurance commissioner must approve proposed bureau or individual insurer rates before they go into effect.

## Role of Rating Bureaus

As of early 1983, every state except Kentucky, Michigan, Oregon, and Texas permits rating bureaus either to develop advisory rates or make rate filings in behalf of their members. Kentucky, Michigan and Oregon permit rating bureaus to develop only advisory "pure" premiums (premiums without expense or profit loadings). In Texas the State Board of Insurance makes the rates. Only 10 of these

Table 1

Types of Workers' Compensation Insurance Rate Regulation, by State, Early 1983

| Jurisdiction | Rating bureaus | | | Deviations permissible | Prior approval of rates required |
| | Bureau rate filings or advisory rates permitted | Membership required | Rate adherence agreements permitted | | |
| --- | --- | --- | --- | --- | --- |
| Alabama | Yes | No | Yes | Yes | Yes |
| Alaska | Yes | No | Yes | Yes | Yes |
| Arizona | Yes | Yes | Yes | Yes | Yes |
| Arkansas (OC) | Yes | No | No | NA | Prior filing only |
| California | Yes | Yes | Yes | No[a] | Yes |
| Colorado | Yes | No | No | NA | Yes |
| Connecticut | Yes | No | No | NA | Yes |
| Delaware | Yes | No | Yes | Yes | Yes |
| District of Columbia | Yes | No | Yes | Yes | Yes |
| Florida | Yes | No | Yes | Yes | Yes |
| Georgia[b] | Yes | No | No | NA | Yes |
| Hawaii | Yes | No | Yes | Yes | Yes |
| Idaho | Yes | Yes | Yes | Yes | Yes |
| Illinois (OC) | Yes | No | No | NA | No |
| Indiana | Yes | Yes | No | Yes | No |
| Iowa | Yes | No | Yes | Yes | Yes |
| Kansas | Yes | No | Yes | Yes | Yes |
| Kentucky (OC) | No[d] | No | No | NA | No |
| Louisiana | Yes | No | Yes | Yes | Yes |
| Maine | Yes | No | Yes | Yes | Yes |
| Maryland | Yes | No | No | NA | Yes |
| Massachusetts | Yes | No | Yes | No | Yes |
| Michigan (OC) | No[d] | No | No | NA | No |
| Minnesota[c] | Yes | Yes | No | NA | Yes |

| State | | | | | |
|---|---|---|---|---|---|
| Mississippi | Yes | No | Yes | Yes | Yes |
| Missouri | Yes | No | Yes | No[a] | Yes |
| Montana | Yes | Yes | No | NA | Yes |
| Nebraska | Yes | No | Yes | Yes | Yes |
| New Hampshire | Yes | No | Yes | Yes | Yes |
| New Jersey | Yes | Yes | Yes | No | Yes |
| New Mexico | Yes | No | Yes | Yes | Yes |
| New York | Yes | No | Yes | Yes | Yes |
| North Carolina | Yes | Yes | Yes | No | Yes |
| Oklahoma | Yes | No | Yes | Yes | Yes |
| Oregon (OC) | No[d] | No | No | NA | Prior filing only |
| Pennsylvania | Yes | Yes | Yes | No | Yes |
| Rhode Island (OC) | Yes | No | No | NA | No |
| South Carolina | Yes | No | Yes | Yes | Yes |
| South Dakota | Yes | No | Yes | Yes | Yes |
| Tennessee | Yes | No | Yes | Yes | Yes |
| Texas | State Board of Insurance makes rates, no deviations | | | | |
| Utah | Yes | No | Yes | Yes | Yes |
| Vermont | Yes | No | Yes | Yes | Yes |
| Virginia | Yes | No | No | NA | Yes |
| Wisconsin | Yes | Yes | Yes | No | Yes |

SOURCE: Derived from information supplied by the American Insurance Association and the National Council on Compensation Insurance.

a. Unless above rates approved by the commissioner.

b. Effective January 1, 1984 Georgia will substitute an open competition rating law for its present approach. Bureaus will be permitted to publish advisory rates.

c. Effective July 1, 1983 Minnesota will enter a transition period that will lead to full open competition by January 1, 1986. After that date the bureau will not even be permitted to publish advisory pure premiums. It will be able to publish aggregated loss data, trend factors, and loss development factors. Prior approval will continue with respect to upward deviations from these pure premiums until July 1, 1986 when it will cease completely. (In late May 1983 Minnesota advanced the beginning of complete open competition to January 1, 1984.)

d. Advisory pure premiums only.

43 jurisdictions (Arizona, California, Idaho, Indiana,Minnesota, Montana, New Jersey, North Carolina, Pennsylvania, and Wisconsin) require all workers' compensation insurers to belong to a rating organization, but the practice in most other states is for most, if not all, insurers to become bureau members. Although bureau membership is not required in most states, all but 14 of the 43 states that permit bureau rate filings (Arkansas, Colorado, Connecticut, Georgia, Illinois, Indiana, Kentucky, Maryland, Massachusetts, Michigan, Minnesota, Montana, Rhode Island, and Virginia) permit bureaus to require adherence to the bureau rates. In these states that prohibit such adherence agreements, however, most insurers have until recently elected to use the bureau rates. Among the 29 states that permit agreements to adhere to bureau rates all but seven states (California, Massachusetts, Missouri, New Jersey, North Carolina, Pennsylvania, and Wisconsin) permit insurers either (1) to deviate from the bureau rates after securing the insurance commissioner's approval or (2) a much less common option, to charge lower rates without securing any prior approval. Such deviations seldom occurred in the past except for specialized classes for which some insurers may have developed some special expertise or associations. They have become more common in recent years through the filing of deviations from class rates or of scheduled rating plans. Only five states require all insurers to belong to a rating bureau, permit agreements to adhere to the bureau rates, and prohibit deviations from these rates.

In most states the National Council on Compensation Insurance is the rating organization. The exceptions are as follows:

Workers' Compensation Insurance Rating Bureau
  of California
Delaware Compensation Rating Bureau

Hawaii Insurance Rating Bureau
Indiana Compensation Rating Bureau (administered
    by the National Council on Compensation Insurance)
Workers' Compensation Rating and Inspection Bureau
    of Massachusetts
Workers' Compensation Rating and Inspection
    Association of Michigan
Workers' Compensation Insurers' Rating Association
    of Minnesota
New Jersey Compensation Rating and Inspection
    Bureau
New York Compensation Insurance Rating Board
North Carolina Rate Bureau
Pennsylvania Compensation Rating Bureau
Virginia Compensation Rating Bureau
Wisconsin Compensation Rating Bureau

The National Council provides many of these independent rating bureaus with statistical services.

All states with independent rating bureaus except Indiana, Minnesota, and Virginia permit these bureaus to require adherence to their rates. Of the seven states that prohibit deviations from agreements to adhere to bureau rates, all but Missouri are states with independent rating bureaus.

Georgia and Minnesota will soon become open-competition states. In Georgia insurers will be permitted to develop advisory rates. In Minnesota rating bureaus will at first be permitted to develop advisory pure premiums, but starting in 1986 (changed to 1984 in late May 1983) they can publish only actual loss costs plus loss development and trend information.

Connecticut, New Jersey, and New York are all rating bureau-prior approval states. However, Connecticut does not require insurers to belong to the bureau and forbids agreements to adhere to the bureau rates. New Jersey requires insurers to belong to its independent bureau, permits agreements to adhere to the bureau rates, and prohibits deviations from those rates. New York does not require insurers to belong to its independent bureau, but it permits agreements to adhere to bureau rates. However, deviations from the bureau rates are permitted. Connecticut and New Jersey, but not New York, permit insurers to waive the advance payment of a full deposit premium.

## Prior Approval Requirements

As table 1 shows, all states, except the six open-competition states, require insurers to file their proposed rates and wait until the state insurance commissioner approves them. Usually the commissioner must act within a stated period after the rates are filed. If he or she fails to act within that period, the insurer can use the rates.

In two open-competition states (Arkansas and Oregon) an insurer cannot use rates until they have been on file for a designated period. In the other states, insurers are permitted either to use the rates and then file them or to file their rates and use them immediately.

Georgia and Minnesota will soon become open-competition states. Georgia will not require prior approval; Minnesota will require approval only of upward deviations from the bureau advisory pure premiums until 1986 (changed to 1984 in late May 1983) after which time insurers will be able to use their rates immediately and file them later. Connecticut, New Jersey, and New York are all prior approval states.

## Important Regulatory Issues

Three regulatory issues that have been the subject of intense debate in recent years are (1) open competition versus the rating bureau-prior approval approach, (2) the effect of insurers' investment income on the profit loading in their rates, and (3) the excess profits approach as a supplement to either open competition or prior approval.

## Open Competition Versus Rating Bureau-Prior Approval Approach

Traditionally workers' compensation insurance rates have been more restrictively regulated than other property and liability insurance rates. Although a few states have erased or reduced these differences, workers' compensation rates continue in most states to be more rigidly controlled. For example, 21 states are generally considered to be open-competition states with respect to property and liability insurance. Only six states (soon to be eight states) have open-competition workers' compensation laws. However, several other states have considered such legislation in recent years. The arguments advanced in the legislative debates on this issue are summarized in the next two sections.

### Arguments Favoring Open-Competition Laws

Those who favor open-competition laws argue that the rating bureau-prior approval approach stifles or discourages price and service competition. In the early days of workers' compensation, this approach made sense because only a few states had insolvency funds that would protect employers and injured workers against insurers who became insolvent because of competitive pricing pressures or undercapitalization. Furthermore, few insurers had developed enough experience or expertise to establish their own prices. Today such guarantee funds exist in every state; insurers are now more highly capitalized and better managed, and many insurers, with the aid of data advisory organizations, can establish their own rates with confidence.

A prior approval requirement, in their opinion, is a misguided, inefficient use of regulatory resources. Insurers are subjected to costly delays, decisions that are influenced too often by political pressures instead of objective evaluations, and in some states expensive hearings. Regulators are required to make decisions that would frustrate Solomon and are better left to the marketplace. Consumers lose because insurance availability problems arise when insurers believe the approved rate structure is inadequate, and because for some insureds the approved price exceeds the competitive price.

Rating bureaus by definition set an average price that is too high for some insurers, too low for others. The expense allowances included in the rates are typically based on the average expense experience of nondividend paying stock insurers, which tend to have higher expenses than the other groups of insurers. Without rating bureaus or prior approval requirements, they argue, insurers will compete more vigorously for business. Both price competition and service competition will intensify, producing better services and lower prices. Much of the service competition will consist of improved loss control advice and assistance and more effective claims management, both of which will reduce claims costs. Price competition will cause the premiums to be lower on average and more responsive to the loss experience of groups of insureds with similar exposures and of individual insureds. Groups of similar insureds and individual insureds will in turn have more incentive to better their own performances in controlling losses and managing claims. Admittedly, some intense price and service competition does exist under the rating bureau-prior approval approach, but according to open-competition supporters, this competition benefits almost exclusively larger employers who might otherwise self-insure.

Open-competition laws will also force insurers to make more independent decisions regarding workers' compensation insurance instead of delegating so much of this decision-making to the rating organization. Currently, insurers tend to assign their most able employees to other lines involving more decisions. Open-competition laws will cause more of these employees to become concerned about workers' compensation problems; the result will be some innovative approaches.

Finally, open-competition advocates argue, in those states where open competition has been tried price competion has been intense, no serious insolvency problems have developed, insurer services have not suffered, and insurance has become more readily available through standard channels.

### Arguments Against Open-Competition Laws

The opponents of open-competition laws argue with equal intensity that it would be a serious mistake for most states with rating bureau-prior approval laws to move to open competition. Workers' compensation insurance, they argue, is different. Workers' compensation insurance is social insurance. With a few exceptions, workers' compensation is the exclusive recourse of the employee against the employer. The benefits, prescribed by statute, are to be paid on a no-fault basis. Unless employers secure permission to self-insure their financial obligations under this statute, they must purchase workers' compensation insurance. Consequently, the public is much more concerned about the solvency of workers' compensation insurers and how they establish their prices than in the solvency and pricing practices of other insurers. Consequently the public is best served by (1) a pricing mechanism that permits a rating bureau to apply its expertise to the pooled experience of many insurers and promotes rate stability and (2) prior approval which involves the regulator more actively in the pricing process.

These opponents deny that permitting rating bureaus to exist and requiring prior approval stifles price and service competition as much as the open-competition advocates claim. In the typical prior approval state, competition takes many forms. Insurers need not belong to the rating bureau; they may develop their own rates. The bureau is permitted to require members to adhere to its rates, but the members may secure insurance department approval to deviate from these rates. Schedule rating plans that permit such deviations on the basis of subjective evaluations have become much more commonplace. Dividends provide another avenue for price competition. Prior approval, they agree, could be a problem if rigidly and unfairly administered, but they believe this is not the case in most states. The trend is toward more flexibility and reliance on market forces. Furthermore, price competition is not the only kind of competition that is possible. Under prior approval, insurers have even more incentive to compete on the basis of services rendered.

The second line of thought pursued by the opponents of open competition is that this approach will itself produce some adverse effects. For many insureds, especially small employers, prices will rise in the short run and probably the long run. Price competition may become so intense that the solvency of many insurers and the viability of guarantee funds may be threatened. Small insurers especially will be adversely affected by the inability of the rating bureau to develop rates to which they can simply agree to adhere. Because smaller insurers may be less able to compete effectively under open competition, the market may soon be controlled by a few large insurers; this growing concentration would weaken the degree of effective competition. The proponents of open competition, they assert, have greatly underestimated the quality of the insurer and rating organization personnel who are currently involved in workers' compensation insurance. The rating practices, loss control services, and claims management services match in quality those associated with any other line of insurance.

Probably the most serious concern of open-competition opponents is that the data base used to calculate workers' compensation rates will be less reliable. Unless all insurers use the same rate classes, or subclasses that can be combined into a uniform set of rate classes, their experience cannot be pooled to establish a credible yardstick for measuring the fairness of the class rates. Open-competition laws are likely to generate heterogeneous classifications that will substantially reduce the volume of experience that can be meaningfully pooled.

In any event, these opponents say, it is too early to evaluate experience under the open-competition laws in force. None of these laws has been in effect for more than a few years. Even if one leans toward the concept of open competition it is better to liberalize the administration of a prior approval state and to "wait and see."

Some opponents of open-competition laws simply deny that price competition in workers' compensation insurance is effective enough to justify such heavy reliance on the marketplace. These opponents are much more opposed to removal of the prior approval requirement than to prohibiting rating bureaus.

### A Brief History: 1980-83

The trend toward open-competition workers' compensation laws was stimulated by the adoption in December 1980 by the National Association of Insurance Commissioners of a model open-competition rating law. This model bill, which was considered to be a regulatory alternative for those states favoring the open-competition approach to rate regulation, dealt with most types of property and liability insurance, but one of its most controversial parts was the section on workers' compensation insurance rates. For two years rating organizations could publish advisory rates, but insurers would not be required to join the organization and would be prohibited from agreeing to adhere to the advisory rates. Insurers would have to file new rates before they used them, but these rates would not be subject to prior approval. After two years workers' compensation insurance rates would be treated like most other property and liability insurance rates. Rating organizations could develop only advisory pure premiums. Insurers could use new rates before filing them.

In December 1982, in response to some objections to the December 1980 model bill treatment of workers' compensation insurance rates, the NAIC adopted a separate and different model open-competition workers' compensation act. Under this bill, data service organizations can develop only advisory pure premium rates. A major provision requires insurers to report their loss experience under a uniform statistical plan approved by the state insurance commissioner.

During 1982 at least eight states debated vigorously but did not act on open-competition workers' compensation statutes. Fewer states have thus far seriously considered this possibility. This slowing down has been attributed primarily to the development of, and more liberal regulatory response to, scheduled rating plans and other deviations from bureau rates, but some observers believe the real cause is a "wait and see" attitude.[4]

### Investment Income and Insurance Rates

Employers and others have expressed intense interest in recent years in whether workers' compensation insurers have adequately recognized in their pricing the investment income they generate from writing workers' compensation insurance. This section will describe (1) why insurers generate investment income from writing workers' compensation insurance and (2) how this investment income is recognized in the profit loading in class rates.

### How Insurers Generate Investment Income From Insurance Writings

Insurers generate some investment income from their writings in all lines of insurance because some time elapses between the dates when the insurer collects its premiums and the dates when it pays some of its expenses and most of its claims. For some lines of insurance, such as fire insurance and automobile physical damage insurance, the time lag is short and the investment income generated during this period on the monies held by the insurer is relatively small. For other lines of insurance such as automobile liability insurance and workers' compensation insurance, the time that elapses is long and the investment income generated by the insurer relatively large. For example, according to the most recent rate filing by the Workers' Compensation Insurers Rating Association of Minnesota, on the average only 22.5 percent of the total dollar claims is paid by the time the insured's policy expires, 58.5 percent five years after the policy period starts, 77.8 percent ten years later, and 92.9 percent 20 years later.[5]

### The Profit Loading in Manual Rates

Insurers have for many years recognized investment income in their pricing of workers' compensation insurance. Whether they have adequately recognized such income and whether they should do so explicitly is the real issue. In most states insurers include a 2.5 percent profit loading in their class rates which, if their predictions are correct, will produce an underwriting profit equal to 2.5 percent of the premiums earned. If an insurer's workers' compensation premiums are three times the net worth the insurer allocates toward writing workers' compensation insurance, the 2.5 percent profit loading will produce a 7.5 percent under-writing profit on net worth.[6] Therefore, the insurer's total return on net worth because of its workers' compensation writings would be 7.5 percent plus its investment income ex-pressed as a percent of net worth.

The underwriting profit loading has not always been 2.5 percent. In 1915 the national underwriting profit loading was 0 percent. The loading was raised to 1.5 percent in 1917 but dropped again to 0 percent in 1920. Despite underwriting losses insurers did not try to increase this 0 percent profit loading again until 1934. According to C. A. Kulp, insurers did not seek a higher profit loading during this period because (1) workers' compensation insurance was a favorite wedge or business-getter for more profitable lines and (2) workers' compensation time lags provided substantial funds for investments.[7] Other considerations were the threat of state funds and the social insurance characteristics of workers' compensation. In the early thirties, however, in-vestment income disappeared or turned into losses and underwriting experience worsened. In 1934 the National Association of Insurance Commissioners approved a profit loading of 0 percent to 5 percent, depending upon how the insurers' cumulative losses in the state since 1933 compared with the portion of the premiums collected since 1933 that was supposed to cover these losses. If the cumulative loss payments equaled the cumulative loss allowances in the rates, the approved profit loading was to be 2.5 percent. If the cumulative payments exceeded the cumulative loss allowances, the profit loading could be more than 2.5 per-cent but not more than 5 percent. If the payments were less than the allowance, the loading could be less than 2.5 percent but not less than 0 percent. Because underwriting experience improved markedly during the next few years, during the forties the loading under this rule soon became 0 percent for all but a few states.

In 1949 the National Council on Compensation Insurance included a 2.5 percent profit loading in its rates, which by 1957 had been approved in most states. One argument in favor of including a 2.5 percent profit loading in workers' compensation insurance rates was that in all other property and liability insurance lines the profit loading was at least 2.5 percent. In 1951, however, a subcommittee of the National Association of Insurance Commissioners had recommended that the loading be only 1.5 percent. The subcommittee argued that a 1.5 percent profit loading plus investment profits should provide a reasonable rate of return on net worth. The NAIC, however, approved a 2.5 percent profit loading.

In recent years a few states have required insurers to include a smaller profit loading than 2.5 percent because of the presence of investment income. For example, on April 21, 1981 then Minnesota Commissioner of Insurance Michael Markman issued an order disapproving the request of the Workers' Compensation Insurers Rating Association of Minnesota for an average 28.6 percent increase in workers' compensation rates. Instead he granted an average increase of 11.8 percent effective June 1, 1981.[8] The principal reason why the Commissioner recommended a much lower increase than requested was because he disagreed with WCIRAM's 2.5 percent profit loading in the proposed rates. He argued that if rates were increased 28.6 percent, the combined underwriting and investment profits of insurers would exceed 30 percent, which would be excessive. He based this finding on several assumptions, including a 14-year payment period for losses incurred during the policy year, net worth during those 14 years equal to one-third of the loss reserve established at the end of each year, and a 7 percent after-tax investment return on assets corresponding in amount to the loss reserves and associated net worth. Commissioner Markman argued that the reasonable rate of return was 18 percent and that, under the assumptions noted above, insurers could attain this objective with a -10 percent profit loading in their rates. Depending on the assumptions used this approach may produce a profit loading above, below, or equal to 2.5 percent.

Only three other states have reduced the 2.5 percent profit loading to reflect investment income—Georgia to 2 percent, Massachusetts[9] to -12 percent, and Oklahoma to 0 percent. The effect of investment income on total insurer profits has been cited in two or three other states as one of the reasons for reducing recently requested rate increases, but the profit loading was not explicitly reduced. In Connecticut, New Jersey, and New York the profit loading is 2.5 percent.

### Excess Profits Statutes

Another approach to rate regulation that may supplement either a prior approval or an open-competition law is an excess profits statute. Six states (Florida, Georgia, Hawaii, Minnesota, New York, and South Carolina) have excess profits statutes applicable to automobile insurance.[10] Only one state, Florida, has such a statute applicable to workers' compensation insurance.

Excess profits statutes require insurers to return to their policyholders profits in excess of a specified threshold. In theory the threshold is the long-run reasonable rate of return from all sources plus an allowance for short-run fluctuations around that reasonable rate of return.

The Florida statute requires workers' compensation insurers to return to their policyholders any underwriting profit that exceeds the profit loading in the rate by 5 percent.

Currently, therefore, the threshold is 2.5 percent plus 5 percent or 7.5 percent. Instead of applying the test to each year's operations, however, the statute orders the state insurance department to test the average underwriting profit over the past three years. Investment income does not affect the allowance for short-run fluctuations, but the department is supposed to consider investment income in approving the basic profit loading.

Excess profits statutes first appeared on the scene during the early seventies when several states passed automobile no-fault statutes and a gasoline shortage existed. Both of these events were expected to reduce insurance costs, but opinions differed widely on the extent of those reductions. Excess profits statutes were passed to protect consumers against large insurer windfall profits. Florida's workers' compensation statute had a similar stimulus—the conversion of permanent partial disability benefits to a wage loss benefit. Insurance costs were expected to decrease because of this change with the possibility of large windfall profits for insurers.

Excess profits may make open-competition statutes more acceptable because insureds have some protection against excess insurer profits. For the same reasons regulators might be able to also administer prior approval statutes more flexibly. On the other hand, excess profits will occasionally require insurers to return profits to their policyholders even if their long-run rate of return is equal to or even less than the reasonable rate of return. Furthermore, determining the excess profit threshold is a difficult process involving several highly subjective assumptions.[11]

None of the three regional states has an excess profits statute applicable to workers' compensation insurance. New York, however, is one of only two states, the other being Florida, that has implemented such a statute applicable to automobile insurance.

## Concluding Remarks

Workers' compensation insurance rate determination and regulation vary widely among the states. A trend exists toward more reliance on competition through the passage of open-competition laws or, more commonly, through more flexible administration of rules permitting class rate deviations and schedule rating. A few prior approval states have reduced the 2.5 percent profit loading in the rates to reflect insurers' investment income. Open-competition states expect competition to reduce insurers' total profits. One state has an excess profits statute.

The three states represented here illustrate this diversity. All are rating bureau-prior approval states. All authorize a 2.5 percent underwriting profit loading. In Connecticut membership in the rating bureau is optional and rate adherence agreements are prohibited. New Jersey, on the other hand, forbids deviations from the rates developed by its rating bureau to which all insurers must belong. New York is much closer to Connecticut than to New Jersey in its rate regulation, but is somewhat less flexible. Both Connecticut and New York have seriously considered open-competition laws. New Jersey has not. New York is one of two states in the nation to implement an excess profits law applicable to automobile insurance.

Strong arguments exist pro and con for each of these approaches. The opportunity to experiment is supposed to be one of the advantages of state regulation as opposed to federal regulation. The laboratories testing ways of determining and regulating workers' compensation insurance rates have probably never been more active.

# NOTES

1. The National Council on Compensation Insurance periodically publishes a listing of state standard premium rates.

2. Employers whose class premium would otherwise be under some small amount, such as $500, have to pay an extra charge called an expense constant because the expense allowance in the rate does not produce enough dollars to cover the expenses incurred in servicing these very small insureds.

3. The rating formula used in practice is more complicated than the one described here. The results, however, are close to those described above.

4. "Drive for Open Competition Rating Starting to Slow Officials," *Business Insurance,* February 21, 1983, pp. 2, 74. "Trend to Open Competition Rating Slows," *Journal of Commerce* (March 11, 1983), p. 7A.

5. *Exhibit A - Derivation of Overall Average Premium Level Change* (Minneapolis: Workers' Compensation Insurance Rating Association of Minnesota, 1982), Exhibit B-I, p. 39.

6. No generally accepted method exists for determining what portion of an insurer's net worth is devoted to writing a single line of insurance. Indeed, some persons argue that an insurer's net worth cannot be apportioned among lines of insurance; each $1 of net worth is available if needed for all lines of insurance written.

7. C. A. Kulp, *Casualty Insurance,* 3rd ed. (New York: The Ronald Press, 1956), p. 151.

8. For more details, see the original order and C. A. Williams, Jr., "Minnesota Employers' Workers' Compensation Costs: The Short-Run and the Long-Run," *Risk Management and Insurance Issues, No. 1,* School of Management, University of Minnesota, January 1982.

9. The Massachusetts –12 percent profit loading, which became effective January 1, 1983, is currently being contested before a court. Investment income was the major reason for a negative profit loading but no single formula was used to derive –12 percent.

10. For an analysis of these statutes see C. A. Williams, Jr., "Regulating Property and Liability Insurance Rates Through Excess Profits Statutes," *The Journal of Risk and Insurance* 50, 3 (September 1983).

11. For additional arguments for and against such statutes see *Ibid.*

# 9

# The Administration
# of Workers' Compensation

Monroe Berkowitz
Economics Department
Rutgers University

## *Introduction*

Too often comprehensive studies of workers' compensation programs conclude (as will this paper) with the recommendation that workers' compensation programs should be better administered. Certainly no one will quarrel with that, but just as certainly it is a relatively weak recommendation. I am as guilty as anyone, and in a study comparing programs in 10 states I came up with the remarkable conclusion that some states are better administered than others.[1] Yet there is hardly any way to account for the superior performance of the Wisconsin program other than to say that its program has been administered in an active or aggressive manner.

The National Commission on State Workmen's Compensation Laws has had a modicum of success in persuading states to increase benefits and broaden coverage. However, in areas where it is difficult to devise quantitative standards, its success has been less well documented. This is not surprising. In so many aspects of workers' compensation, I have the feeling that the problem is not the law, but the way the law is administered. Unfortunately, we do not have much of a clue as to what an appropriate and proper system of administration of the law ought to be, or any objective way in which to judge whether one law is better administered than another.

At the outset, I might point out that the problem is relatively simple in some states when there does not seem to be any administrative mechanism whatsoever. I am not thinking only of a state such as Louisiana which until recently had no administrative agency of any sort, or states such as Alabama or New Mexico where courts play a major role in the administration of the workers' compensation act. I am thinking of other states which have administrative agencies whose sole concern seems to be the adjudication of disputes.

In most jurisdictions, administration of the act is entrusted to a workers' compensation board or commission. The idea of the disinterested public-spirited commission to administer these laws was a popular idea in the progressive era when workers' compensation acts first were passed. Some 21 jurisdictions have a single administrator, sometimes in conjunction with an appeal board, sometimes housed within a Department of Labor and Industry or some other department within the state government.

I do not believe that the organizational structure of the workers' compensation program is the crucial item to be looked at when analyzing problems of administration. It is the functions which are discharged and the manner in which they are carried out.

## The National Commission's Recommendations

Everyone who has looked at this problem agrees that administration is a crucial variable in judging the program. The National Commission on State Workmen's Compensation Laws stated that the basic objectives of the system, i.e., broad coverage, substantial protection against interruption of income, provision for sufficient medical care and rehabilitation services, and the encouragement of safety, are dependent on an equally important fifth objective: "An effective system for the delivery of the benefits and services."[2] The National Commission recognized that in the beginning the system was thought to be self-administering. It was expected that with the elimination of the fault concept and the prescription of benefits by statute, employees would be able to protect their interests without external assistance. We now know that hope for self-administration was overly optimistic. Few would argue with the National Commission's view that litigation might have been less frequent had state agencies provided enough positive assistance to workers who are unable by themselves to deal with the complexities of the law and that the void has been filled by an active plaintiffs' bar.

The Commission viewed the state agencies as having six primary administrative obligations:

1. The agency must take the initiative in administering the law.

2. It must continually review the performance of the program and request state legislatures amend the law to meet the changing needs of the program.

3. An agency must advise workers of their rights and obligations under the law and assure that they receive the benefits to which they are entitled.

4. Agencies should apprise employers and carriers of their obligations and rights under the law. Other parties in the delivery system, including physicians and attorneys, should also be informed of their obligations and privileges.

5. The agencies should assist in a voluntary and informal resolution of issues.

6. The agency must adjudicate claims which cannot be resolved voluntarily.

In the eyes of the Commission, the key to an effective delivery system is the agency's active pursuit of these administrative obligations. "The thrust of the system should be to create an ambience of protection and mediation rather than adjudication."[3] The Commission delved into the processing of workers' compensation claims, making recommendations on reports, organizational structure, attorneys' fees, methods of closing cases, supervision of medical care, and security arrangements, among other aspects. I do not wish to dwell on administrative organization or structure or even the processing of cases. I believe that the crucial variable is the business of creating the ambience and persuading the agency to pursue an active role.

## The Historical Neglect of Administration

It is confusing to discuss administration because of the lack of information, and frustrating because nothing seems to change in spite of continual detailed inquiries about the nature and quality of administration.

As an example, let me excerpt from a fine inquiry into the problem of administration. It was noted that of three recent investigations, all agreed that the system ought to have administrative hearings with informal procedures, and judicial review upon issues of law only. Two investigations urged control of attorneys' fees and that compensation boards be equipped with a competent medical staff to aid in the adjudication of compensation claims. One recommended impartial testimony with respect to the extent of disability. All made recommendations for a more adequate standardization of the disability schedules. The study concluded that there is substantial agreement as to many of the fundamental problems of workers' compensation. What is frustrating is that this excellent study by Walter Dodd was made in 1936.[4]

These same kinds of recommendations have been cited in conferences, investigating reports, and academic discussions since then. But if things do not change in a half century, it may be that the present system meets the needs of the wider community that supports the system. We must be very humble about making any recommendations for changes in workers' compensation administration.

Yet when we look at the essence of the administrative problem and try to state it in the simplest possible way, it is that workers' compensation is fundamentally a social insurance program with compulsory coverage. Neither workers nor employers have choices in these matters. Although it may not be self-administering in the sense that the earliest proponents of the law believed, nonetheless, the principal rationale for the program is that it would minimize conflict. The concept of liability without fault was to substitute a swift, certain and assured remedy for litigation endemic to tort liability. To assure that objective requires some administrative functions.

## The Workers' Compensation Agency Does Not Pay Claims

What are the essential functions that a workers' compensation administration ought to perform? Before we can answer that question it is well to recognize that the administrative agency usually is not responsible for the payment of claims. Common to all systems of cash disability transfers, be they tort cases, workers' compensation cases, or social security disability insurance cases, is the payment of claims. What is different in workers' compensation is that the administration of the claims management function is the responsibility of the *insurer*, whether it is a private insurance company, an exclusive state fund, a competitive state fund, or the firm itself if it is self-insured. Unlike the Social Security Administration, the workers' compensation agency does not issue any benefit checks, does not pay any benefits, nor does it pay treating physicians or any other provider of services. Yet there comes a time, at different stages of the claims process, depending on the jurisdiction, when the workers' compensation agency is charged with responsibility for administering the claims procedure. At these times the agency's responsibilities are substantial.

## The Public Interest in Administration

It is probably important to pin down why this is so. The patient suing his physician in a malpractice suit can settle for any amount that is agreeable to him, his doctor, and the insurance carrier. If dissatisfied with a proffered settlement, he can pursue his remedies through the court system. No state agency will interfere with a voluntary settlement on the grounds that it is not sufficient. At the opposite end of the administrative spectrum, a person seeking social security disability insurance benefits will receive a benefit amount determined in accordance with his wages as specified in the statute. Valid workers' compensation claims are paid by the insurance carrier in accordance with the statutes, but the exact amounts to be paid, especially in the case of permanent disabilities, is not certain. There is wide discretion in the system which impedes the objective of certainty, and unlike the tort settlement, the amount should not be left to the parties alone. The whole theory of workers' compensation argues that there is a direct public interest in the amount of compensation and the manner and method in which it is paid to those injured at work. It is the administrative obligation of the agency to provide guidance as to the type and amount of such payments, the conditions under which they are to be made, and the medical and rehabilitation services to be provided. It is the very nature of a compulsory social insurance program that such matters are not left to the parties.

## The Basic Administrative Functions

Once we allocate the claims management function to the insurer, the functions performed by the agency in processing the workers' compensation cases can be grouped under four separate headings. These are:

1. Recordkeeping
2. Monitoring
3. Evaluation
4. Adjudication

The *recordkeeping* function is present in all agencies. Each workers' compensation case begins with a report of an injury or disease to the employer, a copy of which is sent to the carrier and eventually to the agency. Each state requires some subsequent reporting about the individual case and its eventual disposition. States will vary greatly as to the kinds of case records the agencies maintain and the diligence with which administrators will follow up requests for reports that do not come to them in the normal course of events. However logical it may be to proclaim a public interest in administrative matters, the total extent of some agencies' involvement may be in recording and filing what the parties themselves have done voluntarily.

Some, and possibly most, states go further and are concerned with the *monitoring* function. The state agency is concerned with the equity and adequacy of the payments made voluntarily by the insurance carrier. The agency may also be concerned with the worker's rehabilitation in cases where his return to work is delayed. The agency may police the carrier's activities designed to maximize the probability of the worker's return to his job. The monitoring function may involve procedures for checking on the carrier's promptness of payment, or adequacy of general performance, advising or penalizing carriers if their performance falls short.

A third group of procedures has to do with what may be termed *evaluation* of the workers' permanent disability. Some agencies have prescribed procedures to evaluate, or to aid the parties in evaluating, the extent of the claimant's disability. In some states, the agency itself will take on the responsibility of determining the extent of disability. In other states, the agencies will do almost nothing in this area; the parties reach some agreement, and if they fail to do so, they resort to the contested procedures.

The fourth function is the *adjudication* function which is universally undertaken by the state agencies. Each agency has procedures to adjudicate disputes between the parties.

## Diversity Among the Three States

What has remained a hallmark in workers' compensation has been the diversity among the various jurisdictions in how they go about any one of their tasks. Nowhere is this better illustrated than in the case of the administration of workers' compensation in the neighboring states of New Jersey, New York, and Connecticut.

As far as structure is concerned, in New Jersey we have no workers' compensation board or commission. A supervising judge has chief administrative responsibility for the administration of the law. The agency employs few, if any, professionals, other than the judges of compensation and persons who participate in one capacity or another in the adjudication process. There is no board of appeals within the state. Appeals from compensation judges' decisions are to the state courts. In contrast, the administration in New York is in the hands of a workers' compensation board whose chairman bears responsibility for administrative functions. In Connecticut, regionalism seems to be the key.

As noted in the Connecticut annual report, the workers' compensation law is administered by a nine-member commission with exclusive jurisdiction to adjudicate disputes under that law. The chairman of the commission has statewide jurisdiction. Each of the seven district commissioners has responsibility over disputes in an area of the state, and the remaining commissioner-at-large is assigned by the chairman to act in any district where needed.

When it comes to *recordkeeping* functions, it is safe to say that no one of the states does a complete job. In all states, the case begins with a report of injury to the employer. A copy is sent to the carrier, and eventually to the agency. Each state does require subsequent reporting on the case. In New Jersey, however, very little is done with these records, other than to report annually on case activity. Almost nothing is done now in analyzing the first reports of injury. Few administrative statistics are kept on the agency activities. New York produces a rather complete set of information about closed cases and some analysis of the first reports of injury. In Connecticut, records as to the number of voluntary agreements, informal hearings, formal hearings and appeals processed by the Compensation Review Division are kept. No analysis of these case statistics is done.

The *monitoring* function also differs in each of these states. In New Jersey, from time to time, there has been some review of the so-called direct settlements where the worker and the employer reach voluntary agreement as to the amounts of compensation to be paid. If, however, some discrepancy was found in that type of settlement, the procedure was to advise the worker of his rights and have him file a formal complaint. In these instances, the matter becomes a contested case. In sharp contrast, New York, at least on a formal basis, has a hearing system in which all cases have the opportunity to have a hearing before the matter is closed out. In Connecticut, lack of administrative personnel prevents any significant monitoring activity. The information for recordkeeping and monitoring purposes may be available in the future. Public Law 81-407 established a Statistical Division effective February 1, 1982, but only in the fiscal year ending June 30, 1983 were start-up funds provided to implement that legislation. Funds were also available beginning July 1, 1983 to implement provisions of the law creating a Division of Workers' Education. Presumably that division would undertake some monitoring functions.

As far as *evaluation* procedures are concerned, none of these states has prescribed procedures to evaluate, or to aid the parties in evaluating the extent of their obligations for payment for permanent disabilities. This can possibly best be seen in the area of permanent partial disability. As pointed out above, in some states the agency takes on the responsibility for determining the extent of the permanent partial disabilities. That is not the case in New Jersey. Nothing in the uncontested procedures aids the parties in determining the amounts that are due. Consequently, very few permanent partial disability cases are closed out in New Jersey, except at the formal level or at steps immediately preceding the formal level. In New York, hearings are held in most permanent partial cases whether scheduled or nonscheduled. Connecticut follows the New Jersey pattern with extensive use of informal and formal hearings to dispose of these matters.

All three states devote major portions of their administrative energies to the adjudication function. Each of these states has a type of substitute court system where workers may have their cases heard and decided with the active participation of the plaintiffs' and defense bar.

Are the systems as they exist in these three states optimal? Are they the most efficient and equitable systems that could be devised? Do those clients who seek out representation from the plaintiffs' bar do better than they would otherwise? Is the fact that the normal procedure is to resort to an attorney in the event of permanent partial or permanent total disability the wisest use of scarce resources?

## Using the Tri-State Conference to Improve Administration

This is the first of what I hope will be a series of annual conferences in which interested persons in these three states convene to discuss workers' compensation problems to their mutual benefit. I am a realist. I do not expect quick results. I know that these administrative problems have existed since the inception of the program, and I do not expect that improvements will be made overnight.

One possible purpose of these meetings is to initiate dialogue and to begin discussions about matters of common concern. Perhaps this first conference might be thought of as a consciousness-raising session. I would raise the question of whether it makes any sense for each of these states to begin to think of improving their recordkeeping, monitoring, and evaluation functions. If I were to plead for improvements in the administrative area, I would first plead for improvements in the data and information systems. I believe data systems are useful. As an example, I would like to be able to compare the litigiousness of New York, Connecticut and New Jersey on some valid basis. Yet I find myself defeated by the fact that the data systems are not complete in any of the states, and they are certainly not comparable.

Take another example: states are presumed to be laboratories of experiment. In these states we have three different ways of administering different laws. Which is more efficacious in the prevention of accidents and diseases at the workplace? I submit that the data systems currently in place do not come close to providing an answer.

But something more than data systems is involved. We need better evaluation and monitoring to decrease the proportion of contested cases. Nothing I have said, nor anything I wish to say, is meant to denigrate the contributions of the plaintiffs' bar. In the same vein as saying "Some of my best friends are members of a particular religion," I say that were I injured at work today, I would find myself a good lawyer before I would move one inch in the State of New Jersey. But as I say it, I resent the fact that it is necessary to resort to representation. In the majority of cases where compensability is admitted, why cannot the state devise an evaluation system such that a claimant would know in a particular case what the obligations of the carrier were? Several states have done this, other states are doing it, and although I cannot point to the exemplary state lest my recommendations be misconstrued, I can say that some states do better than New Jersey, New York, or Connecticut.

Although it is difficult to change the administration of state workers' compensation systems, why not start in this part of the country, in these three states which have a high proportion of the workers' compensation cases? Why cannot the responsible administrative and political officials collaborate to seek ways and means of improving their systems? These three states have the unique opportunity of utilizing the services of three universities, each of which has personnel and units vitally interested in the area of workers' compensation.

Administrative reforms might well begin with the matter of data systems, since it is the least controversial and least threatening to the parties involved. It would be equally possible to begin to think about monitoring and evaluation functions, and about doing simple checks of what workers have received in voluntary settlements, and of devising ways and means by which adequate settlements might be forthcoming without litigation.

In similar fashion, it should be possible to think about sets of evaluation standards which could be widely promulgated, or at least to ask the question of whether it is possible to deal with this issue. I raise only one caution. It is necessary for each of the jurisdictions to accept the fact that administrative personnel are necessary if administrative tasks are to be accomplished. I do not think that these matters can be left solely to chairmen, supervising judges or commission members. It should be possible for these responsible officials to get together to think about these matters and perhaps to go further and devise ways and means whereby desirable objectives can be met.

On July 4, 1983, we celebrated the 72nd birthday of the oldest of these three compensation statutes. But in workers' compensation programs, there is no compulsory retirement age. There may be life left in this program which may not yet be ready for the geriatric scrap heap. Survival depends on evidence of change and vitality, and nowhere can that better be shown than in administrative reform. It is the most difficult of areas to change, but even small improvements can yield great social benefits.

## NOTES

1. Monroe Berkowitz, *The Processing of Workmen's Compensation Cases,* U.S. Department of Labor, Bureau of Labor Standards, Bulletin 310, 1967.

2. *Report of the National Commission on State Workmen's Compensation Laws* (Washington, DC: Government Printing Office, 1972), p. 35.

3. Ibid., p. 101.

4. Walter F. Dodd, *Administration of Workmen's Compensation* (New York: The Commonwealth Fund, 1936).

# 10

# Nominal Costs, Nominal Prices, and Nominal Profits

John D. Worrall

Economics Department

Rutgers University

The Berkowitz, Burton, and Williams papers ask whether costs, prices, or profits in the workers' compensation insurance market differ across "regulated states." The market is regulated in most states, including those they consider in depth: Connecticut, New Jersey, and New York. A central question they ask is what role the state (or its regulatory arm) plays in the process that generates costs, prices, and profits.

Professor Williams gives an excellent summary and description of rate regulation and price determination in both the national and regional workers' compensation insurance markets. He describes how manual rates are determined, as well as the adjustments to manual rates that affect the price actually paid. He describes the environment in both open-competition and prior approval states. He examines the underwriting profit and *contingency* factor, investment income and insurance profitability. Professor Williams is not judgmental. He is simply scholarly. He reports the pro and con arguments for open competition.

I think that given a state workers' compensation law and its basic administration, what Professor Berkowitz categorized as recordkeeping, monitoring, evaluation, and adjudication, the state and its regulatory arm will play little role in the price of workers' compensation insurance or the profitability of the business. I consider one family of exceptions later. First, I present the rationale for my judgment that the state plays a limited role.

For over half a century, workers' compensation insurance was a stable line. The actuarial estimates of program costs were generally on target and the combined ratios predictable. But in the early 1970s at least two major events eliminated this predictability. One was the impact of inflation. The other was structural change in the program, including increased benefits, brought about in part by the National Commission on State Workmen's Compensation Laws chaired by Professor Burton. These events made the accurate forecasting of losses a more difficult art. Medical costs escalated rapidly, as did indemnity claim frequency, and perhaps the durations of disability, as both real and nominal benefits rose.

As Professor Williams pointed out, writing workers' compensation insurance is a leveraged business. Over the 1970s the leverage, the ratio of either net premiums written or reserves to statutory capital and surplus or to net worth, also increased. Obviously, nominal rates of interest rose with inflation, and the nominal investment income earned by insurance companies increased with the rise in interest rates and leverage. The nominal rate of return required by all industries to attract and retain capital also rose. As regulators and others saw insurers earning increasingly larger amounts of nominal investment income, there was increasing pressure to have open competition or to include investment income in the calculation of manual rates in prior approval states.

The workers' compensation insurance market is characterized by intense price and nonprice comptition. The market has relatively easy entry (and exit) requirements. The capitalization requirements are low in many states and insurmountable in none. There are many sellers in the market and, although some are large in absolute size, the concentration ratio (combined market share) of the top four or top eight firms is low. Firms actively in the market must compete with one another, contend with the threat of firms self-insuring and the potential entry of insurers licensed in the state but not active in the market. There are many buyers in the market, and these buyers are businesses with good prepurchase information. The basic coverage sold in the market is mandated by law, and although insurers compete vigorously on claims handling and safety services, the insurance coverage offered by insurance company A is a good substitute for that offered by insurance company B.

Insurers compete vigorously on price. They do so at the beginning of a policy period, at the end of the period, or both. Professor Williams has listed some of the methods insurers use to compete. Insurers offer firms cost-plus insurance, sliding scale dividend plans (rebate of part of the premium based on the safety record of their insured), and *they alter the time flow of the premium that their insured must pay.* In virtually all states, the deposit premium rule has been waived. This means that an insured and an insurer can enter into an agreement to lengthen the time over which the insured can pay a *fixed* nominal insurance premium. For example, assume the nominal price of mandated coverage is $100. The insurer and insured can agree that this amount will be paid in a lump sum today, or in installments over N periods. The latter case could include some initial periods of zero payment. In effect, there is price flexibility *downward.* Prices will vary with the inflationary and real return expectations of the parties to the contract. It is difficult to imagine excessive profits being earned in markets such as the one described above.

Professor Williams pointed out that some critics argue that competition in the workers' compensation insurance markets "benefits almost exclusively the larger employers who might otherwise self-insure." The argument posed by these critics is extremely weak. Firms risk their capital in expectation that they will receive a market return, which includes a risk premium. Firms are not prohibited from writing insurance business for small risks. Many insurers do so. If there is not great downward pressure on prices for the business of smaller firms, it is because insurers do not evaluate the risk involved in writing this business to be commensurate with the rewards for writing the business. Information is available on the loss records of smaller risks (both individually and collectively). If insurers thought they would earn greater than a market rate of return writing this business, they would. Some risks end up in assigned risk pools. These firms do not end up in assigned risk pools because insurers expect to make too much money writing this business. They do not end up in assigned risk pools because insurers are charities. They end up in assigned risk pools because insurers do not expect to earn a reasonable profit writing these risks. Why? Because most states have mandated that the nominal price of insurance cannot exceed a preset limit. Although there is downward price flexibility, prices are not flexible upward. This is one of the exceptions that I mentioned earlier regarding the impact of regulation on workers' compensation prices.

The state can affect prices and profits by arbitrarily setting the price of insurance too low at the beginning of an operating period and not allowing upward price adjustments. States may also delay the implementation of new manual rates. Or regulators may shift interest rate risk to the beginning of an operating period, in effect lowering the manual rates and hence the ceiling price, and forcing more risks from the competitive market. Finally, the state may constrain the taste for risk bearing on the part of some insurers by requiring them to write business at lower leverage than the insurers would desire, or the market would dictate.

Why do workers compensation insurance prices and costs vary across states? In large part because of differences in the state: law, labor market, industrial composition, cost of living and a host of related factors. The benefits paid may differ over states as a result of variations in state workers' compensation laws and state wage distributions. Workers in a state may be willing to bear more risk or to report more injuries and file more workers' compensation claims given higher insurance benefits. Given different benefit structures across states, workers with the same tastes for risk bearing may have different accident and claim filing rates. In addition, with the same level of benefits across states, workers in different states, *and in particular in different industries and occupations,* may have different tastes for risk bearing. The number of occupational injuries and diseases will be a function of the industrial composition of a state. If more risky industries are concentrated in a state, the total cost of workers' compensation insurance in that state will be higher. Similarly, if the costs of accident prevention are higher in one state than another, all else constant, more injuries will take place in the high prevention cost state.

Professor Burton and Mr. Krueger examine the differences in costs to employers across states. In their research, they control for heterogeneity in the state industrial composition. Their paper gives us insight into how much of the variation in the costs to employers is due to residual factors, including regulation, market conditions, and administration. They carefully document the link between the benefits and costs of a social insurance system. Although they do not stress the point in their paper, their methodology also provides one way to compare the cost of public versus private provision of a social insurance. They close their paper with the value judgment, ". . . New Jersey and New York employers had lower workers' compensation costs than did Connecticut employers, . . . their achievement seems more due to parsimony than prudence." It may be that what Burton and Krueger chose to call parsimony is simply political markets working well.

Monroe Berkowitz poses the basic question, why do some states "administer" their programs by letting litigation take place, and others by aggressive and interventionist strategies. I believe political markets work. New Jersey had high permanent partial claim frequency because it was the political consensus to have it. Property rights and their administration at any point in time are reflections of the will of the people (or their power block coalitions).

The political market is the mechanism through which groups attempt to shift the cost burden of disability. Witness the existence of state insurance funds. This same political market has given us state systems for compensating permanent partial disability, and all of the headaches that go with administering such a system. The market has not *yet* given us a full federal system for compensating for permanent partial disability under the social security system. Much of the claimed "administrative efficiency" of that federal program, and inefficiency of state programs, is actually the market at work. And much of the role that I have ascribed to the state, including the setting of ceiling prices and leverage ratios, is simply that magnificent market at work.

# 11

# Federal Occupational
# Disease Legislation
## A Current Review

Donald Elisburg
Connerton and Bernstein
Washington, D.C.

Attending a seminar and discussing the future of occupational disease legislation and compensation systems sometimes becomes an exercise in riding merry-go-round. It is not exactly clear to me why we have suddenly decided to ride the horse again, but I welcome the opportunity. I particularly welcome the fact that there is renewed public scrutiny of this serious social issue.

My purpose today is two-fold: first, to review the background of congressional consultation of this issue; second, to review and comment on some of the major policy issues involved in this particular legislative activity.

I believe we have finally reached a point in our policy development where we can safely say that most of the relevant issues have surfaced, been examined and explored, and been given reasonable public consideration. That is not to say that there is any agreement on where we go and how we get there.

By way of contrast, when the question of occupational illness was first broached during consideration of the Occupational Safety and Health Act of 1970, there was perceived to be an almost complete lack of information on this subject. The number of organizations paying attention to the issue was miniscule. The focus, if any, was on the question of respiratory diseases, principally pneumoconiosis (Black Lung).

The National Commission on State Workmen's Compensation Laws actually commissioned some interesting work on occupational disease. Those studies recognized that there were coverage and other questions which needed to be considered in the reform process. Nonetheless, the focus of that Commission's report was not on the emerging problems of occupational illness and compensation thereof.

Following the Commission's report, the emphasis shifted to concerns about state workers' compensation systems and the process of legislative reform. Very little time was actually spent on how occupational illness would fit into this compensation system, except along the lines of an adjunct to the underlying need to have a uniform system for injury as well as illness. Thus, even though occupational disease has always been a significant element in the policy and political considerations surrounding such legislation, it has not been recognized as such until recently.

Why, one might ask, did this situation exist? It may be attributed in part to the complacency of the state workers' compensation system administrators and the insurance industry, who saw few occupational disease claims, and assumed that the problem in actuality was far less than experiences reflected. Moreover, awareness of toxic substances, carcinogens, and their impact on individuals has only emerged to its true dimensions in recent years. Again, that is not to say that such things were not known, but the focus tended to be on identifiable situations such as Black Lung and not on the whole host of other occupational illnesses for which the existing state laws are generally quite restrictive.

The next plateau in our consideration rests with the work of the Department of Labor's Interdepartmental Task Force, which spent several years and a fair amount of public funds in exploring a number of workers' compensation issues including problems of occupational disease, product liability and third party issues.

Unfortunately, the problems of commissioning an inquiry and ultimately bringing it to fruition can become quite unmanageable. In this case much of the work of that group commissioned in 1975 and 1976 was not completed until 1978 or 1979 and was not published until 1981. I know not how these documents become lost in the Government Printing Office. However, each of these studies has provided invaluable information about the nature of the problem.

One may cut through all of the complexities and come to the realization that this very serious problem of disability compensation can readily be solved if only it could fit within the existing system.

After all, if in this day and age we have reached a state of public acceptance that those who are made ill by toxic substances should be duly compensated and properly cared for, there is no great public consensus to be built on the underlying issue.

We know that the ideal law should cover any and all occupational illnesses arising out of and in the course of employment. We know that the ideal system should deliver prompt, reasonable benefits for permanent and partial disability and should provide full medical treatment, opportunity for rehabilitation and all of the other facets of a "good" workers' compensation program. Unfortunately, we have a few odds and ends of matters about which we have not quite reached agreement—for example, should this be done on the state or national level, should it cover all illnesses and diseases, or should the legislation be disease-specific; what is a "reasonable" level of benefits and who should pay for them; how should benefits be financed; and, who should administer the program?

I do not come here today with any great conceptual framework about which we can gather to create this new holy writ of a disability compensation law. Most of you are aware that there have been several legislative proposals pending in Congress that represent what might reasonably be considered a fresh start to the process.[1]

There are a number of basic elements that any proposed bill should have in order to make a disability compensation system effective. They include the federal role, coverage, benefit levels, claim processing and funding. A review of these elements might suggest that the major issue is over what diseases should be covered by any compensation scheme. However, in my judgment the major issue is really whether an improved occupational disease compensation program should be created as a new system or be part of the existing state compensation systems.

## Federal Role

Some 10 years ago, I was the advocate for a workers' compensation system that would have provided fully for a federal program administered through the state agencies, including a full occupational disease component. At that time Congress, the Executive Branch, and many scholars on the subject suggested that the federal government's takeover of the state workers' compensation systems, if not unconstitutional, was certainly unconscionable. If one learns nothing else over a period of time in our nation's capitol, it is that you cannot climb the same greased pole twice. Accordingly,

I believe that we are now talking about a compensation system that does not impact on the state agency's operations. Indeed, we are looking at a proposal that was too revolutionary for 1973, that is, preempting the state law with respect to occupational disease claims and administration totally at the federal level. The strongest argument for federal preemption is in the interests of uniformity. Judgments about the effects of toxic substances and the causal relation to the workplace are difficult enough for one agency to develop. Spread to more than 50 jurisdictions, the problem becomes quite unmanageable. Moreover, the political interests of many state agencies do not appear to lend themselves to comprehensive treatment of occupational disease and appropriate benefit levels.

## Coverage

What is covered under this new scheme is indeed the second most serious question. It arises because the onset and causality of an occupational disease are simply not as simple as in straight cases of injury. There are, as we know, long latency periods, complications arising from the combination of on and off the job exposure and numerous other scientific and medical problems to solve before one can reasonably suggest that a particular disease did arise out of and in the course of employment. Nonetheless, much is known about many diseases, both in the U.S. experience and elsewhere in the western world. The fact is that to deal with the occupational disease issue in a fair manner, we are going to have to adopt something called "presumptions." Now if there was any single issue which caused more confusion and difficulty than the Black Lung program, it was the question of presumptions.

Somehow we have established in some quarters a view that presumptions are either a) unscientific, b) unfair, or c) loaded against the employer. In the context of the Black Lung program, Congress confused the issue by legislating different kinds of presumptions without fully explaining the particular political purpose for each one. For example, with respect to the presumptions regarding time worked in the mines and indications of Black Lung, one can argue that there was some medical evidence relating to the development of pneumoconiosis after long exposure to coal mining. On the other hand, creating a set of presumptions relating to pneumoconiosis based on affidavits, nonmedical evidence and other criteria in order to provide compensation to widows of Black Lung victims does not rise to the level of scientific support. There is nothing wrong with providing such a political presumption if indeed it is not characterized as medical criteria. My own view is that Congress, in enacting the Black Lung Law, created a hybrid mechanism of some parts medical, some parts compensation and large parts combat pay. The difficulty, aside from the administrative problems of handling that law, is that it was unfortunately characterized as a workers' compensation program, although it had many of the elements of a pension program or a social security compensation system and an insufficient number of the elements of a true disability compensation program. The worthiness of it should not be in dispute, merely the nomenclature under which it was presented through Congress to the public.

In viewing presumptions for occupational disease, the underlying need is to eliminate the concept that in each individual case an entire system of proof need be offered to establish both the illness and its causal relationship to employment. There is no reason to create a system that would thrive on having expert medical testimony repeat and repeat and repeat the same well-known and established fact that certain exposure to certain types of chemicals and toxic substances in the workplace can and will, over a reasonable period of time, lead to the development of certain occupational illnesses.

The mechanism of developing such presumptions is not easy to achieve. It will require some form of impartial handling, and it will involve judgment calls by some form of neutral or independent agency to promulgate the presumptions against which diseases will be compensated. The fact that it may be a difficult mechanism does not make it the wrong way. In point of fact, there are a number of models from the European experience that could be utilized in the way in which the scientific and medical criteria are developed for purposes of creating such a presumption.[2] Indeed, creating a series of properly medically based presumptions or "good" presumptions is the only way in which a comprehensive occupational disease compensation system can function.

## Benefit Levels

The next area that should be addressed in our model compensation system is one involving the appropriate benefit levels. Once again, we are confronted with a serious dilemma in the way in which we approach workplace disability and occupational disease compensation. If we are talking about an income replacement, or so-called wage loss concepts, we approach perhaps half the problem. Indeed, it is not so different from the disagreements which have been raging in other areas of occupational injury for some years. Perhaps a major difference is that the partially disabled worker with occupational disease has a more than reasonable chance of that disease eventually pushing that worker into total disability and death. Unlike most injuries, occupational illness is not necessarily a discrete result.

Consequently, we're looking at an entirely new compensation system. One should not be narrow-minded in looking at benefit levels and levels of compensation. In particular, should there be some provision that goes beyond income replacement or wage loss, and provides some form of compensation for the pain and suffering as a result of the disease? I think the answer is yes. One result of toxic exposure is harm to an organ which does not interfere with work ability. So the equivalent of a "scheduled" award is worth examining. Should benefit levels be higher for occupational disease than for injury? My response would be probably not. But in developing any new law, we should not accept current levels of compensation as the norm, because by and large they are far below reasonable economic protection.

Moreover, we may be procedurally faced with a situation where there is a family trauma and not just an individual situation, because family members may also be affected by the results of the exposure to a toxic substance. Likewise, the question of a maximum level of compensation in order to provide an incentive to return to work may be a somewhat specious criterion when one is confronted with an occupational disease problem where the result is often permanent disability or death, or progressive deterioration.

### Claims Processing

One of the more difficult problems in dealing with an occupational disease compensation system is the question of claims management and claims handling. Always we are confronted with the question of providing appropriate due process and appropriate procedures for handling administrative and judicial review in a fair and reasonable fashion. The question becomes, to some degree, due process for whom? In a preemption situation, we are clearly looking at a uniform federal system in an area where the federal government has not always been known for its clarity of claims handling.

I suggest that the system, whatever it be, become simple, that it be designed to keep adjudication to a minimum and to focus on eliminating controversy and the adversary mentality. Insofar as the medical side of the claims handling is concerned, this area lends itself to the creation of some form of impartial medical evaluation. It may be advisable to create one group of physicians who will determine causality and a different group of physicians who will be the panel to review degree of impairment or disability caused by such exposure.

A major concern about the due process mechanism of any claims proceeding is the determination of who will pay. If some form of a group requirement or group responsibility is created, it then is very important to create a mechanism that does not provide a "super employer" to challenge each and every claim. The concept of super employer is currently embodied in the "pool" arrangement of HR 3175. In that proposal, the pool represents all of the employers and has the right to challenge claims pending before the Department of Labor. If that be the case, it might be better to keep pushing at the states to adopt improved systems of handling occupational disease claims matters, rather than subject individual claimants to the potential of opposition by a single entity representing all employers.

## Funding

In each of these scenarios, one must determine both who should pay and how they should pay it. There are a number of different criteria which have been suggested for a funding mechanism, ranging from assessments to direct taxes to insurance pooling arrangements and a whole spectrum in between. I suspect that as this process continues over the next several years, someone will even invent a voucher system for handling the cost of the compensation program.

On the other hand, in administering such a super-fund program, we may well have reached the point where it would be useful to examine not just the public or the private sector, but also whether we need to create some quasi-public or private agency to handle the paperwork and financial transactions this sort of a fund would entail. Even though the political process of enacting a pool arrangement based on a tax is formidable, I believe it may be the only viable mechanism. The concept of an insurance pool is interesting, but the ability to administer such a process may be beyond our current capabilities.

While I have used up a great deal of verbiage in describing these various components of a disability system, there are at least two more considerations that I would suggest in thinking about the necessary mechanisms for dealing with this problem. First, we have put the cart before the horse somewhat in dealing with these compensation legislation recommendations because we have not emphasized enough the preventive and risk assessment screening programs that are urgently required to protect the workforce against these new and emerging occupational maladies. This is peculiarly an area where investment in prevention, investment in risk assessment and investment in screening will not only pay vast dividends to workers who will be given opportunities for treatment or cure at early stages of their disease, but can also result in enormous cost savings to employers.

Second, having described the basic elements required of any system, I am not at all sure that they constitute the ideal system.[3] I would say to you that while we need to implement this process and have a legislative solution as soon as possible, we ought also consider the longer-range implications of workplace disability, particularly in the occupational disease area.

Because we are confronted with difficulties in causal relationships in occupational illness, there is reason to consider the possibility of an integrated benefit system. It may be time to consider the notion that if one is afflicted with an occupational illness or disease, the question of whether it happened on or off the job is perhaps less relevant than in other compensation systems. One could legitimately view an occupational disease compensation system as the beginning of an integrated approach to disability compensation.[4]

There is an area that I have thus far deliberately not mentioned in this paper. That is the question of whether a program such as I have outlined here should be provided only if it is the exclusive remedy for exposure to occupational hazards in a workplace situation. Under its other name, it is called exclusive liability or elimination of third party liabilities. It may even be one of the criteria for enactment of a product liability statute.

I am not sure that I can add to the many statements made on both sides of this issue.[5] Suffice it to say that it seems to me it is not the relevant consideration for looking at a compensation system that hurdles a problem relating to the employer and employee. In point of fact, the so-called manufacturer is indeed a third party. I would say that the employment contract runs from the worker to the employer. The tort system has traditionally provided a remedy, as between the employer and the manufacturer, or as is now so frequently, between the individual and the manufacturer under various product liability standards. It is indeed strange to see the U.S. Congress, in this area of liability, being forced into denying workers' rights they have yet to receive. I think it is the wrong bargain and the wrong form.

Finally, there is the question of whether or not occupational disease legislation can be enacted. No one ever knows the direction in which the political process will move on a given issue. It is safe to say that there is more interest now in occupational disease than ever in history. There is more interest now in providing a disability compensation system than in any time in recent years. There is also a greater understanding of the scope of certain federal or federally-administered compensation programs such as Black Lung and FECA. These programs have been widely criticized as costly and inefficient. The fact that they were poorly administered and never provided proper funding or management until recently does not mean that they are not fundamentally sound from a public policy and worker protection point of view.

Is all the above feasible? Who knows. But if I can review from the beginning, there is nothing new or novel. There is no lightning rod to come down upon us. The studies have been done. We must recognize that only 3 percent of occupational disease cases are filed through the existing workers' compensation system in the face of vastly more numbers being afflicted. This is the time to be considering such matters. There is an interest now, thanks to the Environmental Protection Agency.[6] There is an interest now, thanks to Johns-Manville and asbestos, asbestos, asbestos.

We do not need any more study commissions or any more large groups to evaluate public policy. We now need to design and implement the program.

# NOTES

1. See, for example, the bills introduced by Congressman Miller and Senator Hart in the 97th Congress (HR 5735 and S 1643). Also note HR 3175 Occupational Disease Compensation Act of 1983, introduced May 26, 1983.

2. E.g., Belgium, Germany, Netherlands, Sweden, U.K. In most of these statutes the descriptions have taken the form of a list of diseases. Once the exposure to a listed disease through a period of employment is established, causation is no longer an issue.

3. Appendix A is a copy of recent testimony of the AFL-CIO that lays out in brief form the way in which these elements could be put togther for a reasonably successful, if not ideal, system.

4. The European systems noted above are examples of integrated benefit programs. Some are all government run and some have strong elements of the private sector. Some, such as in the Netherlands, pay the same benefits regardless of on or off the job illness. Most have some differentials, but none as disparate as those found in the U.S.

5. See generally, DOL Task Force Report, Volume 4.

6. Recent criticism that the Administrator of EPA was not properly enforcing the environmental laws led to a congressional investigation.

# Appendix A

83-55

Testimony in Behalf of the
American Federation of Labor-Congress of Industrial Organizations,
The AFL-CIO Industrial Union Department and
The AFL-CIO Building and Construction Trades Department
Before the Subcommittee on Labor Standards of the
House Education and Labor Committee on H.R. 3175, to Provide
a Program of Compensation for Occupational Disease Victims

June 13, 1983

For the AFL-CIO: Kenneth Young, Executive Assistant to the
President of the AFL-CIO
For the Industrial Union Department: William H. Bywater, President,
International Union of Electrical, Radio and Machine Workers
For the Building and Construction Trades Department: Robert
Georgine, President

Statement of Mr. Kenneth Young, Executive Assistant
to the President of the
American Federation of Labor and Congress of Industrial Organizations

June 13, 1983

The AFL-CIO, the Industrial Union Department and the Building and
Construction Trades Department are appearing today jointly to present
views on H.R. 3175, which would establish a system for compensating
workers and survivors in cases of disability or death caused by occupational exposure to asbestos and other toxic substances.

We thank the committee for this opportunity to appear and we com-
mend you, Mr. Chairman, for your attention and diligent efforts in seeking a solution to a serious deficiency in the workers' compensation
system and to relieve the suffering of tens of thousands of victims of
these diseases.

This legislation, introduced by the chairman and co-sponsored by other members of this subcommittee, offers the Congress, organized labor, the insurance carriers, the manufacturers and processors and other interested parties an opportunity to come forward to discuss this proposal in serious pursuit of solutions to the pressing social, economic, legal and political problems that occupational diseases cause our society. The moral and ethical issues are so serious that common sense tells us that it is time to resolve this problem for the welfare of the stricken workers and their families and for the good of our nation.

We believe that we can agree on several basic concerns:

1. The need for a federal program. State workers' compensation laws governing occupational disease and disability do not provide prompt, adequate and equitable compensation to workers exposed to toxic and hazardous substances. Reform of this inadequate system is long overdue.

2. The need is evident for a system that adequately meets the economic and medical needs of workers stricken by occupational diseases, and for their families.

3. The need is evident for a system that provides swift and certain remedies without delay.

4. The need is evident for a system that provides for expansion of coverage of diseases in an ever-widening world of risk factors and incidences.

5. The need is evident for a system that is adequately financed and properly administered.

6. The need is evident for a system with mechanisms for protecting workers from exposure in the workplace.

Mr. Chairman, none of us is an expert in this field, though we are familiar with the problems and the need for solutions from our direct experience in the labor movement.

While workers' compensation laws in all states cover disability that results from occupational disease, this coverage most often is in name only. There is no uniformity of procedures to determine occupational disease compensability. Many states have in their laws restrictive eligibility provisions or arbitrary compensation standards. Claims procedures are generally too costly and time-consuming. Many occupational diseases are not adequately covered by the workers' compensation system. Thus, millions of workers who suffer the disabling effects of exposure to hazardous agents in the workplace receive no benefits.

The occupational disease effects of new and changing technology are increasingly being borne by workers themselves rather than the system designed to compensate them. Thousands of workers die each year from the effects of asbestos, radiation, cotton dust, vinyl chloride, benzene and hundreds of other hazardous agents to which they were exposed, sometimes many years ago. Millions of workers are at risk of irreversible diseases of the heart, nerves, muscles, bones and lungs. Many of the toxic agents that cause these diseases have found their way into workers' homes and communities, claiming as victims an unknown number of family bystanders as well. Many of these victims are uninformed about the fact that they are at risk as well as about what must be done to reduce the risk.

The AFL-CIO, and our Industrial Union and Building Trades Departments, therefore, have called for the establishment of a federal program to compensate workers and their families for death or disabiity resulting from occupational diseases. Attached to our testimony is the February 28, 1983 statement by the AFL-CIO Executive Council, and the companion Resolution of the Industrial Union Department urging Congress to enact legislation that will establish a comprehensive occupational disease compensation program as well as a program to identify, notify and diagnose workers who are at high risk as a result of occupational health hazards.

There are provisions in H.R. 3175 that we support. However, there are elements of the bill about which we have concerns: specifically, the level of disability benefits, the death benefit, the wage loss provision as well as the procedure for filing and determining claims. While we will not address in our testimony, today, all of these features, we look forward to working with the Committee to resolve the problems of concern and to strengthen this legislation.

At this time I wish to address one problem: the matter of exclusive remedy.

The AFL-CIO has long endorsed the traditional concepts of exclusivity with respect to workers' compensation as between the employer and his employees. The certainty of the compensation payment weighed against the uncertainty of traditional common law actions and defenses has been the cornerstone of the workers' compensation system for more than 70 years in this country.

H.R. 3175 continues this approach by including within the exclusive remedy limitations the employer, insurance carriers, collective bargaining agents and fellow employees.

There is much to argue for this approach. Experience has shown that where workers have had to seek redress in the courts, the time consumed has been extensive, the outcome uncertain and the awards when they come often net the worker very little after lawyer fees and costs.

Also, uncertainty on the employer's part transfers to the worker: If a company does not know its liability, then its workers can have no sense of protection.

There are two points, however, which we would like to make regarding the notion of exclusive remedy. First, in the area of occupational illnesses related to toxic substances, we believe that the exclusive remedy protection granted to employers should not extend to those actions of willful or intentional misconduct which cause harm to employees.

We have seen too many examples of employers with knowledge of the dangerous substances or the dangerous conditions, willfully exposing their workers to these dangers.

Second, we do not believe that the exclusive remedies should be extended to extinguish the traditional third-party rights of actions that employees would have against manufacturers. We believe that these workers should be entitled to their full rights against such manufacturers for additional damages including pain, suffering, loss of consortium and punitive damages as appropriate.

Limiting the manufacturing liability to that of an employer reduces the incentives on that manufacturer to operate with a high standard of testing and production as well as comprehensive warning requirements.

Statement of Mr. William H. Bywater, Vice President and Member
of the Exeuctive Council of the Industrial Union Department, AFL-CIO,
and President, International Union of Electrical,
Radio and Machine Workers, AFL-CIO

Mr. Chairman and members of the committee. On behalf of the Industrial Union Department, AFL-CIO, we are very pleased to be here to testify in support of occupational disease compensation legislation.

As stated in the companion testimony of the AFL-CIO, occupational disease is a many-faceted workplace problem. The focus of public attention has been on cancer and asbestos because of the enormous, well-publicized impact it has had on thousands of workers exposed to that substance. Nonetheless, rubber workers who develop leukemia from benzene, plastics workers who develop liver cancer because they must breathe vinyl chloride, miners who die of lung cancer because of ionizing radiation, electroplaters in my own industry who breathe cadmium fumes and die of prostate cancer—all sicken and die just as easily as men and women exposed to asbestos.

Their suffering and the suffering inflicted upon their families should not be less because their tragedy draws less attention in the media.

Cancer is not our only occupational disease. Cotton dust disease, nerves destroyed by lead, mercury and solvents; all are worthy of our concern.

We hope that the Committee recognizes that the effects of other toxic processes and substances should be covered in the compensation scheme. We believe a mechanism for doing so is essential with respect to some of the requisite elements contained in this Bill.

The provisions contained in Section 16 of the Bill provide a framework for coverage of additional diseases and populations. Fleshing out of these provisions is necessary if this section is to be successfully implemented, and diseased workers compensated. Experience with standard setting for toxic substances and processes under other statutes and legislative history, has shown that absent specific Congressional direction in the statute promulgation of effective standards is seriously hindered.

We are concerned that the legislative directions make clear the Secretary of Labor's responsibility to promulgate a suitable regulation in a specific time frame. It is important that workers not become caught in the cross-fire of inter-agency disputes, and suffer long delays in obtaining relief. For those occupational diseases and populations at risk already recognized and well documented such as byssinosis among cotton textile workers, the Congress should set a maximum time limit for coverage of these diseases and workers under this legislation.

The Bill at a minimum should direct the Secretary of Labor to set standards for additional discrete diseases, populations at risk, and substances or processes which consider exposure criteria, diseases and disease sites to be covered, and diagnostic criteria.

The Bill should also make clear that the criteria transmitted to the Secretary of Labor should contain to the extent feasible specific presumptions relating to causality so as to eliminate the challenges to the eligibility where medical evidence is sufficient to warrant the finding of a connection between the occupation and the disease.

H.R. 3175 already contains such presumptions for asbestos-related diseases. The Bill correctly makes irrebuttable the presumption that asbestosis is caused by breathing asbestos because the scarring of the lung and calcification observed by the physician is typically found among exposed workers. The chance is very small that the same conditions can be found in the absence of asbestos exposure.

The proposal makes a similar presumption for mesothelioma.

In this complex struggle with problems of causation and in understanding what happens to populations and groups of workers, we must deal with scientific information as it emerges and relate this knowledge to the legal formulations in order to accomplish our compensation scheme. The traditional requirement of compensating diseases "arising out of and in the course of employment" can and must be reconciled through appropriate redefinitions and qualifications to reflect the state of knowledge about disease causation. The acceptance of presumptions as a basis for clarifying causation and thereby determining compensation is essential.

Presumptions are a method of recognizing the advancement as well as the limits of science; they are valuable only when used fairly and consistently.

We believe that it will not be difficult for NIOSH to make the same determinations for workers exposed to other toxic substances and processes that reflect the increased burden of risk. Those who have borne this risk and developed cancer or other diseases because they are coke-oven workers, welders, textile workers, uranium miners, painters or oil refinery workers are no less entitled than asbestos workers to compensation.

Consideration should also be given to including a "general protection" provision which would allow claimants to seek compensation for work-related disease even though the specific effects have not been explicitly listed as compensable.

All of those provisions requiring consultation with the insurance pool insofar as it would permit a veto of additional coverage should be eliminated from this legislation. In our judgment the question of additional coverage should be limited to assessment of risk or disease and not confused with a criterion of whether there is an insurance mechanism for funding a particular compensation program. We also believe that there is no need for Congressional review of each new disease regulation.

Mr. Chairman, this is not wishful thinking about problems down the road. As is amply shown in my colleagues' testimony this morning, the need for additional coverage for occupational illness is urgent. There are afflicted workers and their families who need help now. There are a number of groups of workers in high-risk populations which should be covered within a short period of time after passage of this statute. The Secretary's timeframe should be far shorter than one year for promulgation of such additional regulations.

We support the approach taken for the medical considerations in H.R. 3175 because we believe that there is an understanding that this complexity of occupational diseases is not explainable in terms of simple single causes and simple single effects. The language of the proposed statute implies recognition of the concepts of risk factors and thinking in terms of populations which need to be the focus of the process of assessment that delineates work-related illness.

Finally, we would like to make clear that our interest is not just in compensation alone. The basic process of risk assessment useful in a compensation scheme is also important and has application in the reduction of suffering and death.

One of the most important realities repeatedly established for environmentally induced chronic disease is the long period of clinical latency between the onset of effective exposure and the first evidence of the disease. This "silent period" between initial exposure and the discovery of disease is of more than theoretical interest. It offers an opportunity, a possibility that intervention during this time might be successful in breaking the chain of events between exposure to an agent and the onset of uncontrollable disease. For cancer alone, the American Cancer Society estimates that nearly a third of the expected deaths could be prevented by existing clinical methods of early detection and treatment. There is even some evidence of reversing the development of disease before it is found when the exposure has been stopped. Consequently, an integrated program of early detection is an urgent need including the identification and notification of high-risk groups, resources for the diagnosis and verification of disease effects, community and family resources for continuous and lifetime surveillance, and referral and counseling.

We believe that these elements are essential to an effective program of occupational disease prevention. We can not focus totally on compensation without bringing to bear an understanding of this need as well.

Mr. Chairman, the Industrial Union Department joins with the AFL-CIO and the Building Trades Department in underscoring the importance of this legislative effort. We are pleased that you lead the Congressional effort to enact legislation and we intend to spare no effort to help achieve a law that is so needed by our membership.

We are attaching to our statement additional remarks which we ask be included in the record of this hearing.

### Statement of Mr. Robert Georgine, President, Building and Construction Trades Department, AFL-CIO

I am very pleased to join with my colleagues from the AFL-CIO and the Industrial Union Department to speak to this committee today on behalf of the Building and Construction Trades Department.

My belief is that *now* is the time for all of the groups concerned over the problems created by hazardous materials to accept the responsibility for the solution to the ultimate problem—how to make whole, and fully and fairly compensate, the diseased workers, and to eliminate the dangerous work practices causing these diseases. No facet of our society can be complacent because they have solved their individual piece of the problem. This legislation certainly addresses the issue of society's restoration of, and financial restitution to, diseased workers and their families.

This is not a matter of abstract concern to the trade union movement. The effort to design and evaluate a comprehensive approach to the occupation disease problem is urgently needed. I also recognize that as the solutions begin to evolve, the potential for conflict will arise. This is so, because there are so many interested parties—labor, producers and manufacturers of asbestos itself, mining, quarrying, packaging, and the processing of the products using asbestos, plus the builders, the consumers, the insurance companies who underwrite risks, the people who are exposed, and the health and welfare services who must tend the victims, plus governments and courts who must administer, interpret and enforce laws.

All of us in construction remember the decade between 1960-69 when more than 40,000 tons of fireproofing material were sprayed annually in highrise buildings. The estimate today is that more than one million tons of asbestos material remain in place aboard ships, in buildings, and in process industries. We know that asbestos dust fills the air when it is damaged or has to be replaced. Fortunately, through our apprenticeship and training programs we have promoted the use of better work practices, means of isolation, and engineering controls to minimize the exposure during removal or repair of in-place asbestos that is easily crushed and releases fibers readily into the job-site atmosphere. Laborers, Asbestos Workers, Painters, are exposed in rip-out work; I could name every International Union in the Building Trades, and I'm sure that they could provide additional situations of exposure.

Boilermakers, similar to many other craft unions, also have lodges or locals that represent workers in an Industrial setting; but they have worked on construction sites where it has been estimated that 10,000 to 20,000 tons of asbestos were applied annually to pipes, boilers, and other high-temperature equipment in factories, refineries and power plants.

We have tried to control the exposure of construction workers to in-place asbestos during rip-out work by encouraging the development of specialty contractors to do this work, and discouraging the use of contractors without experience and knowledge.

Researchers at the Mount Sinai School of Medicine have estimated that 7.5 million construction workers are at some degree of risk of developing an asbestos-associated disease. Within the next 20 years *annual excess deaths* from asbestos-related lung cancer among construction workers are estimated to range from 1,405 persons to 1,893. When other cancer deaths are projected, it adds an additional 1,000 to 1,500 deaths.

There are other toxic substances which I will talk about for a few minutes. An Ironworker told me recently,

> "We used to bring bottles or cartons of milk with us to do the job when we were welding. We would drink this milk thinking that it would reduce the upchucking when we were welding galvanized steel, or over the surface of steel that had been painted with lead in it."

Of course, we all know that it didn't work very well, but I use this as an illustration of the immediate and violent reaction of a respiratory system that is being overloaded with welding fumes. Apply this to confined spaces, and add Plumbers and Pipefitters and the toxic atmosphere problem is magnified. NIOSH has listed deaths due to respiratory disabilities as the number one cause of death among the occupational diseases.

Painters are exposed to the fumes of paints and solvents in the construction trades. Roofers are exposed to coal and asphalt tar pitch fumes, Tile Setters, Plasterers, Cement Masons, Carpenters, Bricklayers are also exposed to mixtures and epoxies from which toxic fumes can be present. Laborers handle bags, barrels, boxes, cans, drums, cylinders, and other containers which may contain hazardous substances, and all crafts on a construction site are exposed to many kinds of dusts and vapors. Ironworkers, Pipefitters and Plumbers handle materials, cut, shape and weld coverings with paint and anti-corrosive materials that are too numerous to mention. Carpenters, Operating Engineers, Electricians—pick any craft, and you will find a potential group of construction workers for exposure to asbestos and other toxic substances.

It is against this background of danger that a special Building and Construction Trades Department Committee was appointed to study and coordinate efforts with other AFL-CIO departments concerning all occupational disease compensation programs. That Committee developed several basic questions about such a compensation system. They are:

(1)  How will our members, who are potential risks to exposure, gain entry to any system devised to meet their health, economic and social needs? Not only for themselves but their families when they are deceased, or worse yet, suffering a "living death"?

(2)  What will be the mechanisms to identify and to label, as well as to define, the very best procedures and equipment needed to protect those who are presently exposed at their workplace, or may face work assignments in the future that will expose them?

(3)  How can we insure that the delivery system will not be outmoded, and constantly require upgrading in the future to serve the people dependent upon it?

(4)  How can we insure that such a program will be adequately financed?

(5)  How can we insure that it will be properly administered?

(6)    How can such a program be designed so that it will become the catchment basin for *all* such future problems as may arise, and not be done on a piecemeal basis as we have done in the past, and then *only* after there has been great suffering by our working people?

Our Committee report to me indicates that their impression of this Bill now pending before the Subcommittee is that it does not answer all of these questions as specifically as is necessary but it does offer an opportunity for substantial improvement over the present situation, and a great deal of opportunity for real progress towards the day that our country will achieve a comprehensive compensation program for working people who are disabled or die as a result of an unsafe or harmful health environment. Our comments are offered in this spirit.

The testimony of the AFL-CIO has outlined in detail the reason why this legislative effort to provide occupational disease compensation is so critical to American workers.

I would like to comment more specifically on the funding mechanics.

This aspect of the proposed legislation is of particular importance to both construction workers and their employers. Construction is an occupation with a high degree of mobility. Most of our members work for many different employers during their normal career. Our industry long ago set up multi-employer health and pension funds to accommodate this mobility.

With the long latency periods and multi-exposure problems of occupational diseases, we believe that it is essential to have a financing system that will fairly compensate our workers made ill and not place the entire cost on the "last employer," whose involvement may be minimal.

We believe that the responsibility for compensating the workers and their families made ill through asbestos exposure and other toxic substances should be placed squarely on those who are responsible for the harm. Any mechanism for paying compensation should place the burden of payment on the employers or manufacturers of the toxic substance; because of latency and multiple exposure factors it is appropriate that a compensation fund be created that will have an industry-by-industry orientation.

We do not believe that the American public should pay for the workplace disability caused by exposure to toxic substances.

We recognize that there are many possibilities for funding mechanisms, one of which is the insurance pool arrangement embodied in H.R. 3175. This is a complex issue and we would be willing to work closely with the subcommittee to develop a mechanism that will provide certainty of payment, reasonable financing, and fairness of process to the injured workers and their families.

We have serious reservations about the insurance pool arrangement from at least two aspects as it is now constituted in H.R. 3175. First, the pool arrangement gives substantial rights to the pool to challenge individual claims coming before the Secretary of Labor. The claims consideration and adjudication process should be simple as we have stated and principally rest with adjudications by the Secretary of Labor. We do not believe it is appropriate to create a process whereby the pool becomes a "super employer" able to challenge claims. Under the pool arrangement, as currently set forth in H.R. 3175, the various provisions of the pool and claims-handling permitting constant challenge to the claim will create a mechanism that will be litigation-prone and will be an injustice to the workers' interest.

Second, we do not believe that the pool should have any say in whether or not additional diseases will be recognized as eligible for compensation under the statute. The pool arrangement appears to give the insurance industry a veto over whether or not additional diseases will be the subject of compensation. This is not an acceptable process for the workers' interest.

Mr. Chairman and members of the Committee, this is a very serious effort you have started. It means a great deal to our membership in the Construction Industry. As we have stated, it is not an abstract proposition for us. It is an urgent need and we hope the Congress will be responsive to this urgency.

Statement by the AFL-CIO Executive Council
on
Occupational Disease Compensation and Prevention

February 28, 1983
Bal Harbour, Fla.

About 100,000 workers die each year from the accumulated effects of exposure to carcinogens and other chemical hazards. Another one million workers become disabled each year from the same cause.

When occupational disease episodes are publicized, attention is drawn to the tragic situation of the victims of radiation, asbestos, cotton dust, kepone, vinyl chloride, benzidine, and hundreds of other hazardous agents. The vast majority of those who have been harmed are not afforded assistance; often they do not even know that they are at risk. And only a very small percentage of the most severely disabled workers receive benefits from state workers' compensation systems, which are designed to deal primarily with traumatic injury, not disease.

A federal program is needed to compensate workers and their families for death or disability from occupational disease. The AFL-CIO is encouraged in this respect by current legislative initiatives. Both Rep. George Miller (D-Calif.) and Sen. Edward M. Kennedy (D-Mass.) have announced an intention to introduce legislation that would establish a comprehensive federal program to provide adequate and equitable compensation.

Any such legislation: should include generous time limits for filing claims that take account of the long latency periods for occupational diseases; should include eligibility requirements that give workers a fair opportunity to prove that their disabling disease is caused by exposure to a toxic substance; and should cover known occupational health hazards and provide for coverage through administrative action of additional hazards as they become known.

While a comprehensive compensation program is essential, it is not sufficient in itself. A program to identify, notify and diagnose workers who are at high risk as a result of an occupational health hazard is also necessary. Legislation should be developed to authorize the National Institute of Occupational Safety and Health (NIOSH) to carry out medical research to isolate occupational diseases and to assist populations at risk.

We strongly object to the denial to workers on grounds of alleged bankruptcy of compensation to which they are entitled for job-related injury and disease. Legislation should be enacted to correct this injustice.

Working men and women need and deserve a nationwide effort by the federal government to prevent occupational disease and to assist those who are paying the price in pain, in suffering and in the lost ability to provide for themselves and their families for years of inaction by employers and by the states.

Industrial Union Department Resolution
on
Occupational Disease Prevention and Compensation

About 100,000 workers die and one million become disabled every year because of past and continuing exposure to toxic agents in their workplaces. Millions of workers are at risk of irreversible diseases of the heart, nerves, muscles, bones, and lungs. Many of the toxic agents that cause these diseases have found their way into workers' homes and communities, claiming as victims an unknown number of family bystanders as well.

When occupational disease episodes are publicized by the media, attention is drawn to the tragedy and pain suffered by victims of radiation, asbestos, cotton dust, kepone, vinyl chloride, benzidine, and hundreds of other hazardous agents. But when the television cameras are turned off, the vast majority of victims remain completely unassisted. They are uninformed about the fact that they are at risk as well as about what must be done to reduce the risk, and only a very small percentage—10 percent in 1978—of even the most severely disabled workers receive benefits from state workers' compensation systems, which are designed to deal with traumatic injury, not disease.

Past legislative efforts have focused solely on the compensation issue, in recent months focused on asbestos victims. Workers and their families need help to *prevent* disease, those who do develop work-related diseases need assistance, and legislation cannot be restricted to the effects of one or two agents. There must be a mechanism for helping *all* workers made sick by conditions at work.

A comprehensive program to identify, notify, screen, diagnose, aid, and compensate populations of both workers and their families who are at high risk of dying or becoming disabled as a result of an occupationally-attributable disease is critical if we are to end this chronic, massive national epidemic based on ignorance, apathy and inaction.

A two-fold national program is needed. This first part would be administered by NIOSH, which would conduct medical research to identify and assist populations at risk and administer a Risk Assessment Board. Coverage for known populations at risk would be based on an epidemiologic trigger. Additional workers would be included as new information is collected through research.

The second part would be administered by an independent federal agency that would compensate disabled workers and their families through industry trust funds gathered from employers, adjudicate claims, and initiate a national recordkeeping system. Compensation would be virtually automatic where occupation is a factor in causing a worker's disease or disability, on a no-fault basis. Workers and the agency would have the right to sue both corporation and individual corporate officers in cases of criminal and gross negligence, and workers would be protected from exclusion from coverage under existing health insurance.

The Executive Council and Conventions of the Industrial Union Department have adopted resolutions on this issue in the past. These have been confirmed as policy statements of the labor movement by action of the Executive Council and Conventions of the AFL-CIO.

NOW, THEREFORE, BE IT RESOLVED:

That the Industrial Union Department, AFL-CIO, mount a campaign to implement these policies, that the Department call on all affiliates and Departments of the AFL-CIO to join us in a national campaign to correct the injustices of the past.

# 12

# Issues in Asbestos
# Disease Compensation

Donald L. Spatz
Director of Occupational Safety and Health
International Brotherhood of Boilermakers,
Iron Ship Builders, Blacksmiths,
Forgers and Helpers

## The Asbestos Legacy

The relationship between occupational exposure to asbestos and the development of human disease has been extensively studied, both clinically and epidemiologically. Scattered reports of lung scarring among workers in asbestos factories occurred throughout the industrial world in the first two decades of this century. In 1918, one of the first industrial hygiene reports issued by the Bureau of Labor Statistics referred to the adverse health experience of asbestos workers.[1] Population studies among asbestos textile workers in the 1930s showed that these workers experienced a high frequency of lung abnormalities.[2][3]

These first clinical and epidemiological reports focused exclusively on the development of asbestosis. In 1935, the first case reports of the cancer-causing potential of asbestos were published.[4][5] In 1946, the annual report of the chief inspector of factories in Great Britain noted an extremely high rate of lung cancer among workers who had died from asbestosis.[6] Population-based studies confirmed the excess risk of lung cancer among asbestos factory workers in both Great Britain and in the United States. [7] [8] In 1964, Dr. Irving Selikoff and others published findings of an enormously increased rate of death from cancer and asbestosis among users, rather than producers of asbestos products.[9]

Since the mid-1960s, scientists have found similar results among other groups of workers occupationally exposed to asbestos in either production or use of asbestos-containing products. Pleural and peritoneal mesothelioma, a rare and striking disease, began to be diagnosed among groups of workers only casually exposed to the "magic mineral."[10] It could indeed be argued that without the finding of mesothelioma among persons with such varied occupational and environmental exposure, that the tragic potential of asbestos to cause human disease might have been thought to be limited to only those persons with direct and substantial contact.

As mesothelioma was found among shipyard workers, railroad workers, construction workers, those servicing automobile and truck brakes, and among family members who cleaned workers' dust-laden clothes, it brought new awareness of the potentially broad impacts of toxic substances. While black lung was restricted to those who chose to mine coal for a living, and silicosis was confined to a handful of occupations, the effects of asbestos spread across occupational groups and, somewhat, across social classes.[11]

While it appears self-serving for a major insurance company with extensive liabilities at stake to call asbestos disease a "social problem,"[12] it is undoubtedly true that the widespread use of asbestos products has caused enormous suffering and personal loss among workers whose jobs brought them into contact with the substance.

Recently, the most detailed estimates of the number of workers occupationally exposed to asbestos and an assessment of those who, because they were significantly exposed, are at risk of developing an asbestos-associated disease, have been published.[13] There are presently more than 21 million American workers who, in the past 40 years, were significantly exposed to asbestos.[14] From this legacy, it is estimated that 8,200 to 9,700 annual deaths from asbestos-associated cancer plus additional deaths from asbestosis will occur for each of the next 20 years.[15]

Of some importance in understanding the implications of the asbestos problem is the fact that less than one in 17 of these workers was involved in the primary or secondary production of asbestos products. The remainder were involved in using, maintaining, or removing products containing asbestos—primarily asbestos insulation materials. Additionally, initial evidence reveals that workers who had no direct contact but were exposed to fugitive asbestos dust may be at risk.[16]

With this toll of current and future victims of asbestos-associated disease as a backdrop, how well have victims and their survivors fared under our statutory social insurance programs—state and federal workers' compensation—and under common law remedies against manufacturers? While data are not available for members of most groups of workers who have been disabled or killed from prior asbestos exposure, this paper presents information on two groups of asbestos factory workers and asbestos insulation workers in the State of New Jersey.

## Artificial Barriers to Workers' Compensation

The statutory barriers to occupational disease claims in state workers' compensation laws have been well-documented, beginning with the report of the National Commission on State Workmen's Compensation Laws in 1972,[17] continuing with the Inter-Departmental Workers' Compensation Task Force in 1976,[18] and most recently by the Department of Labor in its Interim Report to Congress on Occupational Diseases.[19] Perhaps the best summary of the situation was provided by Larson, who wrote, "a close review of the current statutes can only lead one to believe . . . that their real objective is to deliberately limit the number of cases, especially of the chronic long term (and probably costly) variety, which are admitted into this system.[20]

Recency of employment rules, strict statutes of limitations, and definitions of occupational disease that require peculiarity to a particular trade or exclude ordinary diseases of life, are the three types of artificial barriers which restrict the entry of legitimate claims.[21] Recency of employment or exposure rules are patently unfair in cases of disability or death from an asbestos-associated disease. The progressive nature of asbestosis, in which impairment may progress to disability in the absence of additional exposure, and the latency period for the development of an asbestos-associated cancer, have been documented by Selikoff and others. [22] [23] The negative presumption of work-relatedness created by these rules is not necessary because each state still requires the claimant to carry the burden of proving that the condition arose out of and in the course of employment.

Statutes of limitation have been modified by legislative action and judicial interpretation in many states since the report of the National Commission was released. The liberal discovery rules have mollified the effect of statutes of limitation, but unjustifiable exclusion of claims may still occur.

State laws that continue to require that a compensable disease be peculiar to an occupation or trade make little sense for asbestos-associated diseases.[24] How could a brake mechanic show that mesothelioma is peculiar to the trade? It is a disease peculiar to exposure to asbestos, regardless of trade. Exclusion of ordinary diseases may also act as a bar to asbestos-exposed workers who develop lung cancer or cancers of other sites.[25] When the disease is clinically indistinguishable as to specific cause, the asbestos-exposed worker can only point to the higher statistical incidence of the disease in his trade in seeking compensation.

## Experience in a State Without Artificial Barriers

If the worker is fortunate enough to live or work in a state[26] without artificial barriers to seeking workers' compensation, the claimant still faces the formidable problem of proving causality. Even with expert legal and medical advice, the outcome is less than certain and rarely speedy. Evidence of the difficulties that workers and their survivors have faced, even in a state without artificial barriers, is available from a study of three groups of workers in New Jersey who died of an asbestos-associated disease over a decade, from 1967 to 1976.[27]

The New Jersey workers' compensation statute has a fairly broad definition of compensable occupational diseases and, since 1974, has applied a liberal discovery rule with no other artificial barriers.[28] During the decade from 1967 to 1976, 205 deaths from lung cancer, mesothelioma, asbestosis or another asbestos-associated cancer occurred among the three groups. Other than having suffered from the same occupational diseases, the three groups of workers shared few occupational characteristics. One group consisted of asbestos insulation workers who were members of one of the three New Jersey locals of the Union. These were a subgroup of the 17,800 asbestos insulators enrolled in a nationwide mortality study in 1967.[29] Of these New Jersey locals, 44 men died of an asbestos-associated disease during the next decade.

The second group was composed of 87 persons who died from asbestos-associated disease who had worked at a Paterson, New Jersey asbestos insulation factory that had closed in 1954. These workers came under prospective surveillance by the Mount Sinai School of Medicine in 1961. This is a classic case of short term exposure producing an elevated incidence of asbestos-associated diseases. Detailed information on the mortality experience of this group of workers and its relationship to asbestos exposure has been reported.[30] [31] The fact that the factory closed in 1954 permitted examination of the effect that a break in the employment relationship had on the likelihood that these workers or their survivors sought compensation.

The third group included in the comparative analysis consisted of workers employed in production and maintenance classifications in the Manville, New Jersey plant, the largest asbestos products manufacturing company in North America. From a cohort of workers under prospective observation since January 1, 1959, 74 deaths from asbestos-associated disease occurred between January 1, 1967, and the end of 1975.[32]

Long term mortality studies of each of these groups of workers showed a significantly increased incidence of diseases caused by previous asbestos exposure. Lung cancer was the predominant cause of death among all groups, but many of the workers died of mesothelioma and asbestosis. Cancers of the gastrointestinal tract, the kidney, and other sites accounted for the remaining asbestos-associated diseases.[33]

The occupational histories of each group of workers were considerably different. The insulation workers primarily applied and removed asbestos insulation products, working for a variety of different contractors in the construction industry over their careers. Exposure to asbestos was usually continuous during their employment in the trade. The Manville workers were likewise exposed to asbestos over their working lives at the factory. Employment with this company was stable and, for these workers, usually continuous until retirement, disability or death. The workers at the Paterson firm were different. During the war years, labor turnover at the factory was high, and upon its closing in 1954, the remaining workers dispersed to a wide range of other industries and occupations. With the long latency period of asbestosis, however, short term exposure in this plant three decades previous produced a pattern of disease similar to that seen among the insulation and Manville workers, even though the workers had gone on to various types of other blue-collar and white-collar employment.

## Initiation of Workers' Compensation Claims

There were considerable variations among the three groups in the initiation of workers' compensation death claims. Claims for benefits were filed by only nine survivors of the 87 workers from the Paterson factory. In contrast, among the insulation workers claims for benefits were initiated by survivors in 26 of the 44 deaths. A similar proportion of claims (40 of 74) were filed by survivors of the Manville factory workers.[34]

Among the insulators who remained in the same trade, albeit with different employers, and among the Manville workers exposed continuously at one production facility, the association between asbestos exposure and the resultant diseases was much better recognized. In turn, the knowledge to seek workers' compensation was displayed more consistently by these workers and their survivors than among the Paterson victims. The dissemination of information concerning asbestos hazards and advocacy for compensation were aided by the presence of union representation among the insulators and Manville workers. The Paterson workers and their survivors, because of the closing of the plant, no longer shared an occupational bond or association through which information and assistance could be transmitted.

While the proportion of workers' compensation claims filed by survivors of insulators and Manville workers was rather constant over the decade, reflecting early and continuous recognition of the occupational nature of these deaths, the few claims by survivors of the Paterson workers came only in more recent years. The increase in the number of Paterson survivors filing workers' compensation claims could not be directly attributed to any one factor. Greater public knowledge of the effects of asbestos exposure, awareness through participation in a medical surveillance program, and the elimination of the recency of exposure limitation from the state law in 1974, could all be considered contributing factors. Based on interviews with survivors of Paterson workers who did not file claims, it appeared that lack of recognition of the association between asbestos and disease was not as limiting a factor as was the lack of knowledge that the survivors were potentially eligible for benefits.

The specific cause of death, as well as the accuracy of the diagnosis recorded on the death certificate, had an impact upon whether compensation was sought. The influence of these factors, however, was not consistent across all three occupational groups. Among the insulators and Manville workers, claims for death benefits were filed by survivors in a high proportion of deaths from mesothelioma, yet only one in 13 deaths from mesothelioma among the Paterson workers resulted in a survivor's claim. Somewhat surprisingly, claims for compensation benefits were less often initiated by survivors of those who died of asbestosis. To a large degree, this was found to be related to the worker's age at death and the description of the cause of death on the death certificate. Only among the survivors of the insulators were claims for compensation benefits filed from deaths of less well known asbestos-associated cancers, such as gastrointestinal cancer.

Among all three occupational groups, the age of the worker at death was a consistent factor in whether compensation claims were initiated. In part, the decline in the proportion of claims filed as age at death increases reflected the lesser likelihood of there being dependents to advance claims. Yet the same decline in the initiation of claims was seen among those deaths in which there was still a surviving spouse. Although there were no restrictions on the availability of workers' compensation to survivors of those who died after retirement and whose major source of income was no longer wage earnings, the worker's retirement status at the time of death appeared to be a considerable factor in whether compensation was sought by a survivor. Three reasons might be considered to explain this: workers and survivors have less access to information after the connection to the employment network is severed by retirement; eligibility for retirement benefits reduces the financial need to file a claim; and lack of pursuit of potential claimants by legal advocates when a worker's death occurs at an older age.

## Outcomes of Workers' Compensation Claims

Detailed information on the processing and outcomes of the workers' compensation claims was available from the New Jersey Division of Workers' Compensation for the 26 claims filed by survivors of insulators and the nine filed by survivors of Paterson workers. Less detailed data were available on 40 claims and seven direct settlements among the survivors of the Manville workers. Despite the lack of artificial barriers, only 11 of the 26 survivors of the insulators were awarded full dependency benefits. Eleven claims were resolved through the payment of partial benefits, three through compromise agreement by the parties, and eight others by formal decision of the judge in which dependency was dismissed and posthumous disability awards were entered.[35]

Particularly disturbing was the manner in which claims by six survivors of insulators who died of mesothelioma were resolved. In only one case was the widow awarded full dependency benefits. In other words, in only one of six claims could the survivor meet the required burden of proof that the disease and death arose out of and in the course of employment. In neither the one award, nor the approving settlements signed by the judges, was mesothelioma specifically indicated as the cause of death. Despite the fact that asbestos exposure encountered while on the job was the only plausible cause of these workers' deaths from mesothelioma, this medical reality was not reflected by the decisions and practices under the New Jersey workers' compensation system. The handling of claims resulting from deaths due to lung cancer shows a similar lack of consistency with documented scientific evidence. Half of the lung cancer claims were either dismissed or compromised.

Claims resolved through compromise agreements or in which the judge dismissed the dependency claim and awarded posthumous disability benefits provided considerably less in compensation than if judgments for full dependency had been awarded. New Jersey law provided income benefits for surviving dependents of 50 percent of wages at the time of injury since 1970. Claims paid through compromise agreements in a fixed amount were less than $30,000 in all cases and most likely were less than what a survivor would have received had full dependency been awarded. Yet in an individual case facing long litigation, compromise may have been the only way for the survivors to receive benefits during the immediate time of need.

Among the survivors of insulators the median period between filing a claim petition and its resolution was 19 months. One in three claims took two years or more to resolve. Over the decade under study, there was no indication that the period of controversy was reduced as evidence of asbestos-associated occupational disease became more available and seemingly less subject to dispute.

Among the survivors of the Paterson workers, with the extended period of time between the last exposure to asbestos and manifestation of disease, the lack of recognition of the occupational nature of their husbands' diseases and inadequate knowledge of their possible eligibility for workers' compensation were primary impediments. For that reason only 9 of 87 potential claims were filed. The resolution of these nine claims indicates that the New Jersey system was even less capable of acting in concert with medical knowledge of the etiology of asbestos-associated diseases than it had been with the insulators. Prior to 1974, claims of these survivors were effectively barred because of the recency of exposure limitation in the state law.

Although the Paterson asbestos insulation firm was named as a responsible employer in eight of the nine claim petitions, it was ultimately found liable for payment of survivors' benefits in only two (both deaths from lung cancer). One successful claim had been appealed by the company for seven years before final resolution. The widow was finally awarded lifetime benefits of $34 per week, based on her husband's last earnings with the firm in 1954. The other claim in which the firm paid benefits was a $14,000 settlement reached four and a half years after the worker's death. The only claim arising from a death from mesothelioma was dismissed in 1978 for "failure to sustain the burden of proof."

Despite the scientific evidence of the association between these workers' employment at the Paterson factory and their deaths from asbestosis, mesothelioma and lung cancer, the experience of their survivors, when claims were no longer statutorily barred, indicates that the compensation system was unable to handle the medical fact of latency. These workers, who suffered a pattern of disability and death similar to that of the asbestos insulation workers, found that workers' compensation, even in a state with a long-established and well-regarded system, was incapable of assigning responsibility to an employer who had ceased production more than 20 years earlier.

Less detailed data were available on the manner in which claims from survivors of the Manville workers were resolved. About the same proportion of survivors filed claims and received benefits as among the insulators, reflecting the continued exposure until disability, death or retirement. Survivors' benefits were paid in 19 of 23 deaths of mesothelioma, but in only half of the deaths due to lung cancer. No claims were filed by, or direct settlements paid to, survivors of workers who died of gastrointestinal cancer.

The period of time between last employment and death appeared to be a factor in whether compensation was sought or paid. Of five widows whose husbands had been last employed more than 10 years prior to their deaths, only one received workers' compensation benefits. Of some note was the near uniformity between the death certificate cause of death and that established by review of best evidence for those Manville workers who had died of mesothelioma and asbestosis.[36] The employment of the worker in an asbestos products factory rather than as an asbestos products user led the physicians to more often correctly list these two asbestos diseases as the cause of death.

These three groups of workers may fairly well represent the range of responsiveness that other workers and their survivors faced in seeking compensation for occupational asbestos disease in New Jersey. Clearly, those with continuous and current exposure were more aware of their rights and more successful in meeting the burden of proof. Even so, there were a majority of deaths in which benefits were not sought or in which survivors' claims were dismissed or only partially awarded.

The claim experience of these survivors may be atypical to the rest of the country, but the New Jersey statute (with no artificial barriers) can be fairly considered to be more open to potential claimants than the laws in many other states. Among the nationwide group of asbestos insulators reported by Barth, claims for workers' compensation death benefits were proportionately most often filed in the states of New Jersey, Ohio and Washington.[37] While it was found in the nationwide survey that few claims were ultimately denied and that most resulted in an award or settlement, few details were available on the actual resolution of the claim, as was the case in New Jersey.[38] One might surmise that claims of survivors in other states were reduced to far below their full value, as in New Jersey.

The Paterson workers may be representative of many workers in other industries and trades in which asbestos exposure was intermittent, brief, noncontinuous or truncated for whatever reason. However, many of the Paterson workers had participated in a medical research and surveillance program that provided some understanding of the work-relatedness of the diseases which afflicted the workers. Other victims of asbestos-associated diseases, caused by similar exposure circumstances but without a program of surveillance, can be expected to be even less informed and even less likely to seek and obtain compensation. Based on the outcomes of the claims by survivors of the Paterson workers, the potential for swift and equitable resolution of claims for survivors of workers with similar occupational histories does not appear promising under the workers' compensation mechanisms throughout our country.

The issue of causality and sufficient proof is crucial. The divergence between scientific evidence and actual workers' compensation practice—particularly evident in the handling of claims of insulators from deaths due to mesothelioma, but also seen in lung cancer deaths—suggests that in the absence of specific medical presumptions, compensation is neither certain in amount nor swift in delivery. Nor did the resolution of the Paterson claims reflect the extensive body of scientific evidence documenting the issues of latency, etiology, sufficient exposure and increased incidence of disease among briefly-exposed workers.[39] Clearly, workers' compensation practice in New Jersey, over the decade studied, did not reflect scientific evidence establishing the parameters of the relationship between these diseases and past occupational exposure to asbestos.

Similar findings reported by Barth from the much larger nationwide survey of insulation workers who died of an asbestos-associated disease, aptly described as a "best case" scenario,[40] strongly reinforce the findings from New Jersey on the inadequacies of workers' compensation.

## Product Liability Suits

It was a mere decade ago, in 1973, that a district court in Texas extended the concept of strict liability to include the duty to warn both buyers and users of the product. In this landmark case (Borel v. Fiberboard Products Corporation) the court, in ruling in support of an asbestos insulation worker, wrote "the user or consumer is entitled to make his own choice as to whether the product's utility or benefits justify exposing himself to risks of harm.''[41] Since this case, a veritable explosion of third party liability suits have been filed against manufacturers of asbestos products by those who encountered asbestos in their employment.[42] Beginning with the initial cases of asbestos insulation workers, third-party law suits have been filed by numerous shipyard workers and others involved in use, rather than primary or secondary production of asbestos products.

The experience of the world's largest asbestos producer, Manville Corporation, demonstrates the growth in third-party law suits. In 1976, only 159 cases had been filed against the company.[43] The growth in the number of law suits led the company to file for Chapter 11 bankruptcy in August 1982. In congressional hearings, Manville has testified that they were defending against 16,500 suits, which were increasing at a rate of 500 per month.[44] Financial studies upon which the bankruptcy was based estimated an additional 32,000 suits with a potential total cost of $2 billion by the year 2009.[45] Two additional asbestos manufacturers have also filed for Chapter 11 reorganization, and others are expected to do likewise, depending on the prognosis for the Manville action.

The growing number of third-party law suits and the Chapter 11 reorganization filings have increased the pressure to find a better method of compensating victims of asbestos-associated disease. Third-party suits exhibit many of the same problems encountered by the worker or survivor who seeks workers' compensation. State laws govern these actions, and a uniform product liability law does not exist. Restrictive statutes of limitation exist in a number of states.[46] The recent decision of the U.S. Supreme Court,[47] declining to review rulings by the New York Court of Appeals which dismissed asbestos suits based on a three-year statute of limitations, underscores the pitfalls to workers who seek reparations through product liability suits. Litigation is lengthy, and reargument of causation and state of the art are necessary in each suit. Expert medical and legal advice is necessary in every case.

Statistical data on the efficacy of third party suits for asbestos-associated disease are very limited. Among the survivors of the asbestos insulators the average award or settlement in 60 cases was $71,000, with an average lawyer's fee of $26,900, leaving the plaintiffs an average of $44,100.[48] While the plaintiff's legal fees took approximately 37 percent of the award or settlement, the legal cost to the defendants may be even more. Manville Corporation has reported that in 1982 its costs to dispose of suits was an average of $40,000, $19,000 of which was the cost of defending against the suit.[49]

In addition to these direct transactional costs, extended litigation concerning insurance coverage, pitting members of the asbestos and insurance industries against one another over the question of who is obligated to defend and indemnify the insured, add an unknown cost.[50] There can be little argument that having courts of law decide individual suits for compensation when there is such a large class of current and future injured persons is inefficient. Yet a popular sense of justice argues against restricting diseased workers or their survivors from seeking reparations from whatever source available, especially when workers' compensation is inadequate.

Among asbestos insulation workers, it is known that there was an interrelationship between the filing of workers' compensation claims and the initiation of a tort suit. Of those survivors who filed workers' compensation claims, 25 percent also sought a remedy against the manufacturer.[51] Ten percent of those who did not seek workers' compensation filed third-party law suits.[52] This is not unexpected, as in developing the evidence for a compensation claim, the worker or survivor gathers much of the factual information necessary to pursue an action against the manufacturer. However, it should be strongly noted that among the nation-wide group of insulators, both workers' compensation claims and third-party law suits were brought in only 9 per-cent of the deaths.[53] Whether this same interaction between workers' compensation and third-party suits exists among other groups of occupationally exposed workers is unknown.

An interesting finding from the awarded or settled suits of insulators was the substantially higher average award for vic-tims of mesothelioma, compared to victims of lung cancer. While the average age at death was essentially identical, sur-vivors of mesothelioma victims received an average dollar recovery before legal fees of nearly $100,000, while the com-parable figure for lung cancer was just $60,000.[54] This may reflect the availability of cigarette smoking as a defense in lung cancer suits or reflect a subtle difference in treatment between a so-called ordinary disease of life and one with clear-cut etiology. For whatever reason, the disparate recovery begs for an equitable and uniform compensation program for victims of all asbestos-associated diseases.

Also of some note is that two claims for workers' compen-sation for lung cancer in New Jersey (discussed above) which had been dismissed for failure to sustain the burden of prov-ing a causal relationship, resulted in tort suit settlements for the survivors. Though the burden of proof might be thought to be as stringent, if not more so, in these cases the manufac-turers were willing to settle even though there was a previous denial in workers' compensation proceedings.

## Conclusion

Asbestos is foremost among the causes of a growing number of well-defined occupational diseases for which our current system of workers' compensation has been inade-quate. It has not met the basic *quid pro quo* of speedy and certain awards in exchange for abrogating common law actions against employers. Even in the absence of artificial barriers, victims of asbestos-associated diseases fared poorly in a state with a well-regarded workers' compensation program.

The existence of a limited number of manufacturers of asbestos products and a large number of worker-users rather than worker-producers has created a large pool of potential third-party litigants. The now well-established legal interpretation of strict liability, in which the manufacturer is held to the duty of an expert, has opened up an avenue for those who have received less than fair treatment under workers' compensation to seek further redress. However, the number of suits against manufacturers, even if the current figure of 25,000 is accurate, represents only a fraction of those who have been damaged. The experience of survivors of asbestos insulators in seeking tort compensation shows that although recovery can be substantial in some cases, overall it is inequitable and unavailable.

The detailed estimates of economic losses made by Johnson and Heler[55] for the nationwide cohort of insulation workers clearly show that the losses were primarily borne by the disabled, their survivors and the general public, rather than by employers and manufacturers. For the minority of survivors who received survivorship benefits of some type, workers' compensation benefits accounted for only 27.9 percent, and tort suits and settlements 15.9 percent of total payments. In the words of Johnson and Heler, "the fact that the common law and workers' compensation provide such a small proportion of the payments to the victims of occupational illness from asbestos is a serious indictment of both approaches."

Though the "tort problem" has generated new supporters for an equitable and swift occupational disease compensation program, the past history of asbestos manufacturers does not make it easy to find a method to accommodate competing equity arguments. The evidence that has surfaced in tort suits showing that manufacturers covered up their knowledge of the true hazards of asbestos since at least the 1930s[56] [57] makes it difficult for worker advocates who wish to see an adequate workers' compensation system to support barring suits against manufacturers as a fair *quid pro quo* for a nationally administered occupational disease compensation program. Perhaps such a compensation program could be supported as the exclusive remedy for pecuniary losses and medical care on a no-fault basis if workers retained the right to sue outside the workers' compensation system for additional damages when individuals or corporations knowingly and willfully created an unreasonable risk.

Such approaches are not unknown in other parts of the world. In some Western European countries the employer has immunity from civil suits for normal cases covered by their social insurance scheme. But civil action remains possible where there has been penal sanction (Italy), gross negligence (Norway), or serious fault (Switzerland).[58] In still other countries, civil action remains possible to cover elements of compensation, such as damages for pain and suffering, which are not covered by the statutory scheme. Under the compensation program established for coal workers in the United Kingdom there are lump-sum benefits for pain, suffering, and loss of amenity, together with compensation for lost earnings, acceptance of which is in lieu of the right to seek tort compensation.[59]

The findings in the "best case" examination of the experiences of the insulation workers in New Jersey show the need for an independent agency to investigate and adjudicate claims and the need to develop adequate and workable medical presumptions. The burden of proof must be changed to a burden of disproof on the part of the employer when statistical evidence shows a higher incidence of disease among groups of workers exposed to specific substances, and individual workers meet a minimum threshold of clinical signs and symptoms.

No asbestos compensation scheme will be truly effective unless it creates an outreach program to provide surveillance, notification and assistance to those at risk. This must be directed particularly to older workers who are less likely to seek compensation, even though they are at greater risk as asbestos residency time increases. All artificial bars to entry and recovery must be eliminated, and income and medical benefits must be at a level sufficient for appropriate medical care, a dignified standard of living during disability, and to survivors upon death.

## NOTES

1. F.L. Hoffman, *Mortality from Respiratory Disease in Dusty Trades. Inorganic Dusts.* U.S. Bureau of Labor Statistics, Bulletin No. 231 (Ind. Accident Hygiene Series No. 17). Washington, DC, 1918.

2. W.C. Dreessen, J.M. Dallavalle, T.I. Edwards, et al. *A Study of Asbestosis in the Asbestos Textile Industry.* Public Health Bull. 241, 1938.

3. A.J. Lanza, W.J. McConnell, J.W. Fehnel, "Effects of the Inhalation of Asbestos Dust on the Lungs of Asbestos Workers." *Public Health Report* 50:1, 1935.

4. K.M. Lynch and W.A. Smith, "Pulmonary Asbestosis. III. Carcinoma of Lung in Asbesto-Silicosis." *American Journal Cancer* 24:56, 1935.

5. S.R. Gloyne, "Two Cases of Squamous Carcinoma of the Lung Occurring in Asbestos." *Tubercle* 17:5, 1935.

6. E.R.A. Merewether, *Annual Report of the Chief Inspector of Factories.* London, H.M. Stationery Office, 1947.

7. R. Doll, "Mortality from Lung Cancer in Asbestos Workers." *Br. J. Ind. Med.* 12:81, 1955.

8. T.F. Mancuso and E.J. Coulter, "Methodology in Industrial Health Studies: The Cohort Approach, with Special Reference to an Asbestos Company." *Arch. Environ. Health* 6:210, 1963.

9. I.J. Selikoff, J. Churg, E.C. Hammond, "Asbestos Exposure and Neoplasia." *JAMA* 188:22, 1964.

10. In addition to asbestosis, lung cancer and pleural and peritoneal mesothelioma, asbestos has been shown to increase the risk of death from gastrointestinal cancer (esophagus, stomach, colon-rectum, larynx, pharynx and kidney).

11. For instance, the founder of the modern U.S. asbestos industry and Johns-Manville Corporation (Henry Ward Johns) died from asbestosis in 1898 (his death certificate recorded "dust phthisis pneumonitis") and the current chairman of Manville Corporation (John A. McKinney) has testified that he had been overexposed to asbestos. Testimony before the Committee on Labor and Human Resources, U.S. Senate. September 19, 1978.

12. "Asbestos. A Social Problem," Commercial Union Insurance Companies, Environmental Issues Task Force, May 12, 1981.

13. G. Perkel and W.J. Nicholson, "Occupational Exposure to Asbestos," in Selikoff, *Disability Compensation for Asbestos-Associated Disease in the United States,* Environmental Sciences Laboratory, Mt. Sinai School of Medicine, 1982, pp. 21-52.

14. Ibid., p. 52.

15. W.J. Nicholson, "Cancer from Occupational Asbestos Exposure: Projections 1965-2030," in Selikoff, *Disability Compensation,* pp. 52-73.

16. E.C. Holstein, "Asbestos Disease with Fugitive Dust Exposure," in Selikoff, *Disability Compensation,* pp. 76-93.

17. *National Commission on State Workmen's Compensation Laws: Report (1972);* Compendium (1973); Supplemental Studies (3 volumes, 1973).

18. *Workers' Compensation: Is There a Better Way?* Policy Group, Interdepartmental Workers' Compensation Task Force, January 19, 1977, p. 5.

19. *ASPER: An Interim Report to Congress on Occupational Diseases,* U.S. Department of Labor, 1980, p. 4.

20. L.W. Larson, *Analysis of Current Laws Reflecting Worker Benefits for Occupational Diseases.* Report prepared for ASPER, U.S. Department of Labor, May 1979, p. 12.

21. Recency of employment rules require that a disease manifest itself, cause disablement or be contracted within a certain period after the last day of employment or after the last injurious exposure; statutes of limitation require that claims be filed within a certain time period from the date of accident or injury; restrictive definitions of occupational disease either require peculiarity to a trade, process, occupation or employment, exclude ordinary diseases of life, apply "by accident" concepts or otherwise add qualifiers to coverage.

22. I.J. Selikoff, E.C. Hammond, H. Seidman, "Latency of Asbestos Disease Among Insulation Workers in the United States and Canada." *Cancer* 46:2736-2740, 1980.

23. G. Jacob and M. Anspach, "Pulmonary Neoplasia Among Dresden Asbestos Workers," *Ann., N.Y. Academy of Science* 132:536, 1965.

24. In 1979, 21 states continued to require that a disease be "peculiar to" an employee's trade process, occupation or employment. See Larson, *Analysis of Current Laws,* p. 12.

25. In 1979, 30 states excluded "ordinary diseases of life." See Larson, *Analysis of Current Laws,* p. 13.

26. Alaska, California and Wisconsin are examples of states using broad definitions of occupational disease in the workers' compensation statutes. Larson provides the definitions and time limits for all states in Appendices A and B. Table 2.1 provides information on limitations in occupational disease definitions (see *Analysis of Current Laws).*

27. D.L. Spatz and I.J. Selikoff, "Workers' Compensation Experience Among Three Groups of Asbestos-Exposed Workers in New Jersey," in Selikoff, *Disability Compensation,* pp. 293-328.

28. Although the New Jersey statute includes the phrase "characteristic of or peculiar to a particular trade, occupation, process or employment," it also includes "diseases [which] are due to the exposure of any employee to a cause thereof arising out of and in the course of his employment." This latter condition is why the New Jersey statute is con-

sidered to have a fairly broad definition of occupational disease. (*New Jersey Rev. Stat. Art.* 34:15-31, 1978.)

29. Selikoff, I.J., E.C. Hammond, and H. Seidman, "Mortality Experience of Insulation Workers in the United States and Canada." *Ann., N.Y. Academy of Science* 330:91-116, 1979.

30. H. Seidman, R. Lilis, I.J. Selikoff, "Short Term Asbestos Exposure and Delayed Cancer Risk," Proc. *Third International Symposium on Detection and Prevention of Cancer.* H.E. Niebergs, ed. Part I. Vol 1. New York, 1977, pp. 943-960.

31. H. Seidman, I.J. Selikoff, E.C. Hammond, "Short Term Asbestos Work Exposure and Long Term Observation." *Ann., N.Y. Academy of Science* 330:61-89, 1979.

32. W.J. Nicholson, I.J. Selikoff, H. Seidman and E.C. Hammond, "Mortality Experience of Asbestos Factory Workers: Effect of Differing Intercities of Asbestos Exposure." *Environ. Res.* (In Press).

33. Spatz and Selikoff, "Workers' Compensation Experience," Tables 6-3, 6-5, 6-7 and 6-8.

34. Data on workers' compensation claims of the asbestos insulators and Paterson asbestos factory workers were collected through review of records of the New Jersey Division of Workers' Compensation and by personal interviews with their survivors. Data on compensation claims among survivors of the Manville factory workers were provided by the company and were not verified against Division records.

35. In these eight claims, the judge ruled that the claimant had not proved that the death arose out of and in the course of employment, and instead awarded benefits (to the survivors) for permanent partial disability and/or permanent total disability. In essence, the cause of death was judged not to be due to employment, yet the worker was found, posthumously, to have been disabled at the time of death. With a dismissal of the dependency claim and a posthumous award of disability, benefits were limited to a definite period of weeks rather than until the survivor's death or remarriage.

36. For each cohort, the cause of death was characterized both as it was recorded on the death certificate and after review of other available medical and pathological reports (best evidence). For a review of the methodology, see I.J. Selikoff, E.C. Hammond and H. Seidman,

"Categorization of Causes of Death Among Asbestos Workers," in Selikoff, *Disability Compensation,* pp. 197-203.

37. P. Barth, "Compensation for Asbestos-Associated Disease: A Survey of Asbestos Insulation Workers in the United States and Canada," in Selikoff, *Disability Compensation,* p. 254.

38. Ibid., pp. 265-273.

39. Comprehensive references can be found in I.J. Selikoff and D.H.K. Lee, *Asbestos and Disease,* Academic Press, 1978 and G. Peters and B. Peters, *Sourcebook on Asbestos Diseases,* Garland Press, 1980.

40. Barth, "Compensation for Asbestos-Associated Disease," p. 289.

41. Borel v. Fiberboard Paper Products Corporation, 493 F. 2nd 1076 (5th circ. 1973), cert. denied, 419 US 879 (1974).

42. *Wall Street Journal,* March 16, 1981. *New York Times,* February 14, 1982.

43. S. Solomon, "The Asbestos Fallout at Johns-Manville," *Fortune,* May 7, 1979, pp. 196-206.

44. *Occupational Safety and Health Reporter,* (Vol. 12, No. 16, p. 324) Bureau of National Affairs.

45. Ibid., Vol. 12, No. 14, p. 283.

46. D. Lawson and L.W. Zempel, "Product Liability," *Victim Compensation: The Policy Debate,* Government Research Corporation, pp. 42-46. Washington, DC, 1983.

47. Rosenberg v. Johns-Manville (No. 81-1614) and Steinhardt v. Johns-Manville (No. 81-1615), U.S. Supreme Court, 1983.

48. R. Nagle (with I.J. Selikoff, D.L. Spatz and A. Bale) "Tort Litigation for Asbestos-Associated Disease," in Selikoff, *Disability Compensation,* p. 345.

49. *Occupational Safety and Health Reporter* (September 2, 1982) Bureau of National Affairs, Washington, DC.

50. P.G. Engel, "Insurers Dodge the Asbestos Trap" (May 16, 1983) *Industry Week,* pp. 25-27.

51. Barth, "Compensation for Asbestos-Associated Disease,"p. 277.

52. Ibid.

53. Ibid., p. 278.

54. Nagle, "Tort Litigation,"p. 348.

55. W.G. Johnson and E. Heler, "The Costs of Asbestos-Associated Disease and Death." *Health and Society Millbank Memorial Fund Quarterly,* 61, 2 (1983).

56. B.I. Castleman, "The Case for Criminal Sanctions in Preventing Occupational Diseases." Exhibit A: *Asbestos. Dangerous Properties of Industrial Materials Report* (Sept./Oct. 1980).

57. G. Miller, *Asbestos Compensation Statement.* Subcommittee on Labor Standards, U.S. House of Representatives, May 2, 1979.

58. F. Morganstern, *Deterrence and Compensation: Legal Liability in Occupational Safety and Health.* International Labour Organisation, Geneva, 1982, pp. 38-39.

59. Ibid.

# 13

# Problems in Occupational Disease Compensation

### Leslie I. Boden
School of Public Health
Boston University

The papers presented in this section cover an important set of issues in workers' compensation for occupational diseases. First, we are presented with data indicating that the current state systems have serious problems compensating victims of asbestos-related diseases and, by inference, other occupational diseases which are even less well understood. Then, we are given proposals for solving the problems of compensating occupational diseases, solutions proposed to be implemented at the federal level.

Spatz's paper presents a "best case" picture of occupational disease compensation in the United States. He chooses a state system with no artificial barriers to compensation; the most well-known occupational disease agent; and workers who had been under study and were therefore likely to be more aware of the occupational origin of their diseases. In spite of these favorable conditions, Spatz documents serious problems faced by survivors of insulation workers who died from asbestos-related diseases. The issues are familiar ones, echoing those discussed by Barth and Hunt,[1] and by Barth[2] in his recent study of asbestos insulation workers. In Spatz's study, workers' compensation claims for asbestos-related disease were generally controverted, resulting in long delays, high legal expenses, and uncertain outcomes. Most claimants were not paid the full dependency amount, but received a smaller award, a settlement, or no award at all. Survivors of insulators waited a median period of 19 months to have their claims resolved.

Spatz concludes that "our current system of workers' compensation has been inadequate" in its handling of occupational disease. He and Elisburg provide suggestions for altering state workers' compensation systems which, in their views, will improve the compensation of occupational disease victims and their survivors.

These comments will focus on one aspect of occupational disease compensation, the uncertainty that leads to many of the problems presented in Spatz's paper. Before that, I would like to list some basic criteria by which the adequacy of occupational disease compensation can be judged.

### Criteria for Judging Occupational Disease Compensation Systems

Elisburg presents some of the basic goals of workers' compensation: (1) complete coverage of injuries and illnesses arising out of and in the course of employment, (2) prompt delivery of benefits, (3) a "reasonable" level of benefits, including full payment for medical benefits and rehabilitation. I would like to add to this list: (4) efficient delivery of benefits, i.e., a low expense-to-benefit ratio, and (5) certainty about what injuries and illness are covered. In addition, one could suggest: (6) minimal compensation for injuries and illnesses that are not work-related.

Spatz's work suggests that the first five goals have not been met for asbestos-caused deaths. Survivors often do not apply. When they do apply, their claims are often controverted. Settlements are partial, decisions are apparently capricious, substantial legal costs are incurred, and awards are delayed for many months. These problems lead quite naturally into a discussion of reforms designed to improve compensation for occupational diseases. While Spatz does not address the sixth goal, the history of the federal Black Lung compensation program gives us fair warning that altering the workers' compensation system does not necessarily lead to unambiguous improvement.

## The Nature of Uncertainty About Occupational Disease Causation

There are many problems involved in occupational disease compensation, including the artificial legal barriers to compensation and the apparent widespread ignorance of workers and their spouses about the workers' compensation remedy for occupational diseases. In these comments, however, I would like to focus on one type of problem, the *uncertainty* surrounding occupational illness compensation.

There are several types of uncertainty which affect the ability of workers' compensation to function effectively. Uncertainty about the agent that caused the worker's illness appears to be the primary distinguishing factor. Uncertainty about workplace exposures that occurred many years ago creates additional problems. Some common characteristics of occupational disease that contribute to this problem are:

1. The signs and symptoms of a chronic occupational disease are usually not related to a unique occupational exposure. Medical and epidemiological knowledge may be insufficient to distinguish a disease of occupational origin from one caused by nonoccupational exposures.

2. A disease can have several causes, both occupational and nonoccupational. A worker who smokes and has been exposed to ionizing radiation at work may develop lung

cancer. Since both cigarette smoke and ionizing radiation are risk factors for lung cancer, neither can be considered the unique cause. Moreover, it may not be possible to determine the contribution of each exposure to the risk of developing the disease.

3. Even where there is scientific evidence about disease causation, the evidence will be presented in an adversarial setting, and there is no guarantee about how that evidence will be interpreted at hearing, or that all cases with the same factual base will receive consistent decisions.

4. The disease may develop years after exposure began, or even after exposure ceased. Because of this, records establishing employment and exposure may be difficult or impossible to obtain, and memories of events and exposures may be unclear.

5. Records of exposures to occupational hazards may never have existed. Only in recent years, with the promulgation by the federal government of health regulations, have exposure data been collected regularly for health hazards other than ionizing radiation.

Only rarely can a physician diagnose a disease as definitely arising out of and in the course of employment. These exceptions occur when the disease has a unique causative agent to which there is a documented occupational exposure. Unfortunately, few occupational diseases fall into this category. Mesothelioma is apparently one that does, but lung cancer and other lung diseases, hearing loss, low back pain, etc. may be caused by both occupational and nonoccupational factors. It is often difficult or impossible to determine which of these factors caused the disease in a specific case, or even to determine their relative contribution. This is not caused only by the inexactness of the few available epidemiological studies of occupational disease. Even when epidemiological studies are able to accurately determine excess risks of disease in *populations,* they are not able to determine which *individuals* in those populations would not have developed the disease without occupational exposure. In many cases, this uncertainty cannot be resolved.

## The Impact of Uncertainty on the Administration of Occupational Disease Claims

Because it is necessary to demonstrate that an injury or illness occurred "out of and in the course of employment," uncertainty about the etiology of certain diseases implies uncertainty about whether those diseases are compensable. This uncertainty will often mean that a claim, if filed, will be controverted. This controversion, with ensuing delays and expenses, is the proximate cause of the symptoms of a poorly functioning system, namely, long delays and high legal and administrative costs.

Suppose that out of a group of 1000 workers it was known that 30 would eventually develop stomach cancer, but that, because of occupational exposures, 65 workers actually developed cancers. It is not possible to determine clinically which of the workers would have developed the cancer in the absence of occupational exposure. There are a number of toxicological and epidemiological studies that indicate that a substance is a carcinogen, but estimates of its potency vary. In addition, exposure records are not available on the workers. Reasonable and informed workers with stomach cancer will attempt to collect workers' compensation, and reasonable and informed insurers will controvert their claims. The probable outcome is that settlements will be reached for substantially less than would have been paid if the workers won, but much more than they would have received if they lost. The process of negotiation may take over a year and cost both claimants and insurers a great deal in legal expenses. Neither side will be completely satisfied, but both will prefer settlement to the uncertainty of a hearing.

A profit-maximizing insurer or self-insured employer will controvert a claim when the expected gain from controversion is greater than the legal and administrative costs. As the probability of winning at hearing increases, and as the value of the claim increases, the advantage to the insurer of controversion grows. For occupational injuries, there is generally nothing to be gained from controversion.[3] For occupational diseases, where uncertainty is high and disabilities are often permanent and severe, the stakes are high. An insurer would be poorly serving its shareholders and customers if it did not controvert many of the cases brought.

## Proposed Legislative Remedies

The extensive controversion of occupational disease claims makes it impossible for workers' compensation systems to meet the goals enumerated above, or to follow Elisburg's excellent prescription: "I suggest that the system . . . be designed to keep adjudication to a minimum and to focus on eliminating the adversary mentality."

Elisburg suggests two types of legislated changes in the administration of workers' compensation designed to reduce adjudication by eliminating the *legal* uncertainty about whether diseases are occupational in origin. These changes are: (1) the promulgation of legal presumptions and (2) establishing expert, impartial medical boards to determine the cause of, and to evaluate the degree of impairment due to, the claimant's illness. Spatz also suggests the use of presumptions. He suggests rebuttable presumptions that consider the claimant's burden to be met when "statistical evidence shows a higher incidence of a disease among groups of workers exposed to specific substances."[4]

### Occupational Disease Presumptions

Workers' compensation presumptions can specify a set of conditions that determine when the burden of persuasion is shifted from the claimant to the defendant. Experience with presumptions is not limited to the federal Black Lung program. A number of state workers' compensation systems have presumptions linking exposure to hazardous substances and illness, linking job and exposure, and even linking job and illness.[5] New York law (Section 47) provides that any exposure to harmful dust for a period of 60 days or longer is presumed to be harmful in the absence of substantial evidence to the contrary. Thus, a worker with lung disease who was exposed to silica dust for longer than 60 days would be presumed to have silicosis, unless the insurance carrier or employer could demonstrate otherwise. Kentucky has a similar presumption, which states (Section 342.316(5)) that for a worker with pneumoconiosis and employment exposure for 10 years or more to an industrial hazard that is a cause of pneumoconiosis there is a rebuttable presumption that the disability or death is compensable. In several states, including New York, employees in specified jobs are presumed to be exposed to hazards associated with those occupations, even if there is no evidence to support this assertion. In New York, any workers who develop anthrax while working with, or immediately after handling, wool, hair, bristles, hides, or skins, are presumed to have anthrax caused by their work.

The assumption of the papers by Spatz and Elisburg is that presumptions are favorable to the claimant. This may not be the case. Twenty states have *negative* presumptions for some diseases. The typical negative presumption states that there must be minimum exposure to the relevant hazard for compensation to be paid. About half of these negative presumptions are rebuttable, while in 10 states there is no opportunity for workers with less than the mandated exposure to receive compensation.

Presumptions, whether stringent or liberal, should reduce uncertainty. For claimants who meet the criteria of the presumption, more cases may be brought, since the presumption will serve to educate workers and attorneys about the possibility of successful claims. In addition, the rate of controversion for these claims will be lower, since the probability of the claimant's winning at hearing would be quite high. As a result, claims should be paid more rapidly than now, and there should be lower legal costs. Where there are settlements, the amounts will probably be higher. The existence of presumptive criteria may also serve to discourage prospective claimants who do not qualify, even if there is no explicit negative presumption. The criteria would reflect legislative policy in workers' compensation, and are likely to influence decisions even in cases to which they do not directly apply.

A presumption may be relatively generous to claimants, or quite restrictive. And herein lies the problem. Any presumption is likely to include in its scope workers without occupational disease, and is likely as well to exclude workers with occupational disease. Occupational disease experts can evaluate and summarize knowledge about the relationship between occupation, exposure, and disease, but they cannot decide on the basis of their scientific expertise whether to compensate fewer occupational disease victims in order to compensate fewer "undeserving" claimants.

The fact that such political decisions must be made does not, however, mean that future occupational disease presumptions will suffer from the same problems as the Black Lung program. Apparently, states with occupational disease presumptions have not experienced an explosion of successful claims as a result. Given current knowledge, one can only speculate on what would happen. While the concern of employers and insurers is understandable, most statisticians would be hard pressed to make predictions on the basis of a single observation.

Existing presumptions in state programs have not appeared to dramatically reduce litigation and substantially increase compensation of occupational disease claimants. The Black Lung program appears not to have distinguished adequately between occupational and nonoccupational disease. If any conclusion is supportable from these sparse observations, it is that the drafting and administration of presumptions is very important, and that their mere existence means little. The politics of legislation and of implementation are critical.

### Medical Boards

The same may be said for medical boards. While the principle of impartial, expert evaluation appears to be a good one, achieving that goal may not be easy. In the highly contentious climate surrounding occupational disease compensation, expert medical boards have several drawbacks not shared by presumptions. First, they do not provide clear and objective guidelines to claimants and defendants *prior* to the decisions about filing and controversion. In addition, decisions over time and by different medical boards may not be consistent. On the other hand, consistent decisionmaking over time by medical boards may help to narrow the range of dispute and thus reduce the costs of resolving occupational disease claims.

### A Bolder Approach

The development of workers' compensation early in the twentieth century created administrative systems where legal systems had previously existed. Certainty increased for employers and workers; transaction costs declined. While coverage of all workers and adequate benefit levels have remained important issues in the compensation of workplace injuries, the system has clear advantages for all parties over the tort system.

This argument is more difficult to make for occupational diseases. While workers' compensation handles over 90 percent of injury cases administratively, with resultant certainty, speedy payment and efficient delivery of benefits, well over half of chronic occupational disease cases are controverted. Proposed reforms are uncertain in effect and arbitrary in nature.

Perhaps it is time to accept this fact and consider reforms in occupational disease compensation that focus on the most seriously disabling and fatal diseases, creating an administrative system that reduces or eliminates the requirement of demonstrating specific workplace causation. Such an approach would be more like mandatory first-party disability and medical insurance than workers' compensation. As long as such a program were carefully phased-in, with appropriate general funds, similar to second-injury funds to handle pre-existing disease, it could greatly reduce uncertainty and get payment quickly and efficiently to people who need them. An excellent argument for a mandatory first-party insurance scheme for occupational diseases has already been put forth by Peter Barth.[6] Barth proposes such a program, but limits it only to deaths from cancer. While this is a reasonable place to start, it is not apparent why the same arguments for covering deaths caused by cancer should not apply as well to cancer-induced disabilities, and to deaths and major disabilities from other chronic illnesses with occupational causes.

Removing these diseases from workers' compensation coverage would eliminate uncertainty to workers, employers, and insurers caused by the difficulty of determining work-relatedness. Administrative and legal expenses would be lower than the current system, although at the cost of compensating workers with nonoccupational diseases. On the other hand, such a program has several potential drawbacks.

First, it may be very costly, if not constrained to a limited number of chronic diseases and only to deaths and major disabilities. Second, to the extent that there are incentives to reduce workplace hazards in current workers' compensation for chronic occupational diseases, such incentives would be reduced or eliminated.

The incentive effect would be small, in my opinion, since incentives for prevention appear ineffective under the current system of occupational disease compensation. The first problem is potentially the more serious. In some sense, the Black Lung program provided coverage for total disability and death from respiratory disease similar to the plan discussed in this section, but was more narrow in coverage of diseases and populations. This fact alone serves as adequate warning of the dangers of a plan that reduces or eliminates the necessity of demonstrating work-relatedness. As in the case of other reforms, the precise structure of the program, its implementation and its administration, would determine whether its costs were limited and its benefits targeted in a manner acceptable to workers, employers, and insurers. The political process would once again play a critical role.

## Concluding Comments

The apparent unfairness and inefficiency of workers' compensation of occupational diseases arises in great measure from the inherent uncertainty about whether many chronic diseases are work-related. Changes in workers' compensation that attempt to cope with this uncertainty must, by their nature, be arbitrary. In creating legal certainty from essential scientific and factual uncertainty, violence must be done to both the science and the facts. Some reforms, like presumptions, have the potential to increase efficiency and fairness. However, the implementation of reforms occurs in the political arena, and experience with the Black Lung program has left many observers with grave doubts about whether the political process can devise any reforms that adequately address the goals described in the first section of this paper.

There may be no satisfactory resolution to the problems of compensating occupational disease within the traditional workers' compensation framework. Since the limitations of the work-relatedness criterion are so great, more serious attention should be paid to reforms that attempt to remove occupational disease compensation from the workers' compensation umbrella. Such a move would be in the spirit of the change from the tort system to workers' compensation. At first, many employers objected to the idea of automatic payments to injured workers when the employer was blameless. Others were probably concerned about the costs of compensating all workplace injuries, regardless of fault. Yet the change from the tort system to workers' compensation is, I believe, a positive one. Similarly, research and experience may validate the utility of an analogous step for compensating occupational diseases.

## NOTES

1. Peter S. Barth with H. Allan Hunt, *Workers' Compensation and Work-Related Illnesses and Diseases* (1980) Cambridge, MA: M.I.T. Press.

2. Peter S. Barth, "Compensation for Asbestos-Associated Disease: A Survey of Asbestos Insulation Workers in the United States and Canada," Chapter 5 of I.J. Selikoff, *Disability Compensation for Asbestos-Associated Disease in the United States* (1983) New York: Mt. Sinai School of Medicine.

3. The notable exception to this is controversion over the degree of permanent disability. Because of the difficulty of measuring permanent disability prospectively, and the substantial value of permanent disability awards, this issue is often disputed. It often complicates the settlement of

occupational disease claims as well, since many of them involve permanent disability.

4. This raises a more general question about the proper use of statistical evidence in workers' compensation proceedings. See, e.g., Michael Dore, "A Commentary on the Use of Epidemiological Evidence in Demonstrating Cause-in-Fact," *Harvard Env Law Rev* 7, 429 and Khristine L. Hall and Ellen K. Silbergeld, "Reappraising Epidemiology: A Response to Mr. Dore," *Harvard Env Law Rev* 7, 441. A matter of substantial importance is the degree of excess risk needed to satisfy such a presumption.

5. For a more detailed discussion, see Lloyd W. Larson, "Analysis of Current Laws Reflecting Worker Benefits for Occupational Disease" NTIS Report No. ASPER/PUR-78/4385/A (1979).

6. Peter S. Barth, "A Proposal for Solving the Problems of Compensating for Occupational Diseases (1983) (unpublished paper, delivered at Workers' Compensation Conference, Orono, Maine).

# 14

# On Efforts to Reform
# Workers' Compensation
# for Occupational Diseases

Peter S. Barth

Economics Department

The University of Connecticut

## Background

In very recent years, the topic of occupational diseases has become a subject of discussion at the various conferences and seminars that are held on workers' compensation. This reflection of the considerable interest in the adequacy of the state workers' compensation systems in terms of diseases associated with the workplace represents a dramatic change from the disinterest in the subject that characterized the period before the mid-1970s. The reasons for the remarkable growth in attention to this subject need not occupy us here. What is of interest, however, is that the context of these discussions seems to be, invariably, the problems and difficulties of providing a sound, adequate and fair public program to compensate victims of such disabling and killing diseases. In the presence of such widespread concern, much discussion has focused upon efforts to reform workers' compensation. The purpose of this essay is to describe the essential questions that potential reformers must resolve as they design alternative mechanisms that seek to improve the functioning of the compensation system. Most of the efforts to broadly change occupational disease compensation have not been successful. This failure is partly due to the complexity of these questions and to the broader implications of the possible answers.

Efforts to reform occupational disease compensation cannot be analyzed *in vacuo*. Beginning in about 1969, a variety of steps were taken that were designed to fundamentally alter the nature of state workers' compensation laws. In the wake of the Farmington, West Virginia coal mine disaster, Congress enacted the Coal Mine Health and Safety Act that year. Title IV of the law dealt with the widely perceived inability of state laws to compensate victims of coal workers' pneumoconiosis by creating a federal compensation program, with coverage ostensibly limited to a single disease, for a single occupation, and with eligibility limited in several important respects. For example, benefits were to be paid only for death or permanent total disability, thereby totally excluding any direct involvement with temporary disability or partial disability.

The Black Lung program initially attempted to split up compensation by paying benefits out of federal general revenues to victims with "old cases," and by turning over to the states newly developing cases after a short period of transition. The law was significantly amended in 1972, 1977 and 1981. For our purposes, it is sufficient to observe that it has become a permanent federal program, one whose presence serves as a constant reminder of federal activity in the workers' compensation field.

The second major impetus for reform in that era was the Report of the National Commission on State Workmen's Compensation Laws issued in 1972. The Commission owed its existence to Section 27 of the Occupational Safety and Health Act of 1970. More specifically, it was the product of several persons in the Congress who believed that such a body would unlock the gates that historically had kept the federal government out of the domain of state compensation systems (Black Lung aside). It is a mark either of this group's optimism, or of its total frustration born of an inability to breech these gates till then, that its hopes rested with an essentially conservative Commission appointed by President Richard Nixon.

The Commission found many areas in need of overhaul. Of its 84 recommendations for reform, 19 were deemed to be essential ones. Most significant for our needs, the Report urged the states to act as soon as possible to clean up their laws and to comply at least with the "essential recommendations." Issued on July 1, 1972, the Report added that the Congress should step in and act if the states had not complied (at least broadly, presumably) by July 1975. The Commission supported the principle that the Congress should impose a set of minimum standards on each of the states if there was a lack of compliance with the "essential recommendations" in the three years. The 19 recommendations were the key to the potential standards.

It is instructive to observe the reform experience since July 1972. Clearly, no federal legislation of any sort dealing directly with state workers' compensation laws has come close to congressional passage. State-by-state progress has not been the cause of federal inaction. While many states did enact legislation since 1972 that moved them closer to the Commission's goals, the average state still meets only about two-thirds of the "essential recommendations." The hope that states would largely comply of their own accord by July 1975, obviating the need for federal minimum standards, has clearly not been met. What factors explain this apparent inability to achieve full-scale reform, either through voluntary state action or by the federal government?

At the state level I would point to several developments that made full compliance with the "essential recommendations" particularly difficult to achieve. First, the reforms were seen as being expensive, thereby raising insurance costs to employers. Such increases were difficult for state legislatures to justify in the decade following the Commission's Report, when state unemployment rates were reaching and holding levels not experienced since the outbreak of the Second World War. Interstate competition for jobs made such reforms unattainable on a state-by-state basis.

Many states did at least partially implement some reforms, and a number of these changes led to higher employer compensation costs. These changes, occurring as system utilization expanded, served to place limits on the extent of reform by the various states. The unexpected cost increases even led some advocates of the "essential recommendations" to withdraw their support of them.

At the federal level, efforts to enact minimum standards failed even more completely. The same fears about costs, particularly in the economically stagflated environment of the 1970s and early 1980s, contributed to congressional inaction. That aside, three other factors in particular deserve some note, though the list of the causes of failure is longer than this. First, any effort to enact federal legislation must contend with the various interest groups that have developed within the states during the decades that these programs existed. The issue goes beyond simply the reluctance to accept change by those individuals and organizations accustomed to earning a living from the compensation system. It is the sheer number of such groups and the inability to fashion compromises when so many parties have a stake that makes any federal reform legislation so difficult to achieve. Recall that substantial clout can rest with not only labor and management, but that it may reside also with state administrators, the plaintiff and defense bars, several elements within the insurance industry, the health professions, municipal officials and others. This is not to suggest that this kind of numbers problem exists solely when federal reform efforts emerge. It also exists as a problem when efforts for reform are made at the state level.

A second source of difficulties is the nature of the standards that can be administered by the federal government. It is quite apparent that those types of standards that are quantifiable are simpler to set, easier to target on for states, and less likely to be controversial when their compliance is evaluated. By contrast, a variety of possible standards involving a qualitative character would pose considerable difficulty in monitoring for a federal agency. As an example, employers and insurers that might be attracted to some federal involvement as a means of achieving reform often speak of the need for an improved "delivery system" in workers' compensation. Whatever is meant by this, it represents a qualitative sort of change that the federal government is not well equipped to impose on the states. Consequently, the relative ease of raising benefit levels, and the difficulty of assuring a better delivery system, have meant that orchestrating compromises aimed at legislating federal standards are necessarily harder to achieve.

The greatest stumbling block en route to any federal minimum standards has been the inability to find a mechanism whereby the federal government can enforce compliance. The experience under OSHA and Black Lung apparently have left many persons somewhat wary of "temporary" federal takeovers of existing state programs. Since there is no existing federal support of state compensation agencies or programs, the threat of a withdrawal of federal government monies has no meaning for the states. Moving claims into the already overburdened federal courts from state agencies or courts is also highly problematic.

Behind all these difficulties is the obvious aversion of Congress to making workers' compensation a federal program. It is hard to believe that the widespread extent of this view in Congress does not derive, in part at least, from the problems encountered in administering the three federal workers' compensation programs, Black Lung, the Longshore and Harbor Workers' Act and the Federal Employees Compensation Act. These programs serve as a constant reminder that nothing guarantees that a federal compensation program will operate more effectively than a state program.

## The Need for Reform
## in Occupational Disease

While a large variety of potential reforms have been proposed, the most frequently cited ones are relatively few. Surprisingly, there appears to be little disagreement among most of the parties about the nature and the desirability of these most obvious areas of reform. This is not to minimize the differences of views when one leaves the general for the specific, nor the reluctance of the parties to hold back their endorsement of reforms as part of a bargaining strategy. Instead, this is to suggest that the substance of the reforms that have been and will be proposed are well understood.

There exist a variety of limitation rules in some state laws that can serve to bar otherwise obviously worthy claims. As such, they render affected workers or survivors unprotected under this social insurance program. Such rules take several forms. One such barrier requires that a claim be filed within some time period after the last workplace exposure to the source of the disease. A second sort of unrealistic requirement might deny eligibility unless the worker has been employed and exposed to the hazard for at least a minimum specified and arbitrary period of time. The limitation may be medically unsound, having no justification in terms of how the disease is contracted. A third barrier involving timing may require that a claim be filed within a relatively short period of time subsequent to the development of the disease, even if the worker is not immediately disabled by the illness or aware of its presence. Such statutes of limitation may also bar claims from survivors who are not immediately aware of the work-relatedness of the killing disease.

A second cluster of barriers arises from the character of workers' compensation historically, as a mechanism for dealing with injuries caused by accidents. Such limitations have made it more difficult to receive compensation, and have even eliminated the possibility where the claimant could not demonstrate that an "accident" gave rise to the disability. Related to such barriers has been the denial of claims where a disease is thought to be an "ordinary disease of life," providing the claimant with little or no opportunity to prove that the specific instance was work-caused.

Another area in need of change involves the benefit structure. It is hardly possible to justify differential benefits for victims of industrial injuries and diseases, either in terms of compensation or medical-health treatment. It is also difficult to justify benefit payments for workers or survivors that are based on earnings levels at the time of (last) exposure, when the disease develops one or two decades later. The combination of inflation and productivity gains render such historically-based benefit levels hardly worthy of the extended and costly controversy that can follow the filing of a claim.

Another set of problems that is widely acknowledged to exist for certain claimants involves the burden of proof needed to sustain a claim. It is not possible in so short a space to indicate the myriad difficulties that (potential) claimants may have in establishing what hazard caused the disease, or that the disablement or death from disease arose out of and in the course of employment. In many instances the problem of proof relates even to the diagnosis of the impairment. This was the foremost issue that led to the passage of the Black Lung law, and this remains a central problem in claims for asbestosis and byssinosis.

## Problems in Reforming
## Occupational Disease Compensation

Earlier in this paper a number of reasons were cited as to why workers' compensation reform efforts have encountered difficulties and why no federal legislation has been adopted of the sort recommended by the National Commission on State Workmen's Compensation Laws. All of these reasons exist as well, and impede progress toward reform in occupational diseases. Additionally, a variety of other problems exist that must be resolved if the process of reform is to be successful. In this section of the paper four sets of issues on which there is little agreement are described. They are treated in the context of possible federal legislation.

### A. Coverage Issues

Any attempt to reform workers' compensation for occupational diseases immediately confronts issues of equity, costs and politics as it relates to coverage. At one pole are those proposals that would specify a single disease, or set of diseases attributable to a single hazard, or a single occupation or industry as the target of legislation. The advantages of so narrow a focus are thought to be political. By strictly limiting coverage in some such a manner, the costs of such a program will likely be more modest, an unambiguous virtue in an era of governmental austerity, at least as it might affect new programs. The other principal political virtue is that narrow and tightly bounded programs are seen as less threatening in the long run to those who advocate the retention of fully state-controlled workers' compensation systems.

The most obvious disadvantage of such narrow coverage is the inability to provide horizontal equity (equal treatment of equals) to those not covered. For example, the same disease that is compensable to a worker who loads a train with coal at a mine may not be compensable under the federal law for the worker unloading it at the electric utility or steel mill. How does one justify compensating an insulation worker with lung cancer but not a worker with the same disease who was formerly employed on the top side of a coke oven? The answer, clearly, is based primarily on the pragmatic assessment of what might get through the U.S. Congress, and not on the disparate excesses in standard mortality rates for the two groups of employees.

At the other pole in terms of proposed coverage are the schemes that would pull all occupational disease cases out of existing state workers' compensation systems and put these under some federal program. This proposal also violates the principle of horizontal equity, as it differentiates between workers with work-caused injuries being covered by the different state programs, leaving those with diseases subject to the federally determined criteria for eligibility and benefits.

Far more problematic is the question of how and where the line is drawn between disease and injury. It takes almost no effort to identify the many areas of ambiguity that arise when one seeks to cover all occupational diseases with a separate statute. In which grouping would one place the disabilities resulting from cumulative trauma? Are "back cases" instances of injury or disease? Where would hearing loss cases fit? Even where these grey areas are anticipated by the drafters of a statute, what logical criteria would they employ so as to explicitly place a category of harms under or outside of coverage? A wealth of experience exists to suggest that no reasonable degree of foresightedness will be sufficient to prevent considerable litigation and uncertainty from arising over the issue of the appropriate jurisdiction for specific cases.

Somewhere between these polar positions on coverage is the one whereby the statute would cover only one or two diseases initially, but would allow for possible expansion subsequently, without the need of new legislative action. An approach of this sort, as found in Congressman Miller's proposed bill, has the apparent political virtue of compromising between those who would support occupational disease reform legislation only if coverage were very limited and specific, and those who would opt for very wide if not all-inclusive coverage. By initially moving only asbestos-caused (work-connected) diseases to the federal arena, but leaving open the possibility of future expansion of coverage of other specific classes of disease, the question of appropriate coverage is not eliminated but is simply transferred to a less direct and obvious position.

Once one allows for possible future enlargement of scope, the subsidiary issues begin with determining *who* shall decide when and if coverage is to be broadened. Shall it be the Secretary of Labor, the head of an autonomous commission, the National Institute of Health? Presumably, congressional veto will not be available to assure those who fear that decisions about future expansion could run amok if left exclusively in the hands of the executive branch. The U.S. Supreme Court has made this sort of assurance useless. In any case, the core of the question is, shall the expansion of future coverage be primarily in the hands of scientists and health professionals, or will it be left to those more sensitive to the political winds. One could design such a scheme where both types have an input, but one cannot avoid confronting the final step of some such process where it will be either the politicians or the epidemiologists who must decide.

Aside from the question of who shall decide what future coverage will be, a number of secondary questions must also be faced in preparing such reform legislation. Given some decision about *who* shall decide, one has to define *what* possible issues can be considered. For example, suppose the Secretary of Labor is given the responsibility to decide what new coverage may be. Would the Secretary be empowered to consider specific areas based solely on his/her own discretion? Could others force the Secretary to review certain issues? Could anyone block the Secretary from considering the review of possible areas of extension? Would the same rules apply for expanding coverage as for cutting it back? To what extent would possible expansion parallel the protracted and litigation-filled model of the OSHA standard-setting process?

Behind all these questions is the accumulated experience of all the interest groups in dealing with the federal government in the areas of workers' compensation and in occupational health. From the vantage point of organized labor, there is the frustration of not having been able to get any sort of federal involvement in state workers' compensation programs (Black Lung aside). Additionally, there is a sense that OSHA standards have been too few, too slow and difficult to develop, and too timid. All the parties are aware also, that since the passage of OSHA in 1970, the law has not been amended at all. For labor this suggests that the need is to do more than to pass a marginally acceptable piece of legislation with the hope of accomplishing one's basic goals in subsequent amendments.

From the vantage point of industry, the asbestos sector aside, there is considerable concern about the federal government's possible expansion into broader areas of disease. The Black Lung experience is repeatedly cited as an example of politics dominating sound judgment. The extent to which Congress allowed the program to expand in the 1972 and

1977 amendments serves as a red flag to those who would prefer either no federal role in occupational disease or a narrowly defined one with no opportunity to widen it.

A different question regarding coverage that any reform must tackle is the range of exigencies for which benefits can be paid. While most proposals call for benefits to survivors in deaths from occupational disease, as well as benefits for permanent total disability, there is less agreement among supporters of reform beyond this. Potential areas for benefits include "medical only," temporary disabilities, and permanent partial disability. If a federal occupational disease bill provides coverage for any of these, the administrative burdens become far greater as the potential number of claimants is much larger in any of these categories than in death or permanent total disability. Further, compensating permanent partial disabilities can be especially difficult, whether it be for diseases or for injuries. If one takes the expedient route and does not cover such cases, however, serious problems develop in aligning the federal and the state programs where jurisdiction is based on subjective and widely varying estimates of the extent of impairment or disability.

A final question of coverage that needs resolution is the treatment of "old cases." Specifically, to what extent would a new federal reform law seek to deal with deaths and disabilities that occurred in earlier years? By covering such old cases, one is assured both that the costs will be higher and that problems of available evidence and proof become more complicated. Organized labor seems adamantly committed to having old cases covered.

If one decides to cover old cases, are all cases formerly under state jurisdiction to be opened or reopened? The Miller bill opts for some compromise by extending coverage to old cases only where no benefits have been previously paid. The potential for problems and for questions of equity are too numerous to detail, but some must be noted. For example, suppose a worker had earlier received a "medical only" benefit through the state law, but was denied any benefits at a later date when claiming to be permanently and totally disabled. Suppose a worker received $500 for a temporary total disability. If the worker later dies, allegedly from the disease, will the survivor be able to claim federal benefits when state benefits are denied in the death claim?

## B. Medical Issues

Once the questions of coverage are decided, a variety of issues emerge regarding eligibility. Specifically, aside from any potential federal legislation operating without the artificial barriers to compensation that have existed in some of the states, what would make a federal program more accessible to claimants than some of the state systems? Essentially, the answer would have to be that more rational or manageable (from the applicant's view) standards of evidence be required in such claims than exist currently.

Several sorts of changes are likely under any federal reform. Most likely there would be some resort to presumptions that would ease the claimant's evidentiary burden. While the presence of presumptions seems likely to be found in almost any reform proposals, a host of questions about them needs to be resolved before incorporating them in new legislation. Just as in the case of coverage, support for reforms will hang on how these are answered.

The most significant questions parallel those raised about coverage. Are presumptions to be limited to what is placed in the original statute, or is there some way of adding to or modifying them administratively? Who is to determine what the presumptions are to be, who can initiate the process of changing them, what is the process to be of setting them, and what challenges to them will be permitted? Are presumptions to be limited to medical issues and exposure questions? Can the presumptions be rebutted or not? The constitutionality of an irrebuttable presumption has been upheld, but the clamor over the single one found under Black Lung has never subsided. In the presence of rebuttable presumptions, the administrative agency will likely determine in the regulations that it sets, precisely how academic it may be to seek to rebut. One possibility is that rebuttable presumptions are *de facto* impossible to rebut. Alternatively, they may be written in such a way that they are of little help to the claimant. In large measure, this issue depends upon whether it is a government agency that is in a position to rebut an invoked presumption, or if it is a private sector employer or insurer that is defending the claim.

A second set of health issues involves the use of medical panels. To what extent is it appropriate to use such panels of objective and technically qualified experts in cases where there is some dispute about a medical question? One of the most controversial issues that arose under Black Lung was the use made by the government of "B" readers to evaluate the quality of and diagnoses from chest X-rays.

There are three basic sets of medical problems that may arise in occupational disease claims. Disputes about them are not equally well dealt with by impartial medical persons. Questions of diagnosis are probably the best ones to be settled by such specialists. Issues relating to etiology are probably much less amenable to resolution by a panel. The third area depends upon the principle of compensation used by the agency in question. Medical panels are ideal for settling disputes regarding the extent of impairment, but they are not at all suited to deciding whether the claimant's degree of disability has been fairly assessed.

Aside from issues of how to use such experts, questions arise regarding their selection, remuneration and tenure. Additionally, some decisions must be made about the ability of the parties in a claim to challenge the findings of such experts.

## C. Financing Issues

Any federal occupational disease legislation that goes beyond simply requiring the states to meet certain standards implies that a new financial obligation will be incurred by some party or other. The need for new funding sources is especially significant where old cases are to be covered. Presently, there appears to be a universal antipathy to having this burden fall on the U.S. Treasury, as was done in the case in the Part B segment of Black Lung.

A variety of possible options have been weighed. On one side are those who wish to apply some variant of experience rating to a funding scheme so as to make only "responsible employers" pay where their employees developed disease. Such an approach has appeal to those who view this as furthering the safety and health goals of a compensation system through the use of appropriate incentives. This sort of funding plan also satisfies the needs of some who want to mete out punishment to responsible employers. A variation of this, as found in the Miller bill, would seek needed funding from an entire industry but not try to establish who the responsible employer was on a case-by-case basis, nor employ any experience rating at the level of the firm.

There are several grounds for objection to either of these funding approaches. The experience under the Black Lung Act demonstrated the enormity of the task of identifying responsible employers, particularly in older cases. Alleged responsible parties challenged and fought almost every single old case attributed to them. In many of the cases the only possible employer (where the worker had been exposed to coal dust) was no longer in business or unable to pay the compensation. Where the workers had been employed by several different employers, the choice of the liable party often could appear to be capricious or a matter of convenience, but not justice. (In a building trade such as insulation work, asbestos workers can work for several different employers within a single year!)

To overcome some of these problems, the Miller bill opts for a sort of superfund, financed by a tax levied on the entire industry from which the disease originated. This approach immediately encounters some immense problems. First, on what basis does one allocate the tax on the industry? Does one use current levels of employment, sales, profits? What criteria are employed to split these among importers, manufacturers, distributors, fabricators, and possibly certain users? What of firms that were formerly in the asbestos industry, for example, but are now no longer involved? And unlikely though it may be, new firms could enter the industry without any past history of usage, thereby having no reasonable probability of generating claims against the fund in the next few years. Are they to be absolved of the tax, and accordingly given a competitive edge on the industry?

Aside from the question of who, specifically, is to pay, there are a number of questions regarding the nature of the fund itself. Either a fund of this sort builds up reserves prior to or as future obligations develop, or it operates on a pay-as-you-go basis. The former approach pushes many of the costs onto the front end of the program and is not attractive to existing firms that would bear the brunt of these costs. The latter approach shifts some of these direct tax burdens into the future and could thereby shift them to other employers. With no basis for determining what the costs of an occupational disease bill will be under a pay-as-you-go basis, revenues would need to be adjusted frequently, perhaps annually, in order to avoid significant surpluses or shortfalls in the fund. All this implies a highly flexible scheme of taxation. Understandably, employers, members of Congress and others are loathe to provide this sort of discretion to set tax rates to a Secretary of Labor or any other political appointee, especially where the rate may not be made uniform in the industry, where the industry is difficult to define, and where exit and entry to the industry by some firms may have an immense impact on the costs borne by other firms therein.

The superfund approach is also not likely to be endorsed by those who seek to use the tax as the source of incentives to employers to maintain a healthy and safe workplace. So long as each taxed employer pays the same rate as other firms in that sector, there is no reason for the firm to reduce the exposure to the hazard in question.

## D. Exclusive Remedy Issues

Efforts to achieve reform of workers' compensation practices in cases of (occupational) disease owe much to the difficulties spilling over from the tort system. It is no coincidence that those employers who have shown some willingness to move toward federal reforms are those now facing huge costs from tort actions brought by (alleged) victims of occupational diseases. Their support for such change emanates from a realization that any options to bar further suits must be accompanied by the guarantee that the remaining remedy, workers' compensation, be made more accessible to potential users. If such a *quid pro quo* were not possible, there would be no reason for those employers who support federal action to do so. Similarly, without such a bargain, organized labor would never willingly accept the principle that workers' compensation be the exclusive remedy in disease cases. Indeed, it will be a challenge for reform-minded parties to move some elements of organized labor to this compromise. If labor cannot be budged from its current public position of seeking to retain the right to sue third parties, however, the prospects for federal reform are reduced considerably.

The difficulty of achieving a compromise between labor and at least some employers is complicated by other factors. Organized labor, particularly at the state level, has never invested significantly in the development of an understanding of the workers' compensation system. There was little apparent need to do so as long as expert opinion was available to them, typically provided by plaintiffs' attorneys familiar with state practices and issues. The interests of such practitioners were generally consonant with those of the unions and their members. On this issue, however, there is considerably less overlap of mutual needs. The trial bar has no apparent interest in having future lawsuits by workers or survivors barred in disease cases. Any promise of a more effective workers' compensation system holds less interest for them than maintaining and expanding the opportunity to sue. If organized labor is to move towards the *quid pro quo,* they will have to do so without guidance or support from their traditional ally and source of expertise.

At the time of this writing, it is probably true that only a small proportion of U.S. employers, weighted by any criterion, are attracted to the *quid pro quo* of reforming workers' compensation through federal intervention, and being absolved of liability under tort in future occupational disease cases. This small group consists primarily of businesses involved with asbestos. There exist, however, firms in other industries that are very sensitive to these issues out of a concern that other industries will eventually be dragged down by third party suits for occupational diseases. For a number of reasons, these firms are loathe to identify themselves or the basis for their interest.

## Other Needs

One of the principal shortcomings of how compensation systems have dealt with occupational diseases is the underutilization of this remedy by potential applicants. The problem is one that appears to be large and well identified. None of the potential reforms noted above bear directly on this issue, at least so far as underutilization has resulted from worker (or survivor) ignorance of their rights to compensation for diseases, or of the cause or nature of the illness. If this matter is not addressed in reform efforts either at the state or the federal level, the reforms will have relatively little impact on the usage people make of the system. Much more is known about the existence of underutilization for these reasons than how to ameliorate it. Perhaps that is why proposed reforms regularly seem to avoid confronting the matter.

# 15

# Accident Compensation as a Factor Influencing Managerial Perceptions and Behavior in New Zealand

Barbara McIntosh
School of Business
University of Vermont

Governments legislate remedies when other segments of society fail, or are perceived to fail, to respond to a particular need. A prime example is in the area of health and safety. The belief that there were excessive industrial accidents was taken as evidence that the private sector was not doing enough with health and safety in the work environment, and remedies were not only insufficient but difficult to secure. Throughout the 1970s sensitivity to the suffering caused by industrial accidents and the lack of recourse led many countries to direct more attention to the problem. In New Zealand, this response resulted in the most extensive no-fault accident compensation legislation in existence today. All persons who suffer a personal injury by accident are compensated, regardless of whether or not the injury is employment-related.

Certainly the intent of New Zealand's legislation is laudable, but it is critical to examine the manager's experience within such a system because legislation does not always result in the intended consequences. For example, rather than reducing lost time from industrial accidents, comprehensive compensation provisions may, in fact, have the opposite effect. Since compensation becomes the accident victim's entitlement and right, there may be an increase in the number of accidents reported and/or the duration of time off resulting from an accident. If the legislation results in this behavior, the economic burden on the employer is greater and this shift may, in turn, cause the employer to reduce prevention program initiation and/or compliance. In this case, the number of accidents may go up and the outcome is opposite the original intent of the legislation to reduce suffering.

Obviously, employers are a critical link in implementing and financing the provisions of health and safety compensation legislation. Thus, one must determine to what extent health and safety legislative provisions influence management's perceptions concerning employee behavior and their subsequent decisionmaking in the health and safety area. Do employers perceive that the provisions facilitate or hinder organizational health and safety activities? Do the legislative provisions shift a greater economic burden onto the employer because employee behavior changes? Are other institutions or groups more influential than the government in the firm's administration of health and safety programs?

The answers to these questions obviously have both management and public policy implications. Management's response within the context of multiple external pressures will affect future legislation as it is modified to achieve the intent of the original law and *vice versa*. Understanding the influence exerted by other factors, including other firms, unions, employee groups, and other government rules and regulations, will also provide insight into the most effective implementation approaches. Not only the government but the employers themselves may be able to use these groups to cooperatively improve health and safety records.

This paper examines employer perceptions and behavior in response to New Zealand's comprehensive accident compensation legislation. In the first section the background of the Accident Compensation Act is briefly reviewed, followed by a discussion of the provisions of the legislation. Provisions for levy rates and incentive rebates under the Safety Incentive Scheme are outlined. The second section examines the current data on industrial accidents in New Zealand, highlighting the data on seven high-risk industries. The third section then outlines the methodology used in collecting survey data on management's perceptions and responses within these high risk industries. The data are reported and, finally, conclusions are drawn.

## New Zealand's Accident Compensation Act

Prior to the 1972 Accident Compensation Act, New Zealand's personal injury remedies under the law were fragmented and generally considered insufficient.

- A victim was entitled to a limited form of compensation payable under workers' compensation legislation but only if the accident or disease arose out of work and in the course of employment.

- A victim could claim damages in the Courts if negligence on the part of some other person could be established.

- A victim could draw on funds administered by the Crimes Compensation Tribunal if the injury was caused by the criminal acts of others.

- A victim could receive social security[1] if none of the above remedies was available.

- Owners of motor vehicles were required under the Motor Vehicle Insurance Act of 1928 to insure against death or injury liability (Fahy 1982).

The litigation and inequitable treatment resulting from this fault-based approach (i.e., that an action in law for damages arising out of personal injury or death could only be sustained if negligence on the part of the defendent was proven or admitted) ultimately led to a Royal Commission of Inquiry on Compensation for Personal Injury in New Zealand report in December 1967 (the Woodhouse Report)[2] and passage of the Accident Compensation Act (ACA) in 1972. The 1972 Act and its Amendments were supplanted by the Accident Compensation Act of 1982 which became effective April 1, 1983. The 1982 Act did not alter the concept of the system but rather simplified previous complex wording and improved administrative provisions (Fahy 1983).

The Royal Commission set down several principles upon which the legislation rests:

- Community responsibility;

- Comprehensive entitlement;

- Complete rehabilitation, which would be encouraged by an award not being revisable downward after an initial assessment;

- Real compensation (adequate benefits); and

- Administrative efficiency (Royal Commission 1967).

The purpose of the Accident Compensation Act is thus to provide accident prevention, compensation, and rehabilitation for every man and woman, and protection 24 hours a day. The compensation itself is governed by the personal circumstances of the accident victim. If there is a loss of earnings or a loss of earning power, the compensation payable under the accident compensation scheme is related to that loss of earnings and earning power. Rehabilitation assistance is also tailored to meet the actual and continuing needs of the accident victim, so the nonearner is covered in this way (Inglis 1982).

To insure this coverage, three schemes have been implemented: An Earners' Scheme for employed or self-employed persons, a Motor Vehicle Scheme for persons injured in accidents involving motor vehicles, and a Supplementary Scheme for persons not covered under the first two schemes, including homemakers and visitors to New Zealand (Dahl 1976). Broadly, the Earners' Fund and the Motor Vehicle Fund are independently financed and self-supporting, and each is charged with all amounts paid in claims which arise under the respective schemes.[3] The Supplementary Fund is financed from money appropriated for that purpose by Parliament.

## Employer's Contributions

Since the focus of this paper is on employer costs and factors influencing their behavior, it is important to examine the Earners' Fund, which is financed by levies on employers and self-employed persons. Through this fund employers finance the earnings-based compensation which is paid to employees who suffer an injury, whether or not such injury arises in the course of employment. The levy paid by the employer is paid at a rate specified for that particular industry activity classification or classifications. All industry, trade, business and professional activities are classified so that the amount of levy collected for each class and the amount of compensation, medical expenses, and other payments provided can be recorded. Work accident accounts are kept by industrial activity classification. A separate nonwork accident account is kept and the costs (compensation, medical expenses and other payments) are spread equally over all industrial activities. It should be noted that industrial activity refers to the employer, not the occupation of the employee. Thus, the nature of the goods produced or services rendered determines the industrial activity under which the leviable earnings of the employees are classified. The levy rate per $100 of wages ranges from $.50 for the provision of actuarial services, the practice of accountancy, the services of administrative agencies, clerical, management activity, etc. to $5.00 for mining underground, exploring, prospecting and development works (natural gas, minerals, oil) in, on, or above the continental shelf, and tunneling (Accident Compensation Corporation 1983). While higher rates are set for more dangerous activities by the ACC Board, there is not a strict multiplicative relationship between the degree of danger and the levy. In other words, as evidenced in the injury rate (see tables 2 and 3) mining is more than 10 times more dangerous than actuarial services. To some extent then, "safe" activities subsidize more dangerous activities.

The Accident Compensation Act does fix a maximum amount of individual earnings on which the levy is payable. The Accident Compensation Order of 1981 (S. 1981/338) raised this maximum to $39,000[4] applicable to payments due May 31, 1983. Prior to this, the maximum amount of individual earnings on which the levy was payable was $18,720. The leviable earnings include wages and salaries, overtime pay, holiday pay, piecework payments, long-service leave pay, bonuses or gratuities, gross commissions, honoraria and allowances for boarding, lodging or housing.

The Earners' Fund gross levy revenue ($149,317,624) made up 62 percent of the total income ($242,388,617) received by the Accident Compensation Corporation for the year ending March 31, 1982. At this time there was a credit balance of $218.2 million in the Earners' Fund, but forecasts indicated that the fund would be inadequate to meet the long term run-off of claims in years ahead. The shortfall was $62.7 million (Fahy 1982). The financial implications of this for employers may be very serious.

While a financing deficit is projected, it is interesting to note, as indicated in table 1, that the number of work accident claims remained fairly constant from 1975 through 1981. The proportion of claims on the Earners' Fund for nonwork accidents, however, has been steadily increasing, from 31 percent in 1975 to 43 percent in 1981.

**Table 1**
**Claims Received by Fund**

| Claims received | 1975 | 1978 | 1981 |
|---|---|---|---|
| Total claims | 105,018 | 132,438 | 128,747 |
| Earners' Fund | 91,337 | 103,481 | 96,652 |
|   Work accidents | (63,212) | (62,826) | (55,607) |
|   Nonwork accidents | (28,125) | (40,655) | (41,045) |
| Motor Vehicle Fund | 9,405 | 11,563 | 11,771 |
| Supplementary Fund | 4,276 | 17,394 | 20,324 |

SOURCE: *ACC Statistics,* Wellington, Accident Compensation Corporation Vol. 1, No. 1, March 1982, p. 12.

NOTE: Not all claims result in compensation being paid—especially those made to protect the claimant's entitlement in the future.

In addition to paying levies into the Earners' Fund, an employer is also responsible for directly compensating employees 100 percent of their earnings on the day of the accident and during the following six days if the employee is unable to work because of an injury arising out of and in the course of employment (ACA & 112). Effective April 1, 1983, the employer's first week compensation liability also includes any overtime the employee would have worked (Fahy 1983). In practical terms, this means the employer must pay the employee the full amount he/she would have received had he/she been working. In 1982 it was reported that the cost of this first week's compensation still averaged about 10 cents per $100 of the leviable payroll (Fahy 1982, p. 32). If the earner is incapacitated for more than seven days the Commission pays the compensation regardless of whether or not the accident arose out of and in the course of employment[5] (ACA & 113).

## Safety Incentive Scheme

The Safety Incentive Scheme rewards those employers whose work-related accident records are significantly better than other employers paying the same industrial activity levy. This is not a no-claims bonus system, but rather is based on actual performance relative to expected performance. In other words, an employer with a perfect record (no accidents for which claims are filed in the period) does not necessarily receive a bonus. If the employer is engaged in low accident activities, no claims would be expected. A significant improvement is thus more likely from employers engaged in activities where the accident rate is expected to be high.

In 1982 the ACC paid out 190 Safety Incentive Bonuses totaling $1,145,661, based on accident and wages information for the period of April 1, 1978 to March 31, 1981. The bonuses were calculated at 12.5 percent of the net work levy paid for the year ending March 31, 1981.

## Accident Rate Data

It is logical to hypothesize that the first week provisions and the Safety Incentive Scheme would provide the employer with an incentive to actively seek health and safety improvements and reduce the accident frequency rate. Unfortunately, it is not possible to make valid comparisons between data published preceding and following the passage of the Accident Compensation Act. Unlike current provisions, claims made under the old Workers' Compensation Act, for example, included first-week incapacities but excluded injuries to the self-employed (notably farmers). Injuries received traveling to and from work were also not included in previous statistics but are now deemed to be "work-related." These last two factors are significant contributors to the "fatalities" now recorded. The exclusion of the first-week incapacity also means that injury frequency and severity statistics are not compiled as in the past (Accident Compenstion Corporation 1982). As shown in tables 2 and 3, an "injury rate" is currently calculated based on the number of compensated accidents per 1000 workers, which does allow comparisons across industries and occupational groups, however.

The industry data in table 2 shows that while the injury rate averages 35 for all industries, it ranges from 86 for mining and quarrying to 5 for finance, insurance, real estate and business services. Manufacturing had the second highest injury rate in 1981, 60, with a total 18,672 compensated accidents. More than one-third of all compensation paid went to manufacturing workers. The highest number of fatalities, 44, was in forestry and fishing but this industry did not have the highest accident rate (compensated claims per 1000 workers) as previously discussed.

By occupation group, the highest injury rate and number of fatalities were recorded for transport equipment operators and laborers as shown in table 3. This occupational group also received nearly two-thirds of the compensation paid in 1981, $21.2 million. Forest workers, fishermen and hunters had the second highest injury rate, 43, with 45 fatalities. Compensation paid to this occupational group totaled only $5.1 million, however.

## Table 2
## New Zealand's Accidents, Injury Rates and Compensation - 1981

| Industry group | Fatal | Nonfatal | Total | Labor force | Injury rate* | Compensation** |
|---|---|---|---|---|---|---|
| All industries | 178 | 46,117 | 46,295 | 1,332,339 | 35 | 33,578 |
| Agriculture, hunting, forestry and fishing | 44 | 6,237 | 6,281 | 144,249 | 44 | 5,084 |
| Mining and quarrying | 2 | 397 | 399 | 4,656 | 86 | 428 |
| Manufacturing | 22 | 18,650 | 18,672 | 311,130 | 60 | 11,719 |
| Electricity, gas and water | 0 | 774 | 774 | 15,123 | 51 | 485 |
| Construction | 13 | 3,411 | 3,424 | 85,737 | 40 | 3,203 |
| Wholesale and retail trade, restaurants and hotels | 14 | 3,055 | 3,069 | 218,439 | 14 | 2,390 |
| Transport, storage and communication | 28 | 4,392 | 4,420 | 107,829 | 41 | 3,769 |
| Finance, insurance, real estate and business services | 6 | 421 | 427 | 91,638 | 5 | 382 |
| Community, social and personal services | 26 | 6,637 | 6,663 | 307,575 | 22 | 4,526 |

SOURCE: Derived from *Summary Report—Compensated Accidents, 1981*, Accident Compensation Corporation, Wellington, New Zealand, 1982.

*Compensated claims per 1000 of labor force (1981 census).

**Reported in thousands as of May 31, 1982.

## Table 3
## Compensated Work Accidents by Occupation - 1981

| Occupational group | Fatal | Nonfatal | Total | Labor force | Injury rate* | Compensation** |
|---|---|---|---|---|---|---|
| All occupations | 178 | 46,117 | 46,295 | 1,332,339 | 35 | 33,578 |
| Professional, technical and related workers | 16 | 2,033 | 2,049 | 183,969 | 11 | 54 |
| Administrative and managerial | 5 | 196 | 201 | 45,993 | 4 | 249 |
| Clerical and related workers | 6 | 1,334 | 1,340 | 214,761 | 6 | 977 |
| Sales | 6 | 1,135 | 1,141 | 127,101 | 9 | 959 |
| Service workers | 11 | 2,911 | 2,922 | 106,626 | 27 | 2,077 |
| Agricultural, husbandry, forest workers, fishermen and hunters | 45 | 6,296 | 6,341 | 146,295 | 43 | 5,143 |
| Production and related workers, transport equipment operators and laborers | 70 | 30,455 | 30,525 | 457,932 | 67 | 21,227 |

SOURCE: Derived from *Summary Report—Compensated Accidents, 1981*, Accident Compensation Corporation, Wellington, New Zealand, 1982.

*Compensated claims per 1000 of labor force (1981 census).

**Reported in thousands as of May 31, 1982.

## Employer Decisionmaking

Given the universal coverage of the Accident Compensation Act, the levy system, the employer's responsibility for compensation during the first week, and the presence of an incentive scheme, it is important to examine the employer's response to this legislative initiative. Specifically, four questions need to be addressed:

- To what extent does the availability of accident compensation and government legislation, in general, influence management's response to health and safety compared to other factors such as the union, other firms, employee concerns, and other government rules and regulations?

- To what extent do employers believe that the provisions of the ACA change employee behavior? That is, does the existence of compensation prolong the absence of injured workers, or are more accidents reported as a result of the compensation?

- To what extent do employers believe that their expenditures in the health and safety area are offset by lower accident rates?

- To what extent are the influencing factors and the employer's cost benefit assessment correlated with actual accident behavior in the organization?

The answers to these questions are all related to one another. In terms of cost considerations, price competition and the employment relationship, the employer is going to be influenced by other firms in the industry, government rules and regulations (as distinct from compensation provisions), unions, and other employee groups. Employee behavior can be expected to be influenced by the benefits provided through the government's accident compensation legislation.

This behavior will in turn affect the employment relationship. The interactive relationship between these factors is shown in figure 1.

**Figure 1**
**External and Internal Factors**
**Influencing Employer Perceptions and Behavior**
**in the Health and Safety Area**

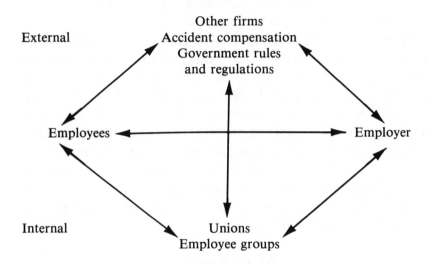

As suggested in the questions above, it is hypothesized that factors influencing an employer's reaction do not have a direct impact; this influence is instead filtered through the employer's overall assessment of the costs and benefits of health and safety activities. This relationship is illustrated in figure 2.

**Figure 2**

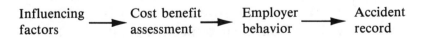

Employer cost benefit analysis moderates the effect of factors influencing employer behavior and resultant accident record.

With respect to costs, economic theory suggests that organizations assume a proprietary strategy and seek to maximize their return. This classical assumption about economic self-interest does not automatically prescribe a particular treatment of health and safety within the organization, however. On one hand, the employer driven to minimize costs has no incentive to invest in safety programs, machine safeguards, new selection procedures, etc. Accident prevention has explicit costs which can be avoided. On the other hand, accidents themselves are an expense. Accidents may involve disrupted production, damaged equipment, lowered morale resulting in overall lower productivity, compensation payments, recruiting and selection replacement costs, and the payment of wage differentials. The employer may thus choose to invest in accident prevention because "the benefits derived from the safety expenditure are costs which are not incurred" (Berkowitz 1979, p. 53). Certainly some investment in health and safety is economically rational, and it is assumed that these expenditures will have an impact on the organization's accident record.

## Methodology

In order to assess the impact of New Zealand's accident compensation provisions in the context of other factors influencing an employer's cost benefit assessment and accident record, intensive information was collected within seven industries, including forestry, pulp and paper, construction, steel, rubber, oil exploration, and chemicals. The distribution of firms between industries was balanced, and within each industry the number of foreign-owned versus domestic firms was also balanced. Data were collected from 19 corporations, as well as from their respective plant operations, for a total of 38 organizations. Eighteen of these organizations were foreign-owned. Six were headquartered in Australia, six in Britain, two in the U.S., two in Holland and two in Japan. Twenty of the surveyed organizations were domestic enterprises.

Two- to three-hour structured interviews were conducted with the corporate president or chair of the board and/or the senior executive responsible for health and safety within the organization. A second copy of the questionnaire was sent to the general manager of one of the organization's operating facilities. This questionnaire was returned directly to the investigator. Employers responded to detailed questions on organization structure and behavior, and perceptions of factors influencing health and safety administration. Health and safety performance was measured by the level of accidents. Employer response was measured by the hierarchical level of the position of the individual charged with primary responsibility for health and safety, and the percent of this individual's time spent on health and safety issues. Perceptual questions about influential factors, union relations, etc., were measured on a 7-point scale.

## Results

It has been suggested that multiple factors moderate the effect of legislation on management's behavior and their perceptions of this effect. Across the industries sampled, government rules and regulations and the provisions of accident compensation legislation were reported as having a very high influence on health and safety decisionmaking within the firm. The mean influence rating for each of these factors was $\bar{X} = 5.21$ and $\bar{X} = 3.77$, respectively, as shown in table 4. Evaluated on a 7-point scale ($1 =$ not at all influenced, $7 =$ influenced to a great extent), employers also reported being influenced by employee concerns and demands ($\bar{X} = 4.08$) and to a slightly lesser extent, the union in the plant ($\bar{X} = 3.52$). Employers did not indicate that employee turnover ($\bar{X} = 1.79$) had an impact on the decisionmaking. The impact of other firms in the industry ($\overline{X} = 2.78$) was also low. This may be explained, however, by the fact that when employers were asked to compare themselves with other firms in the industry, the mean response was $\overline{X} = 5.49$, with 7 indicating that they believed they placed much more emphasis on health and safety than did other firms.

**Table 4**
**Overall Mean Score Evaluation of Factors Influencing**
**Organizational Health and Safety Perceptions and Behavior**

| Influence factor | Mean response $\overline{X}$ |
|---|---|
| National union | 2.13 |
| Plant union | 3.52 |
| Employee concerns and demands | 4.08 |
| Employee turnover | 1.79 |
| Other firms in industry | 2.78 |
| Accident compensation | 3.77 |
| Government rules and regulations | 5.21 |

An analysis of these influential factors by industry, as shown in table 5, revealed that government rules and regulations were most important across all industries. In both rubber and forestry, the accident compensation and the government rules and regulations were linked as the top two influential factors. In the remaining industries, employee concerns and demands constituted the second most important factor. The oil and chemical industries indicated that other firms in the industry was the third most important factor influencing their health and safety decisionmaking, while the other industries, steel, construction, pulp and paper and rubber, rated the union as being the third most influential factor in their respective industries. The mean response in forestry indicated that employee concerns and demands was the third most important factor in that industry.

## Table 5
### Extent to Which Factors Influence Health and Safety Decisionmaking by Industry (mean response on 7-point scale)

| | Rubber $\bar{X}$ | Pulp & paper $\bar{X}$ | Forestry $\bar{X}$ | Construction $\bar{X}$ | Steel $\bar{X}$ | Oil $\bar{X}$ | Chemicals $\bar{X}$ |
|---|---|---|---|---|---|---|---|
| National union | 1.67 | 1.00 | 2.71 | 4.00 | 3.00 | 5.00 | 2.00 |
| Plant union | 4.50 | 3.17 | 2.80 | 4.00 | 3.33 | 5.00 | 3.00 |
| Employee concerns | 4.33 | 3.66 | 3.57 | 4.25 | 3.33 | 6.50 | 4.25 |
| Turnover | 1.33 | 1.00 | 2.88 | 2.75 | 1.00 | NA | 1.33 |
| Other firms in industry | 2.40 | 1.66 | 2.88 | 3.33 | 2.33 | 6.00 | 3.50 |
| Potential law suits | 1.00 | 1.33 | 2.86 | 3.25 | 1.33 | 2.00 | 2.50 |
| Accident compensation | 4.50 | 3.00 | 5.63 | 3.25 | 2.66 | 1.00 | 2.66 |
| Government rules and regulations | 4.83 | 5.16 | 5.38 | 4.75 | 6.00 | 7.00 | 5.00 |

In order to assess the nature of this perceived influence, the question was asked whether the influence exerted by these factors was positive or negative. In other words, did the managers believe that other firms, the union, employees, etc., facilitated or hindered their efforts in the area of health and safety administration. Certainly it would be possible for one of these factors to be exerting a great deal of influence, but in a counterproductive fashion. In fact, in no case did the 34 employers respond that these factors hindered their health and safety efforts. With the exception of the response to government rules and regulations ($\bar{X} = 5.49$), employers viewed these factors as fairly neutral, that is, neither facilitating nor hindering their health and safety efforts. The mean ratings on the other factors were between $\bar{X} = 3.64$ for employee turnover and $\bar{X} = 4.97$ for employee concerns.

## Cost-Benefit Assessment

Obviously one or two factors, whether internal or external to the organization, will not in and of themselves change an employer's behavior with respect to health and safety decisionmaking. These factors interact with each other and organizational factors such as the amount of time spent on health and safety and the position level of the individual with primary responsibility for health and safety within the organization. The employer then considers these aspects and screens their impact in the context of the economic return to the organization.

As previously discussed, legislation affects not only employer compliance behavior but also employee behavior, which in turn has an economic impact on the firm. One reservation about the accident compensation legislation, for example, is the fear that the system will be abused. If employees view the provisions as benefits to which they are entitled, which in fact they are, more accidents which the employee would previously have simply worked through may be reported. It is also possible that the employee will be absent from work longer with a given accident because he or she is receiving compensation. In fact, when the employers were asked, "To what extent do you believe that more accidents are reported as a result of accident compensation?," the mean response was $\bar{X} = 5.31$, with 1 indicating "not at all" and 7 indicating "to a great extent." The mean response to the question, "To what extent does the existence of accident compensation prolong the absence of injured workers," was also high ($\bar{X} = 5.00$).

In order to assess the overall economic impact of accident compensation legislation and other influential factors, employers were asked "To what extent do you believe that your expenditures in the health and safety area are offset by your accident rates?" The perception of worker's absence, given the presence of a compensation system, was not significantly correlated with this overall cost-benefit assessment, but was significantly correlated with beliefs about the number of accidents reported. The greater the extent to which employers felt more accidents were reported, the less likely they felt that their costs in the health and safety area were offset by the benefits. As shown in table 6, the overall assessments of the influence of accident compensation legislation and government rules and regulations were not significantly correlated with the employer's cost-benefit analysis. Other factors influencing health and safety decisionmaking which are significantly correlated with the employer's cost-benefit assessment include the union and employee turnover.

Organizational characteristics which were positively correlated with the manager's cost-benefit analysis at a significance level less than .05 included the size of the corporation measured in terms of number of full-time employees (r = .28 p < .05). If the firm was headquartered in New Zealand, the employer was also more likely to feel that the costs were offset by the benefits or lower accident rates (r = .27 p < .05).

Table 6
**Correlation Between Factors Influencing Health and Safety Decisionmaking and Employer Cost-Benefit Analysis (Pearson Product Moment Correlation Coefficients)**

| Influence | Cost-benefit coefficient |
|---|---|
| National union | .30** |
| Plant union | .27* |
| Employee concerns | −.0 |
| Employee turnover | −.22* |
| Other firms | .21 |
| Accident compensation | −.04 |
| Government rules and regulations | −.01 |

*p < .10
**p < .05

## Influencing Factors, Cost-Benefit Analysis and Accident Record

The impact of legislation and other factors is important not only in terms of the degree of influence on decisionmaking and the employer's subjective assessment of the costs and benefits. More significant is the relationship between these elements and actual accident behavior in the organization. Given the number of factors influencing health and safety outcomes, is accident compensation correlated with lower accident rates, or is the direct effect erased by the economic impact of unintended consequences, i.e., more accidents being reported and longer absences by those who claim compensation?

Table 7 shows that accident compensation legislation, as a factor influencing employer decisionmaking, is positively correlated with the accident rate ($r = .33$ $p < .05$). This finding may simply reflect the fact that the more accidents in an organization, the more likely it will have transactions with the Accident Compensation Corporation. The relationship between government rules and regulations and the accident rate in 1982 was significant and in the expected direction ($r = -.39$ $p < .05$). The greater the reported influence of the government, the lower the accident rate. Another external factor significantly correlated with the accident rate was the influence of the national union ($r = .55$ $p < .05$). The relationship is not in the expected direction. The coefficient indicates that the national union influence was stronger in those organizations with higher accident rates.

**Table 7**
**Correlation Between Factors Influencing Employer Health and Safety Decisionmaking and the Accident Rate in 1982**
**(Pearson Product Moment Correlation Coefficients)**

| Influence | Accident rate in 1982 |
| --- | --- |
| National unions | .55** |
| Plant unions | .09 |
| Employee concerns | .0 |
| Employee turnover | .29* |
| Other firms | .14 |
| Accident compensation | .33** |
| Government rules and regulations | -.39** |
| Other structural variables: | |
| Locus of ownership | -.34** |
| Responsibility level | -.25* |

*$p < .10$
**$p < .05$

As an internal influencing factor, employee turnover ($r = .29$ p$<.10$) was positively correlated with the accident rate in 1982. In other words, the greater the influence of employee turnover, the higher was the accident level and *vice versa*. Other organizational structural variables which were significantly correlated with the level of accidents in 1982 included the locus of ownership and the position level of the person given primary responsibility for health and safety. The locus of ownership variable revealed that New Zealand organizations were more likely than foreign-owned organizations to have accidents ($r = -.34$ p$<.05$). The position level of the individual primarily responsible for health and safety also indicated that for the organizations sampled, the higher this assignment, the higher the number of accidents ($r = -.25$ p$<.10$).

## Conclusion

Accident compensation legislation does not always result in intended consequences. Survey research conducted in 38 organizations shows that the New Zealand Accident Compensation Act is not, in and of itself, perceived as a major influence on employers' health and safety decisionmaking. Government rules and regulations are a major influence, however, along with employee concerns and demands and the plant union.

The impact of the accident compensation legislation is evident in employers' assessments of resultant employee behavior and their own subsequent cost-benefit analyses of health and safety expenditures within the organization. Employers reported that they believe more accidents are now reported as a result of accident compensation ($X = 5.31$ on a 7-point scale) and that the existence of accident compensation prolongs the absence of injured workers ($X = 5.00$ on a 7-point scale). The employer's overall assessment of the costs and benefits of health and safety activities within their organization was significantly correlated with the employers' beliefs about the number of accidents reported, but not with the employers' beliefs about extended absences. This finding supports the notion that the overall benefits derived from comprehensive compensation provisions outweigh the cost. Despite the belief that more accidents may be reported, employers felt that their expenditures in the health and safety area (including the first week compensation requirement) are offset by lower accident rates.

Further evidence of the impact of accident compensation legislation is found in the significant correlation between the influence of this legislation and the level of accidents in the firm. Government rules and regulations and national unions were also significantly related to the number of accidents reported in 1982.

The policy implications of the findings reported here are that government agencies and the Accident Compensation Corporation may be able to strengthen their influence on health and safety in the firm even further, through increased cooperation with the unions. The data show that this effort would be best directed toward the individual plant union organization rather than the national federations. The findings further indicate that efforts to help employers address employee concerns should also prove useful. Across all industries, employers reported a high level of influence exerted by perceived employee concerns and demands. An example of such an involvement would be facilitating policy formulation, such as the New Zealand Employers Federation policy statement on health and safety in the workplace adopted in 1983 ("NZEF Adopts Policy" 1983).

From the employer's perspective, the finding that the stronger the union influence on health and safety decision-making the more likely the employer reported that the benefits outweighed the costs in health and safety administration, suggests that employers may also find it useful to strengthen the union's role in this area. A second recommendation, which fits with working more closely with the workers, is to place management responsibility for health and safety administration at lower levels within the organization. This suggestion flows from the finding that the higher the assignment of responsibility for health and safety within the organization, the higher the level of accidents. A third recommendation is that employers may find it useful to work with other firms on resolving health and safety problems. The majority of firms reported that they believed that they placed more emphasis on health and safety than did other firms. This suggests that organizations may be able to learn from one another. The unions may also be able to provide a mechanism for this linkage.

# NOTES

1. Under Part 1 of the Social Security Act of 1964, injured persons able to qualify under the relevant means test had modest monetary benefits, and all New Zealand residents normally had access to medical, hospital and other related benefits under Part 2 of the Act (Fahy 1982).

2. The Woodhouse Report characterized the adversarial fault system as being cumbersome, erratic, and extravagant in operation. The negligence action was labeled a lottery producing an adequate indemnity for only a relatively small group of injured persons.

3. Prior to the revisions effective in the Accident Compensation Act 1982, the Earners' Fund was charged with all amounts on claims where workers suffered injury in motor vehicle accidents in New Zealand arising out of and in the course of the injured person's employment. Now all compensation resulting from motor vehicle accidents is financed through levies on vehicle owners.

4. New Zealand dollars are reported. The NZ/US exchange rate was approximately $.64 (NZ) per $1.00 (US) as of April 1984.

5. For the individual, the legislation stipulates that the earnings related compensation for all periods of incapacity extending beyond the first week is calculated by reference to the amount of "relevant earnings" (ACA & 104). In December 1978, the limit on relevant earnings determined under S. 104 was removed, however. Instead a limit was placed on the amount of weekly compensation paid. In December 1981, the maximum amount of earnings-related compensation was increased from $288 per week to $600 per week. The ACC may at its discretion fix a minimum amount of earnings for the self-employed, and for the period March 1983 to March 1984 this minimum was set at $12,324 or $237/week. Earnings-related compensation may in general be paid until a claimant reaches the age of 65 years, but where the injured earner is over 60 special provisions apply.

# REFERENCES

*Accident Compensation Act 1982* (ACA). Wellington, New Zealand: Government Printer, effective April 1, 1983.

Accident Compensation Corporation. *ACC Statistics.* Wellington, New Zealand: Accident Compensation Corporation, Vol 1. No 1, March 1982.

Accident Compensation Corporation. *Levies on Employers.* Wellington, New Zealand: Accident Compensation Corporation, April 1983.

Berkowitz, Monroe. *The Economics of Work Accidents in New Zealand.* Wellington, New Zealand: Occupational Safety Trust Board, Accident Compensation Corporation, 1979.

Dahl, Harry. "Injury Compensation for Everyone? - The New Zealand Experience." *Journal of Urban Law* 53 (1976), pp. 925-947.

Fahy, J.L. *Accident Compensation Coverage: The Administration of the Accident Compensation Act of 1972.* Wellington, New Zealand: Accident Compensation Corporation, 1982.

Fahy, J.L. "The ACC in the 80's Meeting the Information Challenge." *Accident Compensation Journal* 1, 2 (August 1983), pp. 1-6.

Inglis, B.D. "Accident Compensation Policy." *Accident Compensation Journal* 1, 1 (November 1982), pp. 3-5.

"NZEF Adopts Policy on Workplace Safety." *The Employer* 81 (June 1983).

Royal Commission on Inquiry, *Compensation for Personal Injury in New Zealand.* Wellington, New Zealand: Government Printer, 1967.

*Summary Report - Compensated Accidents 1981.* Wellington, New Zealand: Accident Compensation Corporation, 1982.